FROM THE THEATER TO THE PLAZA

MCGILL-QUEEN'S IBERIAN AND LATIN AMERICAN CULTURES SERIES
Series Editor: Nicolás Fernández-Medina

The McGill-Queen's Iberian and Latin American Cultures Series is committed to publishing original scholarship that explores and re-evaluates Iberian and Latin American cultures, connections, and identities. Offering diverse perspectives on a range of regional and global histories from the early modern period to twenty-first-century contexts, the series cuts across disciplinary boundaries to consider how questions of authority, nation, revolution, gender, sexuality, science, epistemology, avant-gardism, aesthetics, travel, colonization, race relations, religious belief, and media technologies, among others, have shaped the rich and complex trajectories of modernity in the Iberian Peninsula and Latin America. The McGill-Queen's Iberian and Latin American Cultures Series promotes rigorous scholarship and welcomes proposals for innovative and theoretically compelling monographs and edited collections.

1 Populism and Ethnicity
  Peronism and the Jews of Argentina
  Raanan Rein
  Translated by Isis Sadek

2 What Would Cervantes Do?
  Navigating Post-Truth with Spanish Baroque Literature
  David Castillo and William Egginton

3 The Pen, the Sword, and the Law
  Dueling and Democracy in Uruguay
  David S. Parker

4 From the Theater to the Plaza
  Spectacle, Protest, and Urban Space in Twenty-First-Century Madrid
  Matthew I. Feinberg

FROM THE THEATER TO THE PLAZA

Spectacle, Protest, and Urban Space in
Twenty-First-Century Madrid

MATTHEW I. FEINBERG

McGill-Queen's University Press
Montreal & Kingston • London • Chicago

© McGill-Queen's University Press 2022

ISBN 978-0-2280-1069-2 (cloth)
ISBN 978-0-2280-1236-8 (ePDF)
ISBN 978-0-2280-1237-5 (ePUB)

Legal deposit second quarter 2022
Bibliothèque nationale du Québec

Printed in Canada on acid-free paper that is 100% ancient forest free
(100% post-consumer recycled), processed chlorine free

McGill-Queen's University Press acknowledges with thanks the financial contribution of Baldwin Wallace University towards the publication of this book.

Library and Archives Canada Cataloguing in Publication

Title: From the theater to the plaza : spectacle, protest, and urban space in twenty-first-century Madrid / Matthew I. Feinberg.
Names: Feinberg, Matthew I., author.
Series: McGill-Queen's Iberian and Latin American cultures series ; 4.
Description: Series statement: McGill-Queen's Iberian and Latin American cultures series ; 4 | Includes bibliographical references and index.
Identifiers: Canadiana (print) 20210388773 | Canadiana (ebook) 20210388838 | ISBN 9780228010692 (cloth) | ISBN 9780228012368 (ePDF) | ISBN 9780228012375 (ePUB)
Subjects: LCSH: Theater—Spain—Madrid. | LCSH: Theater and society—Spain Madrid. | LCSH: Public spaces—Spain—Madrid. | LCSH: Lavapiés (Madrid, Spain)
Classification: LCC PN2786.M3 F45 2022 | DDC 792.0946/41—dc23

This book was typeset in 10.5/13 Sabon.

Dedicated to Erin Benay

Contents

Figures and Tables | ix
Acknowledgments | xi

Introduction: The "Kind of Problem a City Is" | 3

1 The Stage of a Nation:
The Urban Theater of Madrid | 25

2 From Lavapiés to Madrid:
The Populist Myth of "*Lo Castizo*" | 63

3 The Global Stage of Madrid:
The Teatro Valle-Inclán and the Rehabilitation of Lavapiés | 96

4 Resisting the Spectacle:
The Practiced City of the Laboratorio 03 | 130

5 The Representational Space of the City:
Lavapiés in the Theater | 167

Aftermath:
Restaging Spanish Politics in the Theater and the Streets | 202

Notes | 213
Bibliography | 251
Index | 275

Figures and Tables

FIGURES

0.1 BollyMadrid. Photo by author | 7
0.2 *Chulapos* in Madrid. Photo by Diario de Madrid. Used under Creative Commons Attribution License 4.0 | 8
0.3 Map of Madrid. Copyright Matthew Feinberg | 14
0.4 Detail map of Lavapiés. Copyright Matthew Feinberg | 15
1.1 Corral del Príncipe. Drawing by Carlos Dorremochea. From *The Reconstruction of a Spanish Golden Age Playhouse, El Corral del Príncipe 1583–1744*. Used by permission of University of Florida Press | 31
1.2 Plaza Mayor. Used under Creative Commons Attribution License 4.0 | 42
1.3 Palazzo Reale. Photo by author | 43
1.4 Kilometer Zero Marker. Photo by author | 51
2.1 La Corrala de Tribulete. Photo by author | 66
2.2 "La Tabacalera a Debate" from 2005. Used by permission of David Rodríguez | 67
2.3 Franciso de Goya y Lucientes *La maja y los embozados* [*The Maja and the Cloaked Men*]. Public domain | 73
2.4 Juan Comba y García, *Los teatros y su público/Theatres and their Audience*. Used with permission from Museo de Historia de Madrid | 86

3.1 Image of the Centro Drámatico Nacional – Teatro Valle-Inclán. Photo by author | 98
3.2 Reflective glass of the Teatro Valle Inclán. Photo by author | 108
4.1 Protest of Teatro Valle-Inclán inauguration. Frame grab from personal video archives of Antonio Girón | 131
4.2 Entrance to the Laboratorio 03 calle Amparo 103. Frame grab from *Laboratorio 03: Ocupando el vacío*. Directed by Fernando Menéndez. Kinowo Media, 2007 | 148
4.3 Protest symbolically closing the Office of Municipal Rehabilitation. Frame grab from *Laboratorio 03: Ocupandoel vacío*. Directed by Fernando Menéndez. Kinowo Media, 2007 | 150
4.4 Eviction protest on Facade of Labo 03. Copyright Julio Palomar / El Mundo. Used with permission | 153
5.1 Image from performance of *Bazar*. Used with Permission from the Centro de Documentación de las Artes Escénicas y de la Música | 182
5.2 Performance of "La vida no es una cárcel/Life Is Not a Prison." May 2009. Photo by author | 186
5.3 Francisco de Goya y Lucientes. *El aquelarre o Gran Cabrón* [*The Witches Sabbath or Great Goat*]. Public domain | 192

TABLES

0.1 Demographics of immigration in Lavapiés. Statistics from 2008 municipal census of residents. Table by author | 12
4.1 Brief chronology of occupied social centers and spaces of self-management (*autogestión*) in or near Lavapiés | 136

Acknowledgments

I am grateful to a number of institutions, organizations, and individuals that supported this work and helped me to complete it.

In particular, I want to thank the Program for Cultural Cooperation between Spain's Ministry of Culture and American Universities, the University of Kentucky Graduate School, the Fulbright Program of the United States Department of State Bureau of Educational and Cultural Affairs, the Andrew W. Mellon Foundation, the Centro de Documentación Teatral of the Instituto Nacional de Artes Escénicas y de la Música (INAEM), and Baldwin Wallace University. I also want to thank the peer-reviewers whose input helped guide the revisions of this manuscript and the editors at McGill-Queen's University Press who made this process so smooth and professional.

Underpinning my work as a scholar and a teacher has always been the inspiration, guidance, and support of my professors and mentors.

From Colorado State University I want to thank Sarah Sloane, Carol Cantrell, John Calderazzo, and Gerry Callahan for all that they taught me about writing, teaching, and interdisciplinary studies. José Luis Suárez-García also bears special mention, since it was his encouragement that led to my pursuit of a doctorate in Spanish – something I never imagined possible before.

At Middlebury College, Brett Millier, Will Nash, and Michael Newbury gave me the freedom to take risks in literary studies as an undergraduate student. Likewise, all my esteemed professors of language and literature at the Middlebury College Spanish Language School in both Vermont and Madrid provided me with a love of the Spanish language and the linguistic tools to carry out this research. Like countless other students over the decades, I was blessed to study with the brilliant Ricardo Doménech so many years ago, an experience that sparked my interest in Spanish Theater. His influence will always remain in my work – may he rest in peace.

At the University of Kentucky, I would like to thank Yanira Paz, Alan Brown, Aníbal Biglieri, Patricia Ehrkamp, Susan Carvalho, and, of course, Ana Rueda for their never-ending guidance and support. I would also like to thank Anderson Stewart, Lee Reyes, Mahan Ellison, Rebecca Kaplan, Alice Driver, Betsy Dahms, Ismael Artiga, David Hoopes, and Michelle Dumais for their friendship.

Susan Larson's support as a mentor, a friend, and a collaborator has been immeasurable. Her work as a scholar in the study of social space in the context of Spain has served as continual inspiration for my work. Her diligent guidance (and many words of encouragement) during the ebbs and flows of this book have been essential to its completion. Thank you.

I am also extremely grateful for the support and friendship of myriad people in Madrid and Lavapiés who welcomed me into their community and guided me in this research. In particular, many thanks go to Carlos Sambricio, Fernando Roch, César Barló, Carlos Vidania, Ana Sánchez, Gloria Durán, Pedro Álvarez González, Laura Corcuera, José Antonio Soler Martínez, Ana Westley, Ángel Moreno Plou, Leire Arietaleanizbeascoa, and Erik Martínez.

Special thanks are owed to Jacobo Rivero for his friendship and support. This book would not have been possible without his help.

The kindness and generosity of the dramatists about whom I write in this work have always been greatly appreciated and valued. Thank you to Juan Mayorga, Jerónimo López Mozo, David Planell, and César López Llera.

I also want to thank Malcolm Compitello, Benjamin Fraser, Stephen Vilaseca, Susan Divine, Rebecca Haidt, Sebastiaan Faber, Leslie Harkema, Max Deardorf, and my colleagues in the Department of World Languages, Literatures, and Cultures at Baldwin Wallace University: Nadia Sahely, Karen Barahona, Christina Svendsen, and Stephen Hollender.

For the love and support that family provides, thanks to Barbara and Paul Feinberg, Avrom Feinberg, Erica Gallagher, Tesher Feinberg, Elliot Benay, Carole Ober, Keith Spielfogel, Susan Tierney-Cockburn, and Chuck Cockburn.

I have to express my sincere gratitude for the love and support of Phyllis Benay and Kelly Feinberg. They are no longer with us, but their spirit endures in my memory each day.

Most importantly, my infinite thanks to Erin, Ari, and Benjamin for blessing each day of my life with smiles, laughter, and love. You are my all.

Matthew Feinberg
Shaker Heights, Ohio.
June 2021

FROM THE THEATER TO THE PLAZA

INTRODUCTION

The "Kind of Problem a City Is"

In March 2020, the streets of Madrid lay empty as a result of the national "state of alarm" declared by Spanish President Pedro Sánchez in response to the COVID-19 pandemic. Soon thereafter, a similar situation would unfold in New York, Paris, and other major urban areas around the world. Images circulated on the Internet of empty plazas and vacant streets across the world. Facebook, Instagram, and Twitter feeds filled with the yearning of urban dwellers for a return to that thing called city life. These events drew attention to the fact that cities are not merely a physical assemblage of buildings. Rather, it is the people that enact the thing we might call the Urban. As French urban theorist Henri Lefebvre argued, space does not merely exist a priori, but rather is produced – as he called it – through the varying ways that people build, use, and imagine it.[1] It is this interplay between imagination, human action, and spatial setting that makes cities so dynamic and perpetually in flux.

With Lefebvre in mind, this book approaches the production of space by considering its resonance with the production of a theater performance. Upon the stage, the scenography and the actions of the actors imbue one another with meaning to produce the drama; this dynamic, in turn, creates meaning for the spectators, without whom the production is not complete. Likewise, cities are built in response to the shifting interests, desires, dreams, and actions of inhabitants as they traverse and interpret the urban stage – whether they be residents, day shoppers, urban planners, commuters, or tourists.

As cities slowly began to reopen in spurts and starts in the months that followed that first state of alarm, both city leaders and residents attempted to chart a new path forward through a future compromised by pandemic, and in doing so have brought renewed attention to ways in which we use cities. Many of the questions posed by this book have been made all the more pressing by these seemingly perpetual images of empty cities: Where, why, and how is culture created in cities in the early twenty-first century? What is public space? Who defines what can and cannot be done there? While much will be written in the coming months and years on the reshaping of the production and consumption of culture in cities in the wake of the pandemic, this book looks backward toward the first decade of the twenty-first century with the hope of illustrating the "kind of problem a city is," as urban scholar Jane Jacobs put it.[2] More broadly though, I pose questions about the ways that these dynamics between culture and city space also inform our understandings of other geographies, or, as I will refer to it in this book, different geographic scales. How can we understand the interplay of culture at the neighborhood level with the way we imagine a city as a whole or its connection with national territory and identity? As the pandemic reshapes these relationships, this book asks that we take stock of these questions in the decades before shelter-in-place orders. This process may help us to understand both what we have lost, and also what we need to consider if we hope to rebuild cities for human connection and engagement.

To explore these broad and (admittedly) abstract questions, I focus on two specific and interrelated locations. The first is Spain's capital city, Madrid, whose role as the administrative center of the Spanish state has always worked in lockstep with its role as a stage for regal power and a symbol of centralized Spanish (read Castilian) power and identity (as aspirational as that symbolism may be). The second location is one of the city's most unique and iconic central neighborhoods: Lavapiés. A diverse and multicultural place, this neighborhood is known as much for its immigrant population and its activist *okupas* (squatters) as it is for its associations with a myth of Madrid's *castizo* identity – a term that loosely means authentically Madrilenian.[3] While the study of these locations seems to imply distinct geographies – one at the scale of the neighborhood and the other the scale of the metropolis – one of the central objectives of this book is to demonstrate the contingent and overlapping nature of these categories as they have intercalated one another both historically and, more recently, in the context of global competition between cities. I contend that it is in the spectacle of urban space where these tensions are best illustrated.

By studying Madrid in its global context, this book builds on recent scholarship that considers Madrid as the site of contestation between two countervailing trends: one defined by policies of privatization and deregulation built around circuits of international financial capital and spatial segregation and the other aligned with efforts to resist this regime through the repossession of space and politics through grassroots organizing and cultural production.[4] For many scholars, these conflicts came to a head with the emergence of the 15-M movement in Madrid on 15 May 2011, a protest movement that then spread to other Spanish cities that summer. Born out of frustration with the lack of an effective political response to Spain's economic crisis, which began in 2008, 15-M not only reshaped the Spanish political landscape, but arguably marked a generational shift in the understanding of Spanish culture. Scholars like Amado Fernández-Savater, Germán Labrador Méndez, Luis Moreno-Caballud, and others have seen 15-M as the end of the "culture of consensus" and the "Regime of 1978" that had dominated Spanish politics since the approval of Spain's constitution in 1978.[5] This book does not seek to explain 15-M nor argue for its significance (that it was significant is not debatable, even if the how and why might be). Rather, it argues that the spectacle of 15-M in all its chaotic mix of local and global politics had been rehearsed in the preceding decade in the struggles over urban space in Lavapiés and the many spectacles produced by those conflicts. Most significantly, I argue that these tensions between local, municipal, and global discourses in Madrid have a long and important history in the capital, and that they have often been expressed on the urban stage of Madrid – both in urban space itself and in the cultural imaginary. The study of this history reveals how dominant power structures, as well as movements of popular resistance, have used spectacles to engage with these layers of meaning in long-standing struggles over the meaning of Madrid – and even of Spain itself. It is these urban spectacles that form much of the primary material for exploring the central questions in this book.

What follows is an examination of the important tensions between institutional and non-institutional cultural production in the formation of cities, which also considers how local expressions of urban culture fit into their global context. This research not only demonstrates to scholars in the Humanities and Social Sciences the material impacts of cultural production on the shaping of cities, but it also brings attention to the development of cooperative approaches to urban cultural production that have emerged in Spain in recent years. It is my hope that readers leave this book with a richer understanding of Madrid's theatrical tradition and a deeper sensitivity to the ways that culture shapes the urban experience.

THE URBAN STAGE OF LAVAPIÉS

In the late afternoon of 12 June 2012, the rhythmic sounds of bhangra beats filled the Plaza Agustín Lara in Madrid's Lavapiés neighborhood as a group of dancers delighted spectators with their Bollywood dance moves on a temporary stage erected in front of the rehabilitated ruins of the old Escuelas Pías school and chapel (see Figure 1.1). For the fifth summer in a row, the BollyMadrid festival had turned public space in Lavapiés into a mini-Mumbai (or someone's simulacrum of Mumbai) to celebrate Bollywood and South-Asian culture in Madrid. Similarly, an event from the year before, called "Tapapiés" had advertised the possibility of going "for tapas around the world without leaving Lavapiés."[6] Both events were intended to consolidate the reputation of this iconic neighborhood as the multicultural heart of Madrid – a well-deserved reputation, since even on a brief foray through the neighborhood today, one might find Bangladeshi and Pakistani residents playing badminton in the Plaza Nelson Mandela (formerly the Plaza Cabestreros), several halal butcher shops on the calle Tribulete, with daily specials written in Arabic, and the smell of delicious *maafe* being served in one of the handful of Senegalese restaurants scattered along the calles Amparo and Mesón de Paredes. While local cultural organizations played an important role in its production, the event in the Plaza Agustín Lara was also the result of years of investment by Madrid's Ayuntamiento (municipal government) to reverse years of neglect and to transform Lavapiés into an alluring symbol of Madrid's international diversity, a goal reflected in the BollyMadrid moniker that referenced not the neighborhood, but Madrid itself. Gone was the dusty, repressed 1960s capital of Franco's Spain; so too was left behind the crumbling and insecure inner city of the 1980s and 1990s. In its place was a dynamic urban spectacle in which the city's working-class immigrant neighborhoods reflected a rehabilitated capital and the emergence of Madrid as a cosmopolitan and global city.

Figure 0.1 | BollyMadrid Festival in the Plaza Agustín Lara, Lavapiés, Madrid, 2012.

Lavapiés also benefited from a number of other features that made it attractive to city planners and leaders for redevelopment. First and foremost, perhaps, was the neighborhood's strategic location adjacent to Madrid's recently refurbished Atocha train station and the city's Paseo del Arte, containing the city's most important (and most visited) museums – namely the Reina Sofía National Center for Contemporary Art, the Thyssen-Bornemisza Art Museum, and the National Museum of El Prado. Secondly, the neighborhood has been a locus for independent theater and bohemian culture in the city since the late 1970s. Finally, Lavapiés was also ideal for these redevelopment plans because it has long been romanticized as one of Madrid's most "authentic," or *castizo*, neighborhoods.

This folkloric *castizo* culture has its roots in Madrid's theater tradition, particularly in the short plays called *sainetes*, written by Ramón de la Cruz in the eighteenth century, which focused on Madrid's lower-class neighborhoods and their inhabitants. Later, these images of Madrid's lower classes would be rearticulated in the nineteenth century in Madrid's lyric theater tradition of the

Figure 0.2 | Enthusiasts dressed as *chulapos* for a street *verbena* in Madrid in 2018.

zarzuela and in its wildly popular short-form, called the *género chico*, or "small genre," that emerged at the end of the nineteenth century and the beginning of the twentieth. These images have come to be closely associated with Madrid, and are often celebrated as expressions of the city's unique culture, particularly on 15 May during celebrations of the city's patron: Saint Isidore the Laborer. During this feast day of San Isidro, many children, adults, and the elderly dress up as *chulapos* and *chulapas*. The men and boys wear the traditional white-and-black-checked newsboy hat, with a carnation tucked neatly into the lapel of a matching jacket or vest, while the women dress in form-fitting floor-length dresses evocative of Andalusian flamenco style, a white scarf on their heads, carefully knotted at the neck, and a traditional *mantón de manila* piano shawl around their shoulders (see Figure 0.2).[7] One might even come across an elderly couple dancing a turn-of-the-century *chotis* in Madrid's Plaza Mayor, a living reproduction of the scenes mythologized by Madrid's theater tradition.

WHAT'S IN A NAME?

Notably, the mythology of Lavapiés extends beyond its associations with *castizo* culture, as the neighborhood's name and origins are draped in mystery and debate. The neighborhood occupies the steep southern slopes of the high, dry *meseta* where, in the late ninth century, Muhammad I, the Emir of Córdoba, attracted by the site's strategic defensive position, constructed a fortification that would eventually develop into modern-day Madrid.[8] Lavapiés itself likely developed around the natural spring formed by the confluence of various streams (*arroyos*) as they made their way down the hillsides toward the Manzanares River that runs south along the city's western edge before sweeping east on its way to join the Jarama River. The neighborhood's name loosely translated means "foot-bath" or "foot-washing," and may have derived, according to chronicler Federico Bravo Morata, from the fact that, during rainstorms, water would fill the *arroyos*, rush down the hill, and fill what is now the Plaza Lavapiés.[9] This etymology of the name Lavapiés emphasizes its physical geography and suggests that common references to the neighborhood as a *barrio bajo* (low neighborhood) allude, in part, to its physical location literally below the central areas of the city – as such, it is the place to which water and other effluvium flowed.[10]

Yet the neighborhood's "low" character historically has also been a reference to the social status of its inhabitants – whether because of social class or religious identity. Bravo Morata, for example, also suggests that the name Lavapiés derived from it being the place where "the bishop would wash the feet [lávase los pies] of the poor on a determined day of the year" – a tradition that was intended to evoke the humility of Christ washing the feet of his disciples (a reference to John 13:1–17).[11] These theories not only attribute a purifying quality to the waters of Lavapiés, but perhaps more importantly they allude to the social status of the inhabitants and the possibility that their impoverishment offered the bishop the appropriate stage for this symbolic act of "humility."

One of the most persistent myths about Lavapiés suggests that it was the location of the city's Jewish ghetto, or *judería*, a theory put forth in the late-nineteenth century by Father Fidel Fita, who suggested that the church of San Lorenzo, located in the neighborhood, was originally the site of the city's synagogue.[12] Unfortunately, as Gonzalo Viñuales Ferreiro has demonstrated, there is little evidence to support this narrative and much evidence to indicate that the synagogue, and indeed the *judería*, was located elsewhere in the city during the late-medieval period. In fact, maps from the period suggest there was little to no settlement in this area near the city.[13] What does seem logical is that there began to emerge a small outlying settlement near the gate of the new enclosure, or *cerca*, that had been built to control the influx of goods and people after Philip II relocated the royal court to Madrid in 1561 and the city's population surged.[14] Whatever the character of this small settlement, it was likely made up of people who, for whatever reason, were not allowed inside the city walls.[15]

Perhaps because of Spain's long tradition of religious persecution, it has often been assumed that this marginal community was either Muslim or Jewish. These assumptions regarding the *judería* have led to the popular belief that the foot washing referenced in the name Lavapiés refers to the ablutions performed by residents before entering the synagogue that supposedly used to stand on the site now occupied by the church of San Lorenzo. Despite this theory's erroneous conflation of Jewish ritual practices and the Muslim foot-washing tradition, it is one that became codified as historical fact in the work of Pedro de Répide, who would go on to become an official chronicler for the city of Madrid in the early-twentieth century. In his *Guía de Madrid* from 1921 – a series of celebratory sketches of the capital published in the daily newspaper *La libertad* – Répide suggests that the etymology of the name Lavapiés derived from "some fountain or basin for ablutions in which, perhaps, it was customary to wash the feet of those that went to the Jewish neighborhood but did not belong to the community and, upon leaving, would wash or purify their feet."[16] Here again, the neighborhood's foot washing remains a fixation, despite the somewhat odd interpretation of the ablutions tradition that assumed that people leaving the neighborhood would purify themselves in said footbaths.

According to Répide, this history also suggests why the neighborhood always historically contained a high concentration of *conversos* – Jews or Muslims that had converted to Christianity.[17] It is because of this (supposed) *converso* population, he argued, that Lavapiés acquired the nickname of *La manolería*, a name that came from "a Jewish preoccupation that caused the families of the *conversos* to always call the first son Manuel, by which, because of the abundance of this name, the neighborhood remained the place of Manueles and, therefore, of the *Manolos*."[18] Any quick Google search about Lavapiés will demonstrate that many of these various dubious theories have been reproduced and informally codified in blogs and travelogues of amateur urban historians and travel writers from Spain, the United Kingdom, and the United States. The very prevalence and persistence of these abundant myths, false histories, and etymologies regarding this historically working-class neighborhood point to the unique place of Lavapiés in the urban imaginary of Madrid.

LAVAPIÉS, CRADLE OF IMMIGRATION

While ambiguity surrounds the origins of the neighborhood, what is clear is that Lavapiés has historically been one of the traditional collection points for immigrants arriving in Madrid. From the waves of rural immigrants arriving from other parts of Spain in the late-seventeenth century through to the international immigrants that began to arrive in the late-twentieth century and the present day, Lavapiés would become the immigration arrival point par excellence.[19] In the cultural imaginary, too, Lavapiés is characterized this way. Perhaps one of the most famous examples can be found in Antonio Nieves Conde's famous 1951 film *Surcos*, which relates the tragic plight of a family arriving in Madrid from Andalusia in the mid-twentieth century. More recently, one might look to the 2002 documentary directed by Basel Ramsis and entitled *The Other Side: A Closer Look at Lavapiés*, which gives voice to the immigrant communities living in the neighborhood. These associations with immigration are significant, because Madrid as a whole, according to David Ringrose, is "a city of immigrants," and within this context Lavapiés has often been perceived as the crucible where the amalgam of Madrid's identity has formed.[20] For example, for nineteenth-century chronicler Ramón Mesonero Romanos, Lavapiés was where *lo madrileño* (the thingness of Madrid) was formed: a fusion "of the boastful Andalusian, of the vivacious Valencian, and of Castilian severity and haughtiness."[21] As people from many different parts of Spain arrived, they were not only integrated into the capital city, but fused their regional differences into some invented idea of Spanish national identity.

Today, this immigration and diversity has taken on a more international flavor, as much of the Spanish working-class population has been replaced by foreign immigrants. Indeed, between 1998

Table 0.1 | Demographics of immigration in Lavapiés. Statistics from 2008 municipal census of residents.

Bangladesh	2,378	14.69%
Ecuador	2,254	13.93%
Morocco	1,271	7.85%
China	1,067	6.59%
Bolivia	864	5.34%
Senegal	808	4.99%

Others include: Romania, Italy, Colombia, Peru, Argentina, Dominican Republic

and 2008 – the period that forms the focus of this book – the foreign population in Lavapiés grew by 351.28 per cent (3,586 in 1998 to 16,183 in 2008) (see Table 0.1). By 2010, this dramatic demographic change made Lavapiés, according to the municipal census organization, the neighborhood in the Centro District with the greatest number of resident foreigners in the city, with 16,183 of the 49,754 total foreign residents.[22] As a result of these numbers, Lavapiés has the highest concentration of immigrants per square meter in Madrid.[23] This diversity includes the high numbers of North Africans that arrived in the early 1990s, as well as the groups that followed, including those from sub-Saharan Africa (particularly Senegal), South America, the Caribbean, other parts of the Middle East (Iraq, Iran), Southern Asia (India, Pakistan, Bangladesh), and, later, from China. It is in this context that Lavapiés acquired its international reputation and by 2010 became an asset for attracting both *madrileños* (Madrilenians) from other parts of the city and international tourists.

Significantly, these high numbers of immigrants – many of them undocumented – contributed to the marginalization of the area during the late 1990s and early 2000s.[24] The presence of other underserved groups – like the elderly – contributed to a general level of neglect in the neighborhood and, by the early 2000s, like much of the historic center of the city, it suffered from a proliferation of degraded housing stock. For example, at the turn of this century, the area in Lavapiés designated for targeted rehabilitation by the city included some 766 buildings with 11, 878 identified housing units. Around 4,969 (nearly 42 per cent) were considered *infraviviendas* (tenements) – that is, barely habitable.[25] It is this setting that should be kept in mind as the story of Lavapiés unfolds in the forthcoming chapters.

During this period of neglect, the low rents attracted other residents. As a result, it was not only the large immigrant population that gave Lavapiés its reputation as an "intercultural laboratory," as sociologist Mayte Gómez has called it. She divides this intercultural character into four components. The first is the very engaged community of activists, including *okupas* (squatters), feminists, liberation lesbians and gays, anti-war activists, and housing advocates, which for years were loosely associated with one another in the Lavapiés Network.[26] Other community organizations complement this cohort of activists. These include more traditional neighborhood associations, such as La Corrala Neighborhood Association, and those formed around ethnic identity, like the Association of Senegalese Immigrants of Spain, the Association of Moroccan Immigrants in Spain, and the very active Bangladeshi Neighborhood Association. In contrast to these more politically active residents, who arrived in Lavapiés starting in the mid to late 1990s, Gómez also describes the increasing presence and influence of *novísimos vecinos*, or newbies, a group of young, middle-class progressives, around thirty to forty years old, with some bohemian or artistic tendencies, that started arriving in the mid-2000s.[27] The wave of international immigrants, activists, and *novísimos vecinos* that began to inhabit Lavapiés markedly changed a neighborhood that had been predominantly occupied by lifelong residents, typically elderly residents known as *los vecinos de toda la vida*. It is because of this mix of immigrants, neo-bohemians, activists, and the elderly that the Film Festival of Lavapiés has used the slogan "one neighborhood, many worlds" since its inception in 2003.

To clearly delineate the limits of this neighborhood for this study, I rely on the work of sociologist Manuel Zárate Martín, whose interviews and surveys with secondary-school students from the neighborhood loosely designate the parameters of Lavapiés. According to these youths, the neighborhood forms a triangular-shaped area within the city center of Madrid that extends southward from the Plaza Tirso de Molina. It is contained to the east and west by the

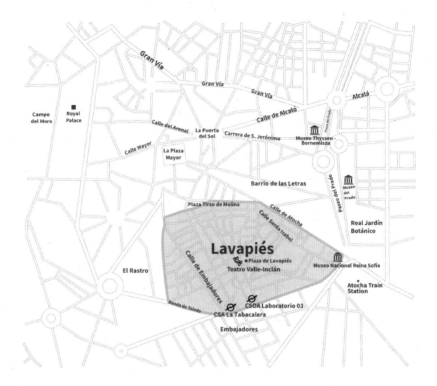

Figure 0.3 | Overview map of Madrid.

streets Santa Isabel and Embajadores respectively, while the southern boundary is formed by the Ronda de Toledo and the Ronda de Valencia as they connect the roundabouts of Embajadores and Emperadador Carlos V (where the Atocha train station is located) (see Figures 0.3 and 0.4). These limits distinguish Lavapiés from the adjacent neighborhood of La Latina and El Rastro to the west and the Barrio de las Letras to the east of the calle Atocha. Of course, these boundaries are fluid – all the more so since Lavapiés is not an officially designated district of the city, an ambiguity that reflects the shadiness of the neighborhood's origins and name. In technical terms, Lavapiés is nothing more than the name of a metro stop and a plaza. Within these boundaries is a neighborhood characterized by a rich historical legacy, cultural diversity, inspired political activity, and, in the last twenty years, the spectacle of intense urban change.

Introduction   15

Figure 0.4 | Detail map, highlighting theater venues and self-managed spaces in Lavapiés.

FROM *BARRIO BAJO* TO *BARRIO COOL*

In September 2018, the London-based media and entertainment company Time Out chose the Embajadores neighborhood of Madrid as the "coolest neighborhood in the world."[28] The article highlighted cultural institutions like the Casa Encendida and the self-managed social center La Tabacalera. It seemed to eschew much of the actual Embajadores district to focus exclusively on attractions north of the Embajadores traffic circle, in what most residents would refer to as Lavapiés. This attention from an international tastemaker only continued to popularize the neighborhood. Perhaps as a result of this publicity, a proliferation of short-term rentals, via platforms like Airbnb and Vrbo, has plagued the neighborhood, as it has other "cool" cities in Europe (like Amsterdam and Barcelona).[29] As Javier Gil and

Jorge Sequera demonstrate, many of these rentals are not owned by local residents, but rather by subsidiaries of international hoteliers like Wyndham Worldwide's Friendly Rentals, which Sequera and Gil suggest own nearly two hundred units throughout the neighborhood.[30] This process has profoundly transformed the real-estate market in Lavapiés and merely accelerated a gentrification process that began in the period that forms much of the focus of this book.

In this period from roughly 1997 to 2011, the unique mix of inhabitants in Lavapiés created a potent combination for speculative real estate. Lavapiés had become a counter-cultural mecca. Its diversity, grittiness, political activism, and connections with a historic past gave, and continue to give, this unique neighborhood a particular "urban *terroir*" – a branded sense of place based on seemingly authentic local culture.[31] By eating in one of the neighborhood's many Indo-Pakistani restaurants along the calle Lavapiés or more *castizo* establishments like the Café Barbieri or the Bar Automático, one might consume the neighborhood's distinct cultural offerings visually, financially, and/ or gastronomically. Alongside this social milieu, there were specific urban-planning decisions that encouraged the "urbanization of capital," to use David Harvey's term, an accelerating circulation of international capital focused on investing in the built environment.[32]

These decisions were the result of a process that began in the mid-1980s, as Madrid's Ayuntamiento began to target Lavapiés for investment and urban change on the heels of the rehabilitation of the Atocha train station from 1985 to 1992 and the inauguration of the Reina Sofia Museum in 1992.[33] In 1994, the Ayuntamiento, the Autonomous Community of Madrid, the Ministry of Development, and private sources entered into an agreement to designate Lavapiés – amongst other areas in the city – a Preferred Area of Rehabilitation (Área de Rehabilitación Preferente – ARP).[34] The objectives of the ARPs were to improve the quality of life, restore the residential character of the neighborhoods, regenerate the social connections, improve the housing and building stock, and encourage citizen participation.[35] When the project was finally put into motion in 1997, it leveraged nearly 120 million dollars from municipal, autonomous, and national governments, as well subsidies provided from the emerging European Economic Community (now the European Union).

The improvements to the infrastructure in the neighborhood included the replacement of sewers and the construction of underground parking in many of the plazas.[36] These projects also included the transformation of the ruins of the Escuela Pías building in the Plaza Augustín Lara into a new library for the National University of Distance Learning, the renovation of the Casino de la Reina park, and a flurry of construction activity associated with cultural institutions and facilities in and around Lavapiés. Amongst these new or renovated institutions there was the architect Jean Nouvel's ninety-two-million-euro expansion of the Reina Sofia museum in 2002; the construction of the Centro Dramático Nacional Teatro Valle-Inclán in the Plaza Lavapiés in 2003; a remodeling of the Teatro Circo Price in 2007; and a shifting series of plans for a new national museum on the site of the iconic Tobacco Factory, or La Tabacalera, a building from the eighteenth century that had been one of the main employers in the neighborhood for many years. This public investment was complemented by the opening of the social and cultural center, La Casa Encendida, by the foundation of the large, regionally owned savings bank Caja Madrid (the fourth-largest financial institution in Spain).[37]

While originally declared in 1994, the ARPs really began to spur action when they were folded into the broader urban plan for Madrid laid out in the Plan General de Ordenación Urbana of 1997 (hereafter known as the Urban Plan of 1997). It was a plan that quite explicitly sought to position Madrid – in the words of former Vice-Mayor Ignacio del Río García de Sola – "amongst the great capitals of the world."[38] Relying on investment in infrastructure, subsidies for housing rehabilitation and construction, and new cultural installations, the Urban Plan of 1997 would position Madrid to compete within a post-industrial economy driven by tourism, advanced services (i.e., finance, accounting, consulting, insurance, etc.), construction, and real estate. Madrid would become a "Global City" – a term coined by Saskia Sassen to refer to large cities like London, Tokyo, and New York that serve as command-and-control centers for the circuits of global capital.[39] While Madrid would never be an alpha city like those global metropolises, it was believed that Madrid could become one of the top beta cities by leveraging its corporate footprint across Latin America and the Mediterranean arc. These efforts were to be bolstered by a major rebranding effort that would culminate – so the plan hoped – in a winning bid for the 2012 Summer Olympic Games (a bid that ultimately was awarded to London). It was to be Madrid's coming-out party in the European arena as a second-tier

Paris or London with the ability to successfully attract international tourists and foreign investment and enough cultural caché to unseat Barcelona as Spain's urban crown jewel.

Within these plans for transforming Madrid, Lavapiés would play a central role. The neighborhood was to become a cultural playground, an urban stage through which domestic and international tourists would pass on their way between the city's other important (and adjacent) cultural sites. In this sense, the seemingly local efforts to rehabilitate the neighborhood deeply intertwined with a broader global competition between cities. What took place in Lavapiés in the first decade of the twenty-first century highlights the complicated nature of urban change in a globalized world. Through its symbolic value, the cultural geography of a neighborhood folds into the scale of the metropolitan; the metropolitan folds into national economic and political agendas; and all of these intertwine within the unfolding of administrative, cultural, and social bodies at the supranational level, like the European Union.[40]

Notably, during this same period Lavapiés also emerged as a locus of local, national, and global resistance movements. As a result, Lavapiés demonstrates what urban theorist Andy Merrifield has called the metropolitan dialectic: the urban is both the site where tremendous inequality is produced (often in the form of gentrification) along with remarkable cultural flourishing.[41] Indeed, it is often the latter that contributes to the former. Thus, to discuss the production of urban space in Lavapiés during the early part of the twenty-first century juxtaposes a wide variety of spectacles – some capitalist, some resistant, but all caught up in the fundamental question of who has a "right to the city," a question that has inspired many of the most important writers and thinkers in urban studies, from Lefebvre and Harvey to Don Mitchell and Manuel Delgado.

These spectacles of protest included some of the most iconic and influential squatted social centers in Madrid. In their emphasis on self-management (*autogestión*), horizontal modes of organization, assembly-driven decision making, and pervasive notions of the "commons," they would be incubation spaces for the tactics, know-how, and ideological orientations of the 15-M protest movement.[42] Without the squatted social centers of the early 2000s, the month-long occupation of space in the Puerta del Sol in Madrid and other plazas in 2011 would not have taken the shape that they did.[43] Notably, the energy of political incubation that began in Lavapiés and flowered in the Puerta del Sol continued to bear fruit beyond that summer of encampments in the form of neighborhood assemblies, various anti-austerity *mareas* (waves), and the emergence in 2014 of the upstart political party Podemos.[44] In short, the physical and discursive reconfiguration of urban space at the local level not only played a key role in a global strategy for rebranding and selling Madrid, but simultaneously activated local protest networks that would later move onto the national and global stage.

SPECTACLES OF URBAN SPACE

What remains consistent between these two seemingly countervailing processes and the central focus of this book is a certain spectacular use of urban space. In other words, these local, municipal, and (inter)national spaces were not only bound together by conflicting approaches to producing the city, but also by a certain theatrical use of the city. These spectacles ranged from theater performances in shiny new theater and museum buildings to new residential construction projects.[45] It also included theater performances in spaces appropriated by *okupas* (activist squatters) as well as theatrical protest tactics in public plazas amongst the manicured facades of rehabilitated historic buildings. Understood together, these spectacles demonstrate how urban space in the contemporary city has become the stage where different actors physically and discursively remake the city – some intended to commodify the city and the practice of everyday life and others that contest that neo-liberal vision.

The interweaving of seemingly local processes of urban rehabilitation with global flows of capital and investment does not make Lavapiés unique – indeed, for urban planners and geographers these issues have been central to their studies of gentrification and urban development in a global frame for some time.[46] Nonetheless, the intersection of the cultural and the material is an area lacking development within the field of Geography. Likewise, the spatial component of cultural production is often ignored by scholars of the Humanities. French urban theorist Henri Lefebvre's theories of social space offer a very useful framework for working across these disciplines because of his emphasis on the dialectic between the built environment and social modes of being, and readers will note the influence of Lefebvre's book *The Production of Space* on the analysis I present throughout this study. Most central to my approach is

Lefebvre's argument that "every society ... produces its own space" and as a result, space should be understood not as an inert stage for human endeavor, but rather as a process.[47] In basic terms, his triad of spatial production suggests a continual dialectical interaction amongst the rhythms of everyday life, the imagination of artists, and the movement of financial capital, as expressed in the constant building and rebuilding of the built environment in response to these various cultural and material vectors.

My approach looks specifically to theater as the means of studying cities and social space because it is the literary tradition that most fully engages with the space of the city: theater arguably requires space and the public to truly exist in a way that other literary genres do not. I also believe that Madrid is unique, because of both its important role in the development of the Spanish theater tradition, as well as its use as a stage for the expression of monarchical power. Thus, it is through the theater that the city's geographical complexity surrounding issues of scale, urban space, and the related conflicts over urban space and territory can best be explored. Therefore, I will demonstrate not only that Lavapiés is deeply connected to broader economic and cultural practices taking place in Spain during the last fifteen to twenty years, but that the urban landscape of Madrid has long been used as a theater for articulating power across various geographic scales. As a means of distilling this Lefebvrian triad into an urban context that allows for both the study of actual theatrical texts as well as theatrical uses of the city, I use the term urban spectacle – a term that resonates with both my interest in theater and the process of urban development.

From Roman processionals to postmodern Olympic games, cities have been the stage for innumerable spectacles throughout history. As a result, I am certainly not the first writer to use the analogy with the theater as a way to discuss the city. From Lewis Mumford's assertion that the city is a "theater for social action" that both "creates the theater and is the theater" to Richard Sennett's explorations of "spectator architecture" in his essay "The Public Realm," the staging of cities and our performance within them has been a continuing theme for writers and philosophers from a wide range of fields.[48] Indeed, in the Iberian context, Catalonian anthropologist Manuel Delgado takes this analogy head-on in his book *El animal público* [*The Public Animal*], questioning its validity for understanding public space and positing instead that the theater of public space, lacking a coherent plot, is merely a series of sketches.[49] Likewise, he also considers the neo-liberal spectacle of the contemporary city in his influential critique of the Barcelona Model.[50] Despite sharing a concern with issues of public space and contemporary cities, I engage with this metaphor in a much different way, because I look to actual theaters, theater texts, and performances to tease out the ways that cultural production has become one of the fault lines between neo-liberal urban development and the urban activism of citizens defending their right to the city.

In articulating the city in terms of its spectacles, readers will also recognize the important influence of Situationist philosopher Guy Debord. Urban space for Debord was fundamentally about spectacle and the tensions between the spontaneity of everyday life and the conversion of daily life in the city into an endless consumer experience. The Situationists did much to map, challenge, and sketch the "psychogeography" of the city through their playful *dérives*, or drifts, through the city, tactics intended to highlight and subvert the everyday rhythms of the modern city, break through the bourgeois spectacle, and rediscover the humanity found in everyday life: children in parks, the elderly on park benches, etc. These playful strolls were complemented by a more radical *détournement*, or monkey-wrenching, of city space, carried out through counter-spectacles manifest in the occupations of buildings and streets.

Debord's idea of spectacles and counter-spectacles provides a key theoretical framework for discussing Madrid and Lavapiés, but this term has a number of layers that require further explanation. In the most general way, I use the term urban spectacle to refer to the physical transformation of the city into a cultural product intended to attract international capital in the form of investment and tourists. Like Debord, I also include the counter-spectacles that accompany this process of urban change in the form of protests, squatting, and encampments that challenge the reification of the city as mere commodity. I argue that, while the urban spectacle of contemporary Lavapiés is instructive about urban development in the twenty-first century, the particularity of the theater tradition in Madrid and Lavapiés forms an important palimpsest – both material and textual – that cannot be ignored.[51] Therefore, as I have stated, I also use it in a more literal way to refer to the theater buildings, theatrical performances, and theater texts where these conflicts over urban space occur.

I look to these very particular types of spectacles because of the deep historical linkages in both Lavapiés and Madrid between theater, urban space, and the cultural imaginary. From royal processions to military parades, Madrid has a rich tradition of serving as a stage for the consolidation of national identities, a fact that will be shown in the early chapters of this volume. Likewise, in Lavapiés, too, the spatial and the imaginary converge in the neighborhood's unique role as both a site and subject of Madrid's theater tradition, a history that is a fundamental and compelling backdrop to understanding contemporary Lavapiés. Importantly, whether as a strategic site in a new redevelopment plan or the subject of popular musical theater, spectacles in Lavapiés have always been embedded within a network of geographical discourses that spanned the local, the municipal, the national, and even the global (depending on the historical moment). Examining a broad historical period in Madrid's history, I argue that theatrical spaces (understood broadly) illustrate the Lefebvrian idea that *"social spaces interpenetrate one another and/or superimpose themselves upon one another."*[52] Thus it is also in this discussion of geographic scale that my "urban spectacle" differs from Debord.

THE PLAN OF THE PRESENT WORK: A LEFEBVRIAN TRIAD

In the coming chapters I will explore the multifaceted ways that the rehabilitation of Lavapiés should be understood as an urban spectacle, while also demonstrating how the symbolic value underpinning this rehabilitation relies in part on a very particular historical legacy. To study Lavapiés in this way draws on a large and expansive body of scholarship, which includes not only the previously mentioned authors, but also the work of scholars like Sharon Zukin, Gerry Kearns and Chris Philo, Jamie Peck, Loretta Lees, and David Harvey, others that have delineated the important connections between the production of culture, capital, and real-estate speculation.[53] Through the study of Madrid's historical connections between city space, spectacle, and power, I demonstrate how the affective meaning of spaces in the city informs the way the city is used and imagined today.

The first chapter focuses on Madrid and the way that theater and theatrical uses of urban space helped to perpetuate a spatial synecdoche, whereby Madrid would take on associations with the entire territory of Spain. I emphasize how the emergence of commercial theater in the late-sixteenth century and the use of public plazas like the Plaza Mayor and the Puerta del Sol were used to reinforce a spatial imaginary, in which Madrid formed the center of the Spanish Empire and (later) the modern State – cultural palimpsests that would later inform the symbolic power of that first 15-M encampment, called the Acampada Sol, which took place in Madrid's iconic Puerta del Sol in 2011. The second chapter narrows this focus by demonstrating how the urban spectacles found in the *sainetes*, or short plays, by Ramón de la Cruz in the eighteenth century and the popular operetta tradition of the *zarzuela* from the nineteenth and early-twentieth centuries reinforced these spatial synecdoches by metonymically linking Madrid and Spain in a *castizo* myth whose referent was the capital's lower-class neighborhoods, most notably Lavapiés.

In Chapters 3 through 5, I use Henri Lefebvre's tripartite understanding of social space as an organizing tool. Chapter 3 focuses on the neighborhood's important role as the focus of the Urban Plan of 1997, paying particular attention to the construction of the Centro Dramático Nacional Teatro Valle-Inclán in 2003. I frame this analysis within Lefebvre's notion of "conceived space" – according to Lefebvre, the space of "scientists, planners, urbanists, technocratic sub-dividers and social engineers."[54] Also called abstract space, it is the terrain in which capitalism articulates its codes, its requirements, its separation of labor, and its separation of reproductive and productive space. In this chapter, I demonstrate how the investment in cultural institutions at the scale of the urban – like this new national theater building – were intimately tied to a broader rehabilitation of Madrid, and the global profile of both Spain and its capital city. Moving from the "conceived space" of institutionalized cultural production in Lavapiés, Chapter 4 analyzes the iconic Self-Managed Squatted Social Center El Laboratorio 03 (El Labo 03). Through the study of manifestos, activity schedules, video documentation of protests, and theater activities, I demonstrate how the Labo articulated a new "perceived" space for the neighborhood – a series of spatial practices that sought to reimagine the social relations within the neighborhood. These resistant cultural practices not only defended the "right to the city" at the scale of Madrid, but also became incorporated into a broad defense of the dignity of everyday life outside the logic of global capital.

The final chapter analyzes the representation of Lavapiés in two contemporary dramas: David Planell's play *Bazar*, which uses

Lavapiés as the setting to explore the challenges confronting the burgeoning immigrant populations of "new" Spain, and César López Llera's *Un chivo en la Corte del botellón o Valle-Inclán en Lavapiés*, a reworking of Ramón María del Valle-Inclán's canonical *Luces de bohemia* (*Bohemian Lights*) to contemplate the dynamic between art and the city in the Madrid of the early 2000s. Reading Lavapiés through these dramatic works reveals one aspect of what Lefebvre describes as the neighborhood's "lived" or "representational" space. Key to this part of the triad is the idea that this representational space is "alive: it speaks. It has an affective kernel or centre: Ego, bed, bedroom, dwelling, house; or square, church, graveyard."[55] If spatial practice refers to the ways that our bodies move through space, and representations of space generate our logical codification of space, then representational spaces account for the emotional and symbolic encounters that individuals have with space.

Through this discussion of representational spaces, spaces of representation, and spatial practice in Lavapiés, I demonstrate how the physical and discursive reconfiguration of urban space by the various "actors" (i.e., urban planners, dramatists, activists, residents, etc.) at the local level of Lavapiés was deeply engaged with broader economic and political processes taking place in Madrid and Spain at this time. Understanding the urban history of both Madrid and Lavapiés through this lens offers insight into the emergence of the 15-M movement, the rise of Podemos, and the economic trends that led to the economic crisis. It is my contention that, through the history of urban spectacles in Madrid, we might better understand how stages in the city and the city as stage have long been implicated in the negotiation of identities and geographies at the local, municipal, and global scales.

I

The Stage of a Nation: The Urban Theater of Madrid

Each spring, on May 15, the streets of Madrid are turned into an urban spectacle dedicated not only to Madrid's patron saint, San Isidro Labrador (1082–1130), but also more generally to the city's folkloric *castizo* culture.[1] While in Latin America the term was deployed in the service of hierarchies of race and caste, in Spain it typically has alluded to a folkloric vision of Madrid's working-class neighborhoods in the early-twentieth century and the street celebrations called *verbenas* and *romerías* that accompanied the annual feast day of San Isidro and other *fiestas castizas*, such as those dedicated to neighborhood saints like La Paloma, San Lorenzo, and San Cayetano. In addition to the liturgical significance, the festival of San Isidro has also become a de facto celebration of Madrid's popular culture in the city's *barrio bajos*, neighborhoods like Lavapiés and La Latina that occupy the steep slopes just south of the city's historic quarter.

This *castizo* tradition owes much of its popularity and perseverance to Madrid's unique tradition of lyric theater known as the *zarzuela*, which rose to popularity in the mid-nineteenth century, but whose roots extend back to the seventeenth century. Scholars like Carmen del Moral Ruiz suggest that these images of Madrid's *barrios bajos* were disseminated so consistently and with such frequency that the myth of Madrid was "forged" by the *zarzuela* and its shorter form, the *género chico*.[2] Given Madrid's heritage as a destination for immigrants from the rural provinces, it was a myth that presented a certain notion of populist authenticity, but in fact synthesized many of the provincial traditions brought from Galicia, Andalusia, rural Castilla, and other parts of Spain during the various waves of immigrants that arrived in Madrid after it was named the site of the royal court in 1561. In this sense, ironically, the contemporary expressions of "authentic" Madrid one might see on May 15 are more or less fabrications.

As Henri Lefebvre has suggested, the production of space is more than merely bricks and mortar and the movement of people. These festival days reproduce this culturally imagined city today, but it is in the actual theaters of Madrid where it has its roots, a subject that forms the focus of this chapter. While it was the popular theater of Madrid that was central to fossilizing these notions of *madrileño* identity in the cultural imaginary of the late-nineteenth and early-twentieth centuries, this process emerged out of a long history of theater production in Madrid in which local, municipal, and (inter)national identities were perpetually interwoven. The following chapter explores this historiography and lays the groundwork for understanding the relationship between theater and urban development in contemporary Lavapiés discussed in later chapters.

It focuses on three key points while demonstrating that, from the early-modern period forward, the theater of Madrid helped to produce both the physical and imaginary city. First, I discuss the significance of Madrid as an urban center of theater production and illustrate the ways in which this theater culture arose alongside concerted efforts by the monarchy to use urban space as a stage for political spectacle. Secondly, I show that these efforts to use city space to project Madrid as the ideological center of Spain would continue as the modern state coalesced in the nineteenth century, albeit through the use of new iconic spaces like the Puerta del Sol. Finally, I discuss how the production of these local identities at the urban scale became imbued with national and international geographies: a symbolic vocabulary that would be utilized for both expressions of autocratic power by the Franco regime and later in the protests of the 15-M movement.

THE URBAN THEATER OF MADRID

Ever since it was named the site of the Spanish court by Philip II in 1561, Madrid has been the point of intersection between urban change and theater. One high-water mark in this history occurred during what is often called Spain's *Siglo de oro*, or Golden Age,[3] a period in which the first permanent commercial theater spaces developed and Madrid became a center of theatrical production. These early theaters relied on the interior central patios of buildings to create *corrales de comedia* (drama corrals). Although technically the first permanent *corral* was built in Seville in 1574, the most influential and paradigmatic *corrales* (namely the Corral de la Cruz and the Corral del Principe) were built in Madrid, and this model would be replicated across the burgeoning nation-state.[4]

From early on, the theater in Spain was intimately connected with the space of the city. It is a relationship that began around the ninth century, with theater's liturgical roots in the performance of "sung tropes" (interpolated phrases), both inside churches and then on the streets.[5] Corpus Christi became a particularly important festival in this regard when the use of floats and *tableaux vivants* were used to perform allegorical morality plays.[6] In the late-fifteenth and early-sixteenth centuries, guilds and *cofradías* (charitable brotherhoods) took over these productions from the churches, and the theatrics and spectacle of the medieval church would shift from interior spaces to the city streets of emerging urban centers – the ensuing spectacles atop horse-drawn wagons becoming a fixture of the processional culture that would develop around important feast days like Christmas, Easter, and Corpus Christi. During the late-medieval and early-modern periods, according to Maureen Flynn, performances for the elaborate rituals of Christianity, like the blood-spattered spectacle of *penitentes* on Holy Thursday, "served the same function as *tragic theater* in ancient times."[7] Often these processions would become an important means for creating the representational space that constructs our emotional relationship with a site. For Margaret Greer, the performance of these liturgical spectacles in these incipient urban environments demarcated "the consecrated heart of the community."[8] The selection of the route and the hierarchical ordering of the various groups within these processionals helped to define the social order. Later, when the administration of these processions fell under the purview of the municipal government instead of the Church, Corpus Christi processions would become expressions of local pride and an arena for early forms of interurban competition – a foreshadowing of the important role of the cultural arts some five hundred years later in the globalized iteration of this type of municipal competition.[9]

Significantly, these public spectacles emerged just as Europe, and Madrid in particular, became increasingly urbanized, a demographic shift that followed the population reductions caused by the Black

Death.[10] In the case of Madrid, the growth might be described as explosive. The city's population almost quadrupled over the course of the sixteenth century, due in part to Philip II's designation of Madrid as the site of the Royal Court.[11] From 1550 to 1600, Madrid saw its population explode from about 20,000 inhabitants to nearly 100,000 (400 per cent growth), and reach almost 130,000 by 1630 (525 per cent growth).

The proto-dramas of the late-medieval period were public events that relied upon an interaction with a public in a developing urban landscape to communicate an ideological message to a generally illiterate public. For example, the shift from the sacred space of the church to the street for the public performance of liturgy caused the dramatic space of the temple to overlay the physical space utilized outside of it. Eva Castro Caridad offers a useful description of this process, citing how "the disposition of places in urban space ... would always respect the orthogonal axis: East (Paradise), West (Hell), North (Christianity), South (Paganism), known already from inside the temple." This organization of the space would convert "all of the plaza ... into a stage space, creating specific places (the Throne, the Heavens, the Mount of Olives, the Castle of Herod, the Doors of Hell)."[12] Eventually this use of the public plaza for sacred performances would be replaced by the more civic spectacles of royal processions and other secular events. The mixing of the sacred and the secular, according to Castro Caridad, would be the "genesis of the city as a stage space in the history of the Spanish theater."[13] Through the processional tradition, urban space developed into a key site for the performance and communication of ideology – both political and religious.[14]

Madrid has a particularly notable history in this regard, because the city was literally an urban stage for the performance of political power: a set piece in the construction of a national identity and the power of the sovereigns.[15] Authors Virgilio Pinto Crespo and Santos Madrazo describe how the traditional processional route began in the convent of Nuestra Señora de Atocha in the southeast corner of the city, on the edge of the grounds of the Palace of the Buen Retiro (now the Retiro park). The royal procession would follow the calle Atocha, skirt the outlying neighborhoods of Lavapiés, and pass through the city gate at Antón Martín. Continuing through what is now the Plaza Mayor (then the Plaza de Arrabal), the procession would end at the Alcázar (now the Royal Palace).[16] At a predetermined place (often the triumphal arch along the calle San Jerónimo), the leaders of the municipality would submit themselves to the authority of the king, while an actor portraying an allegorical image of the town would simultaneously offer the keys to the sovereign.[17] The locality of Madrid subjugated itself to the consolidated centralized power of what might tentatively be called the nation – a body politic represented exclusively by the personage of the monarch.

During the sixteenth century, other forms of performance began to complement these official processions, and the theater began to develop its more modern form (both artistically and economically). Initially, these secular theater productions (performances approaching our modern notions of drama) were limited to private performances, while public space was reserved for religious passion plays (*autos*) and wandering minstrels (*jongleurs*). Influenced by Italian dramas – both in content and business model – Lope de Rueda and Alonso de la Vega organized the first commercial theater companies by combining comedic public performance with elements of the *commedia dell'arte*, a theatrical tradition imported from Italy that already had a popular following.[18] The short one-act *pasos* of Lope de Rueda gave way to the longer and more elaborate dramas of the seventeenth century as a formal industry of commercial public theater began to consolidate. The financing of the theater shifted from the exclusive patronage of religious organizations, municipalities, and the nobility to an institution based on individual ticket sales. This democratization not only subjected the theater to the influence of market forces, but it also broadened its audience and transformed the works of the Baroque period into products for mass consumption.

CORRALES DE COMEDIA AND THE ARCHITECTURE OF EARLY-MODERN THEATER

The rise of commercial theater in Spain led to increasingly more permanent performance spaces. Even as early as the seventeenth century – as will be shown – the representational space of the theater became an important point of articulation between a nascent national sensibility and a municipal identity. The theater – understood broadly – would be implicated in what Lefebvre describes as the abstract space of the city and help to leverage the urban landscape as a tool for the projection of power across a range of geographic scales.[19] The *corrales de comedia*, as they were known, became ground zero for the veritable theatrical boom that took place during the seventeenth century. It is in part because of the remarkable number and quality of the works produced during this period that the early-seventeenth century earned its "Golden Age" moniker – a term that makes reference not only to the presumed high aesthetic quality of the works, but also the literal gold from the Americas that was (barely) funding the crown. In the theaters of the period, playwrights began to negotiate the new geographical boundaries of an embryonic nation-state by contemplating the changing power dynamics of the period.

The term *corrales* refers to the central patio that was a mandated part of new residential construction in the Madrid of Philip II. The royal decree intended to take advantage of the long, narrow parcels of land into which the city had been subdivided in order to meet the housing needs of a swelling population.[20] Because of their enclosed nature and the built-in hierarchy of seating created by the two levels with inward-facing balconies, these domestic spaces converted easily into commercial spaces for performances of theater (see Figure 1.1). Originally, these theater spaces were owned by religious charitable brotherhoods called *cofradías*, and were used to raise money for hospitals for the poor. The theater companies would lease the space from the *cofradías*, who in turn received a cut of the box-office profits, money that they would subsequently use to fund their charitable projects. The architecture of the *corrales* allowed the operators to more easily control access to the interior patio through the use of tickets.[21] As the system of *corrales* developed into permanent spaces specifically designed for theatrical productions, they also became more commercial. With concerns over both the content of the works and the behavior of the patrons (particularly the attendance of women), the Council of Castile (basically the municipal government) became ever more involved in the management of the spaces and maintained tight controls on the frequency and duration of performances. As the *cofradía*'s distribution of profits began to include the city's General Hospital, this close oversight only grew more pronounced, since the managers of the *corrales* reported directly to the Protector of the Hospitals, an important figure because of his status as a member of the City Council.[22] In this way, the municipal government's involvement in the management of the spaces grew, particularly as the theaters became a major source of revenue for the city treasury – a fact that helped insulate the theater industry against moralist objections.

Figure 1.1 | Drawing of Corral del Príncipe.

The most famous of these *corrales* – the Corral de la Cruz built in 1579–80 and the Corral del Príncipe constructed in 1582–83 – were built by a joint venture between the Cofradía de la Pasión y Sangre de Jesucristo and the Cofradía de la Soledad de Nuestra Señora.[23] In contrast to the makeshift *corrales*, living spaces converted into commercial theater spaces, these two *corrales* would be constructed with a permanent stage and seating, as well as an awning to protect the audience. The cities would take a percentage of the profits from the door, with the monies eventually making their way to the various hospitals around the city. But the city was not the only beneficiary of this new commercial enterprise, as the adjacent buildings to these permanent *corrales* were not owned by either the city or the *cofradías*. As a result, the owners of those buildings began a side business selling tickets to access the windows that looked down upon the performance space. Often, these owners even went so far as to construct box seats that would extend into the space of the *corral*. In many cases, the purchase of an adjacent "room with a view" was seen as an investment opportunity, and some owners, such as the Almirante de Castilla, invested in five or six boxes as a way to generate income.[24] In each case, the owners of these buildings would give a cut of their profits to the theater companies producing the performance. Thus, a snapshot from the seventeenth century of one of these two principal permanent *corrales* reveals a spatial collage of private and publicly owned spaces devoted simultaneously to the production of theatrical performance and financial capital.

It was in these two theaters where one of the greatest flourishing of theater production in the history of Spain (and, arguably, Western Europe) would occur. They were, in short, an architectural testimony to the significant role that the *comedia* came to play in the Madrid of the sixteenth and seventeenth centuries.[25] The volume of works produced was astounding. Morely and Bruerton attribute eight hundred plays to Lope de Vega, four hundred to Tirso de Molina, and 180 to Calderón de la Barca.[26] By comparison, William Shakespeare, writing at about the same time, is given credit for thirty-seven plays. Some estimates suggest that, in the seventeenth century alone, the Spanish theater industry produced some ten thousand plays and one thousand *autos*.[27] There was, to say the least, a remarkably strong market for the production and consumption of theater from the late-sixteenth to the middle of the seventeenth century.

Significantly, it was during this time of rich and varied cultural production that Spain's fortunes as the most powerful empire in Europe began to decline, as its imperial project unraveled.[28] In the midst of a series of national crises, the *comedias* not only played an important role in altering the uses of urban space in Madrid, but they also contributed to an emerging sense of national identity by producing a shared cultural vocabulary of dramatic figures and plots. Within this line of argumentation, Melveena McKendrick suggests that, faced with a culture of crisis, "the *corrales* responded with a national drama of epic achievement and individual self-assertion that allowed the Spaniard, when he gazed for a while into its mirror, to burnish his self-image and go away reassured."[29] The sheer volume of works produced and consumed in Madrid, combined with their affordability, broadened the influence of the *comedia*.[30] If, for Benedict Anderson, the "imagined communities" of modern states were formed partially from the public sphere found in an emerging print culture, then, based on the sheer numbers of people consuming the *comedias* and the socio-economic diversity of that public, one can conjecture that the dramatic representations of the *corrales* may have contributed to an emerging sense of collective and – we might even venture – national cultural identity.[31] It is perhaps here that the populace of Madrid would begin to "imagine" itself a community capable of constituting the modern Spanish nation.[32]

At the minimum, the theater played a key role in developing the cultural influence of Madrid. As James Casey argues, the support of the monarchy contributed greatly to the growth of the theater industry, allowing its influence to broaden substantially. Madrid became capable of reproducing its own hegemonic influence as not only a center of culture and power, but also through the use and influence of the Castilian language.[33] The commercial theaters arose alongside other emerging spaces for artistic and cultural production, such as printing shops and painting academies. Within this context, particular notions of power and culture, like the monarchy, the role of the nobility, and honor and revenge, would find constant reinforcement in the *comedias* of the period, an idea advanced by a number of scholars.[34] If the *corrales* played no role in forming the idea of the nation, they certainly helped to reinforce the values that would come to be associated with that nation.

The dramatic innovations of the *comedias* helped to plant these seeds of the modern state. Underpinning these innovations was a fairly rigid structure that had emerged from the pervasive influence of the Italian theater tradition. According to Nancy D'Antuono, the Italianate quality of the Spanish theater made it palatable to seventeenth-century Spanish audiences because dramatists like Lope de Vega had codified many of the structural components of the *commedia dell'arte*: a three-act structure, balance, and duplication in plot and characters.[35] Central to this "standardization" was the use of *tipos-personajes*, or character-types, that recurred throughout *comedias* of the period and made these works both easy to write (hence the remarkable volume) as well as easy to consume. In his influential *History of the Spanish Theater*, Francisco Ruiz Ramón identifies these principal "types" as the *galán* (young man), the *dama* (the maiden), the *rey* (the king), the *gracioso* (the fool), the *caballero* (the knight or gentleman), the *villano* (the villain), and the *poderoso* (the powerful lord).[36] These *tipos* were at times not mutually exclusive and could be overlapping, but they did create certain expectations for the public that could then be exploited by the dramatists. The fact that audience members generally knew what to expect from each character's *tipo* and how they would behave offered clear clues about how and when the social order would or wouldn't be restored. It was this reliance on *tipos* that made many Baroque *comedias* so effective at playing with the ambiguities between reality and appearance.

Other innovations in the Spanish *comedia* included a resistance to the Aristotelian division between comedy and tragedy, a change that led to the inclusion of kings and commoners as protagonists on the same stage. As these categories began to blur in the Spanish theater, the innovation would bring "the figure of the king down from his Greek association with divinity and heroism, set above other men, to the position of an ordinary mortal, having to deal with the conflicts, passions, and obstacles of life on earth."[37] The king became a man amongst other men, with the power previously invested in his persona now derived from elsewhere, an external fountain of power that would eventually become the state. Nonetheless, absolutism was ascendant politically from the seventeenth century until the late-eighteenth century, but, ironically, also implied the need to consolidate power against old rivals for power like the Church and the increasing influence of the aristocracy, the guilds, and a developing middle class. Campbell emphasizes that the rise in absolutism that occurred during this period "operated not through the unrelenting imposition of their authority, but through a process of negotiation and cooperation with existing powers."[38] The world of the *comedia* problematized the relationship between the king and the people by placing them as dramatic equals in many of the stories they created, while also reinforcing social values and mores like honor and duty.[39] Despite the unsettling of the social hierarchy occurring outside the *corrales*, more often than not the king's authority and role as *deus ex machina* remained unquestionable.

One dramatic work which helps illustrate this tension between an emerging populist politics and steadfast conservatism is Félix Lope de Vega y Carpio's canonical *Fuente Ovejuna* (1619). While the themes are relevant to my argument, the example is also compelling, because it is one of the most important plays written by perhaps *the* most important dramatist of this period (with all due respect to Pedro Calderón de la Barca). The play's central argument describes an actual historical event that took place in a small village near Córdoba:

the popular uprising in the town of Fuente Ovejuna in 1476. As in the events that inspired the play, the military, political, and religious overlord of Fuente Ovejuna, el Comendador Fernán Gómez, is killed by the local villagers in retribution for tyrannical acts of rape and theft against the townspeople. In the drama's third and final act, these tensions between tyranny, sovereignty, and the collective will of the people come to a head when a judge sent by King Ferdinand and Queen Isabella arrives to investigate the brutal murder of Gómez. In what is perhaps the drama's most compelling scene, the judge confronts the villagers, demanding to know who killed the Comendador. Resident after resident approaches to declare: "It was Fuente Ovejuna, Lord" – one after another refusing to name any one individual, each asserting that the town collectively perpetrated the crime. In the play's finale, the intransigence of the townspeople forces the judge to appear before the King and Queen and explain that they must accept the transgression as a collective act and either pardon the collective or kill them all. The monarchs, although held up as the final arbiters of justice, and therefore the ultimate legal authority, are really left with no option but to recognize the collective will of the people, forgive the crime, and restore order.

The work is notable in its almost modern vision of the "People" as a force capable of exerting its will against the ruling class. To temper this threatening vision of popular uprising, Lope de Vega goes to great lengths throughout the work to demonstrate the town's fealty to the Spanish king and queen. Indeed, even as the mob descends on the Comendador, the shouts of "¡Fuente Ovejuna! ¡Long live King Ferdinand!" ring out, and even as the bloodthirsty mob decapitates him, they continue reiterating "¡Our lords are the Catholic Kings!"[40] Likewise, in the final scene, as the townspeople appear remorsefully before the Spanish monarchs, they continue to proclaim their allegiance by celebrating the glory and beauty of the King and Queen of Spain. The fact that the dramatic action of the play takes place in the historical period after the death of Henry IV of Castile and the onset of the War of Castilian Succession is also potentially important to the play's overall ideological vision. With several scenes of Ferdinand and Isabella planning to take Ciudad Real from forces sympathetic to the King of Portugal, the play represents a Spain just on the cusp of territorial and political coalescence. In a separate plot line of the play, the armies of the Catholic Monarchs defeat a rebellion by military leaders in Ciudad Real. As a result, the monarchs are able to bring stability to

Castile and the Iberian peninsula. In very basic terms, it is the origin myth of the Spanish nation and presents the monarchs as forces of justice and stability that stand in stark contrast to the tyranny of Fernán Gómez; they are the benevolent rulers that restore justice not only to the town of Fuente Ovejuna but to the broader "national" terrain over which they rule. In this sense, the work is often viewed as highly monarchical in its ideological orientation – a reading that aligns with the view that most seventeenth-century theater merely promulgated the interests of the state and the elite, while nibbling around the edges of critique through thematic interest in false appearances and a culture of *desengaño*, or disillusionment.

In contrast to the image of monarchical stability offered by Lope's play, at the time the work was written – sometime between 1610 and 1619 – affairs in Spain, as mentioned earlier, were moving in the opposite direction. With this historical context of crisis in mind, McKendrick suggests a more ambivalent reading of Lope de Vega's drama. She argues that instead of seeing Lope's vision within these king-plays, as she calls them, as monolithic, there is a "systematic campaign of demystification and a concerned and penetrating dialogue about the relationship between men and the institution of monarchy."[41] Antonio Carreño Rodriguez echoes this line of reasoning by arguing that Lope's *comedias* should be understood as "allegories of power" that reject dominant modes of conduct by offering both positive models (like the Catholic Kings) and contrarian examples (like Fernán Gómez) of how to rule.[42] These are views that situate seventeenth-century drama, and the work of Lope in particular, more firmly within the crisis in which Spain found itself at the beginning of the seventeenth century.

Indeed, as McKendrick and Carreño have suggested, despite *Fuente Ovejuna*'s quasi-nationalist vision of the monarchy, the play is perhaps more astutely read as engaged in a contemplation of political power and sovereignty. It warns of the dangers of tyranny and the power of the people on the one hand, while on the other it presents a world held together by the strength of the Spanish monarchs. Significantly, the play makes clear that violence, or the threat of violence, underpins all the acts of power and justice in the play. This body politic built on violence evokes the work of sociologists Thomas Hansen and Finn Stepputat, who have argued that the "hard kernel of modern states" – as they call it – is found in "the internal constitution of sovereign power *within states* through the exercise of violence over bodies and populations."[43] In other words, sovereignty relies on the legal and *legitimate* use of violence by the state against its own people, an understanding that runs contrary to more popular notions of sovereignty that focus on the defense of one's territory against foreign incursions. That kings and feudal lords might use violence against their own people is, of course, nothing new, but Hansen and Stepputat's approach emphasizes that the state constitutes itself via this violence by disciplining – in the Foucaldian sense – the populace to accept this violence as a legitimate expression of authority. In its most basic terms, they suggest that the sovereign state to which an individual belongs is determined mostly by who has the legal right to enact violence on that individual.

What is compelling in *Fuente Ovejuna*, though, is the way that the use of violence is inverted and appears to flow both ways. Though the violent retribution by the townspeople requires an intervention by Ferdinand and Isabella – an intervention that situates them as the arbiters of justice – the violence that is committed on the body of the Comendador by the people of Fuente Ovejuna demonstrates that authority is not a power derived from birthright, but rather from the potential to enact violence on the body. Although the incipient state in the form of the monarchy has the authority to absolve and implicitly approve of the people's revolt, this power is in part granted by the people in their willingness not to revolt and carry out tyrannicide against the monarchs. It is this mutually constitutive equilibrium of violence that constructs the linkages amongst "state-territory-sovereignty."[44] Considering when it was published and the decadent state of Spain's imperial project, *Fuente Ovejuna* clearly seems to be firmly ensconced within more generalized discourses of the era that attempted to theorize the monarchy and its relationship to the state.[45]

In a more historical frame, it is this same negotiation of power between an absolutist monarchy and a people's movement that forms the focus of the opening case study in urban sociologist Manuel Castells's book *The City and the Grassroots*, a groundbreaking work that spans multiple geographies (Spain, the United States, Ireland, France, Chile) and time periods (from the sixteenth to the twentieth century).[46] His research on the revolt of the *comuneros* in Castile in 1520–22 reveals that nearly a hundred years preceding the publication and production of *Fuente Ovejuna* there had been "a citizen movement for local autonomy ... challenging the feudal order ... in search of a modern constitutional state."[47] Importantly, this research also reveals that, even as early as the first decades of the sixteenth century, the city functioned as both a technology of resistance as well as power. It is not only the place where power was consolidated, but also the stage for reforming the developing state. The impact of the *comuneros*, according to Castells, was profound, in that it transformed medieval cities from a "spatial form into an urban culture and a political institution."[48] This was a revolutionary development, in that the *comuneros* envisioned a new socio-political organization for society – "both in the cities themselves (the commune) and in the overall state (the parliament) as a representation of free cities."[49] It is perhaps exactly this anxiety and tension that is explored in *Fuente Ovejuna*. In the burgeoning metropolis of Madrid, the king's hold on power was perhaps seen as somewhat tenuous.[50] Given the fact that the *corrales* were attended by individuals of all social classes – including at times the king and the nobility – it was perhaps a pragmatic move by Lope de Vega to leave the political content of his work open to interpretation. Nonetheless, Lope could not stray too far from a vision that maintained the social order of the monarchy.

But even if the content of Lope's work and that of other dramatists of the period were ambivalent in their political content, the urban circumstances of theater production allowed the *corrales* to be one of the few forms of "mass" media available in the early-modern period, particularly for a general populace that was largely illiterate. Juan Aguilera Sastre suggests that the pragmatic utility afforded by the management of the *corrales* was not lost on officials in the city. For this reason, he writes, "in Spain the majority of the *corrales de comedias* in the seventeenth century were managed by official decrees – typically municipal – that guaranteed and controlled this important cultural instrument as a true weapon of political action in all of its social, economic, and ideological derivations."[51] The censorship in the *corrales de comedia* was one of the tools by which the city leaders, in conjunction with the church, sought to manage social behavior and "educate" the masses.

URBAN SPECTACLE AND THE SPACES OF THE MONARCHY

The pervasive influence of theater culture and spectacle in Madrid during the late-sixteenth and early-seventeenth century was not limited to these burgeoning theater spaces. The very urban fabric of the city contributed to the establishment of a "theater state," as José Antonio Maravall has called it.[52] While the ideologically conservative dramas performed in the Corral del Príncipe and the Corral de la Cruz produced the representational space of the cultural imaginary, the spaces of representation – that is, the spaces produced by urban planners and the practice of everyday life – were to be found in the material spectacle of the city's architectural landscape. In this sense, the proliferation of urban theater occurring in the *corrales* was merely one component of a broader drama in which the city itself became a stage on which to enact spectacles of power – demonstrations of pomp and circumstance that were intended to convey the authority of the crown and an emerging state apparatus. Notably, this multivalent urban spectacle was produced within the municipal space of everyday life, but was deeply enmeshed with signs and signifiers of the expansive Hapsburg empire. In other words, the presence of the Court made early-modern Madrid a variegated space that used the municipal scale to convey the global reach of the Spanish monarchy.

For scholars like Enrique García Santo-Tomás, this perspective has its limits, because it implies a fixed and immobile set piece, projecting power upon passive inhabitants. As he details so carefully in *Urban Space and Literary Creation in Philip IV's Madrid*, his important work on the interplay of the theater and the city in the seventeenth century, this view of early-modern Madrid ignores the ways in which new smells, different clothes, new foods, and even tobacco from the New World were reshaping the relationship between public and private life. Indeed, he suggests that Madrid was more a place of contradictions, where an emerging modernity was beginning to butt up against older power structures: "a place of the new and old, like a recurrent palimpsest."[53] The dynamic between an emergent urban experience and the city imagined on the stage, as well as the broader artistic milieu of bookstores, printing shops, and schools of painting, generated a certain amount of cultural discord and melancholy. It was the type of urban alienation that would later become the central concern of urban scholars and philosophers.[54] Thus one should not understand this "stage of power" to be all encompassing and the city's inhabitants merely passive recipients. For example, readers familiar with Madrid of this period will recall the famous *casas de malicia* [houses of spite] scattered throughout the city, which were constructed with the illusion of one story in order to skirt the royal decree that had made mandatory the housing of functionaries in houses of two stories or more.[55] Rather, it should be seen as an attempt to quell the very fissures that García Santo Tomás describes. The Baroque city would communicate power, stability, and solidity – the sense of social decadence countered by the force of imperial architecture.

The work of Jesús Escobar on the shaping of Baroque Madrid is particularly informative in this regard, particularly on the role of the Plaza Mayor as an urban stage for enacting the power of the state. The distinct architecture that would come to characterize the Hapsburgs conveyed this authority, a style best illustrated by the iconic Casa de la Panadería, which hems in the plaza's northern edge. Although this building was completed in 1607, the vision for the Plaza Mayor had begun much earlier, during the reign of Philip II, as he began to build the architecture of a global empire. Commencing in 1582–83, the demolition began of the irregular and uneven blocks of housing surrounding the Plaza de Arrabal – as it was formerly known – because of its location on the periphery of the medieval city. In its place would be a more open public space fit for royal festivals and processions, a space whose uniform architecture and unbroken lines would not only replace the old unsightly housing that had tarnished the appearance of the plaza for decades, but would also provide a reassuring image of rational organization that could provide a backdrop for the spectacles of monarchy.[56] Escobar emphasizes that in this context of monarchical spectacle the Casa de la Panadería would be imbued with immense symbolic value because of its central role in the city's network of bread distribution.[57] During Corpus Christi, when *cofradías* continued the medieval tradition of producing mobile *autos sacramentales*, people would linger in the Plaza Mayor, still under construction, while the Casa de la Panadería framed the scene – a bread market that communicated the benevolence of the monarchy while perhaps also alluding subtly to the spiritual power of communion.[58] Given that a bread crisis in 1589 had informed the rationale for constructing a centralized bread distribution center, the Casa de la Panadería stood as a symbol of the king's ability, as Escobar puts it, "to nourish his people." [59] Like the messages of good governance being communicated in the theaters of the time, the space of the city, too, served as a medium for producing the social space – to put it in Lefebvrian terms – of the urban environment in early-modern Madrid.

For this reason, this visually arresting building also evoked the monarch's power and reach. The mix of Flemish towers, the interplay of red brick with granite, and the rectilinear array of balconies astride uniform undulating porticos, evoked the architectural motifs of Philip II's palace-monastery El Escorial, a symbol both then and now of the imperial Catholic power of the Spanish monarch. The Casa de la Panadería brought into the city center a hybrid style that would be reproduced across the city in buildings and plazas like the Palacio de Santa Cruz (now the Office of Foreign Affairs) and the Ayuntamiento building found in the Plaza de la Villa, as well as others. García Santo-Tomás emphasizes how this architectural style became a source of pride for locals in the early-seventeenth century – especially after Philip III abruptly and briefly moved the court to Valladolid (1601–06) – and points to this nostalgia as an illustration of the sense of distinct urban identity that was emerging in Madrid.[60] The people had become *madrileños*.

In addition to fomenting a sense of municipal identity and fealty, the Hapsburg style also played a role in the projection of Spain's image as an international power – and, by association, Madrid as the center of that power. In Naples, Italy, for example, the Spanish viceroy Fernando Ruíz de Castro oversaw the construction of the Palazzo Reale by architect Domenico Fontana. Begun in 1599, this building, though far removed from the Spanish mainland, still maintained visual reference to Spanish influence and power in its dual towers, classical arcade, and use of pink stucco evocative of the contrasting brick and granite of the buildings in Madrid and El Escorial (see Figure 1.3). The ubiquity of this style across the major buildings of the city, combining Spanish, Italian, and Netherlandish architecture, as Escobar points out, "spoke to the concept of empire and the international realm of the Spanish Hapsburg monarch."[61] In the local domain of Madrid, the architectural symbols of the monarchy expressed the geography of empire, one so expansive that it included the Iberian peninsula, Flanders, Naples, the wide expanse of the Americas, and even the Philippines.

Yet the monarchy did not just use the Plaza Mayor as a stage for seemingly passive architectural spectacles like the Casa de la Panadería. The plaza was also converted into an actual theater space for the aforementioned mobile *auto sacramentales* of Corpus Christi, as well as for performances on temporary stages within the confines of the plaza. As a result, the surrounding buildings served not only a

Figure 1.2 | Plaza Mayor of Madrid.

residential purpose, but also as seating for the spectators. The Plaza Mayor was basically converted into one large *corral de comedias* for spectacles of both the church and the crown. The city built graded stands that rose up to the balconies lining the Plaza Mayor. In this "theater" with a capacity of nearly five thousand people, the prime seating for these events was as expensive as those of the theater houses. During the course of its history, the Plaza Mayor has served as a public site for everything from bullfights to the public spectacles of the *Santo Oficio* [Holy Office; i.e., the Spanish Inquisition]. From the sixteenth to the nineteenth century, the Plaza Mayor functioned as a municipal stage for performances of national and proto-national power. These changes redirected social and economic activity from the old quarter of the city and commercial spaces like the Plaza de la Paja, the Plaza de la Villa, and the Plaza de la Cebada out toward Madrid's evolving limits.[62] The reshaping of the Plaza Mayor into a space for spectacle also had a ripple effect on the city as a whole, as streets and traffic patterns had to be reconfigured to accommodate the new plaza.

Figure 1.3 | Palazzo Reale di Napoli. Naples, Italy.

As the final stop of processions that had navigated through carefully selected routes in the city, the Plaza Mayor also fit into the broader objective of transforming the whole city into a stage. For Ringrose, these urban transformations were focused on one goal: "converting the city into an immense and integrated physical decor that not only emphasized the message of the civic ceremonies, but rather was in and of itself the materialization of the power of the sovereign."[63] Thus the city was reorganized – blocks were demolished, streets straightened, facades improved – to convey a message of uniformity, a value that, during the late-sixteenth and early-seventeenth centuries, was closely associated with notions of good governance.[64] Likewise, the planning and construction of royal buildings and monuments were selected for their strategic locations along the city's ceremonial axis, providing permanent reminders of the authority evoked by the recurring yet ephemeral displays of royal power – a de facto placing of the city under the "royal gaze."[65]

Other spectacles were more diffuse and less focused. When Philip II designated Madrid the site of the Spanish court in 1561, it not only moved the administrative and bureaucratic functioning of the empire to the new capital, but created a space where individual performances of power and acquiescence translated into actual influence – a process that would reach its epoch during the reign of Philip IV.[66] It was the place to see and be seen for nobility and other hangers-on jockeying for power and influence. With the growth of the Spanish empire over the course of the sixteenth and seventeenth centuries, there was a commensurate growth in the size of the bureaucracy to manage it. To maintain control over a growing city and expansive kingdom, the king needed the assistance and cooperation of the local elites. By incorporating these nobles into the bureaucratic system, "the local elites from all parts were integrated into a web that made the king the focal point of the city."[67] It was a system of social organization that had impacts on the spatial organization of the elites, since the ability to gain physical proximity to the crown related directly to one's ability to receive the titles and positions that shaped a shifting social structure driven by bureaucratic power and influence. The largesse of royalty was to be found as a functionary of the crown as much as by owning large tracts of land. In short, as Ringrose suggests, "the goal was the Court, which implied residing in Madrid,"[68] the stage for the procurement and expressions of power. At times, the life of the Court spilled into the street, seizing any minor excuse to celebrate with *fiestas de máscaras* (costume parties) and equestrian events in public plazas. These public displays of the Court not only functioned as "mechanisms for maintaining or earning royal favor," as Pinto Crespo emphasizes, but also helped to reaffirm the control of urban space by the court and the monarchy.[69] The space of the city was both the stage for the grand spectacle of the monarchy, but also the place to rehearse the practice of everyday courtly life.

But the relationship between the court and the theater went beyond mere extravagance on festival days. María Luisa Lobato argues that "the theater served a pedagogic function in the society of the period," not just because it showed members of the court how to behave, but in many cases because members of the court actually participated in the stage performances as actors.[70] The members of the court participated both literally and figuratively in a spectacle of manners to impress each other and the king. In a similar vein, Patrick Williams cites the ways that both the Duke of Lerma and the Count-Duke of Olivares employed theatrical performances during festivals as a means of attracting court attention and creating a courtly orbit around themselves.[71] Indeed, the Buen Retiro Palace on the eastern edge of the city was built with this purpose in mind: to entertain the King and keep him far away from the levers of government found in the Alcázar across town.[72] The performances achieved such a level of extravagance that famous naval battles were re-enacted on the lagoon in the palace grounds. From the Plaza Mayor to private performances in the palaces of the nobles, Madrid was a city built both literally and figuratively on a theatrical tradition and spectacles of power.

In addition to the impact that these urban spectacles had in shaping the physical spaces and the cultural imaginary of Madrid in the seventeenth century, the drama of this period continues to resonate today. For example, in Juan Aguilera Sastre's extremely detailed history of the Teatro Español and the establishment of a national theater building in Spain, the author suggests that "the recuperation of classical theater had been, since its inception, the central theme in the polemic over the National Theater."[73] Sastre elaborates by summarizing that this emphasis on the role of the *Siglo de Oro* stemmed from the belief held by many commentators in the early-twentieth century that "the classics ... are the enduring patrimony of the national culture."[74] This example alludes to the fact that, throughout much of the twentieth century, the dominant discourses promulgated by Spanish academics and critics regarding this period have often linked Madrid, the theater, and the *Siglo de Oro* to a national cultural legacy in Spain. In this way, the theater and theaters of Madrid continue to produce ideological space for the Spanish nation.

MADRID, CASTILE, AND FASCIST SPECTACLE

In more modern and contemporary contexts, this close association between national identity and the theater of this period can be found in both scholarly and institutional contexts. For example, in Ruiz Ramón's previously mentioned history of the Spanish theater, written in 1964, he entitles his chapter on this period "The National Theater of the *Siglo de Oro*."[75] In line with this nationalist discourse, the former Ministry of Culture (since 2011 now a part of the Ministry of Education, Culture, and Sport) devotes one whole national theater company exclusively to the production of classical Spanish theater, a focus that implies the importance of the work of this period.[76] The codification of the late-sixteenth and early-seventeenth centuries as the high point of Spanish cultural production has resulted in the canonization of several important dramatists from Madrid. Calderón de la Barca, Lope de Vega, and Tirso de Molina have become almost synonymous with the literature of the *Siglo de*

Oro.[77] In this vein, it is no surprise then that city leaders organizing the culminating event in Madrid's bid to be selected as the European Cultural Capital for 1992 chose to recreate a Baroque *auto sacramental* as a way to represent not only Madrid's cultural heritage, but – given the international character of the event – Spain as well.[78]

Carey Kasten's work demonstrates how the canonization of Baroque theater culture, and particularly the *auto sacramental* – typically associated with Corpus Christi – became an important tool of the Francoist cultural regime, during the Civil War as well as after.[79] For Francoist intellectuals like Giménez Caballero, the mystery of the *auto sacramental* provided the most effective means of fusing the holy and the national.[80] More broadly, it brought the associations between the genre and the conservative values of the regime to the streets and plazas of Spain's towns and cities. The names of dramatists like Calderón de la Barca and others were used to form a cultural link with Spain's imperial past and its role as the strong arm of the Counter-Reformation. The use of the *auto* also simultaneously celebrated the period's cultural flourishing and alluded to the second cultural Golden Age that was to begin anew – so the logic went – now that the nation was again in the hands of the "righteous" guardians of National Catholicism.

On a grander scale, this fascist penchant for spectacle was merely a continuation of the regime's strategic use of urban space at the end of the Spanish Civil War in 1939 that sought to re-establish Madrid as the symbolic center of the Spanish state. As in the early-modern period, these national and imperial discourses regarding Madrid would rely on those Lefebvrian dynamics between representations of space and spaces of representation by relying on both discursive production and the organization and use of urban space. This process was particularly notable on the official final day of the Civil War, when Franco and his forces used Madrid as a stage from which to proclaim victory. The fact that the capital had been in the hands of the democratically elected Republican government during most of the war certainly added to the symbolism. It was to be the realization of a strategic objective that could not be achieved earlier in the conflict. From the outset of the war, Franco and his rebel forces had hoped that, by taking Madrid in the first days or weeks of the invasion, they would not only take advantage of Madrid's strategic position in the center of Spain – controlling passage to and from the Guadarrama mountains – but would also gain a symbolic victory that would re-establish Madrid as the heart of the Spanish empire. The failure to achieve this objective would only increase Madrid's value as a symbolic totem over the course of the war.

It should also be noted that Madrid carried significant symbolism for those fighting against the fascists. Indeed, the struggle for Madrid – a siege that would last nearly the entire Civil War – would come to be seen as a synecdoche of the broader struggle for Spain as a whole. When communist leader Dolores Ibárruri Gómez famously declared in the summer of 1936 *"no pasarán"* ("they shall not pass"), she saw Madrid as the metonymic line in the sand upon which Spain's fate would lie. The slogan became a rallying cry not only for the Republican militias, but also for international fighters like those of the Abraham Lincoln Brigades, who saw the fate of Madrid as a stand in for the broader fight against fascism in Europe.

If for the Republicans Madrid symbolized resilience and enduring resistance, for the Fascists, the synecdoche of Madrid fit into a more regional nationalist discourse – a weaving together of geographies, whereby Madrid might overlay the national territory. Thus, the conquest of Madrid was a means of imposing both ideological and territorial control. As Franco and his cohort both physically and symbolically appropriated Madrid, it became beneficial to elide Madrid's urban identity, an identity associated with the very working-class activism and leftist intellectuals that had so aptly challenged him during the Civil War.[81] To mitigate this threat, the notion of *castizo* Madrid began to lose its urban character and was replaced by a rural nostalgia for Castile (the general region where Madrid is located), what Nil Santiáñez calls "the *ur-topia* of Spanish fascism and the point of departure for a new (fascist) production of space."[82] This geographical emphasis on the high plains of Spain's *meseta central* was an intellectual project, advanced in part, according to Randolph Pope, "by the philological and Castilianist historical school which reduce[d] the history of Spain to that of Castile."[83] Within this ideological framework, as David Herzberger has aptly pointed out, Castile was seen as the heartland of Spain, a region closely associated with Isabella and Ferdinand and the "spiritual foundations of Spanish imperialism and conquest."[84] This foundational narrative of Spanish nationalism privileged Castilianist linguistic and cultural hegemony and was held in place not only through the work of Francoist historiography, but also through the direct prohibition of Spain's other regional national cultures – and, in particular, their languages: Catalan, Galician, and Basque. Castile was seen as both exceptional – thereby limited to the central region of Spanish territory – as well as spiritually all encompassing; it was to be understood as the heartland of the Spanish nation.

Therefore, it was essential to control the urban heart of Castile – literally the Kilometer Zero of Spain – for the production of fascist space. Echoing the tactics of the Hapsburg monarchs, Franco used the urban space of Madrid as one of the key stages from which to project his complete seizure of power and terrain at the end of the war. This process was enacted both through the ephemeral spectacle of an elaborate victory parade on 19 May 1939 – the culmination of a series of parades carried out in cities across Spain – as well as in the new vision of fascist Madrid expressed in urban planner Pedro Bidagor's General Urban Plan of 1942.[85]

The victory parade in Madrid was a dramatic demonstration of force, as Santiáñez describes in detail. The sheer magnitude of the event contributed to the spectacle, with nearly 15 per cent of the armed forces accompanied by some 150 tanks, 450 aircraft, and an assortment of other heavy equipment, such as artillery and military trucks.[86] Like the processions of the sixteenth and seventeenth centuries, the parade symbolically reconfigured the urban terrain through both the timing and selection of the route – a consolidation of city space and national space in the view of Santíañez. Beginning near what is now the Nuevos Ministerios complex and ending in the Plaza de Canóvas, it began in a "space representative of a yet-to-be established political power," passed through the heart of the Spanish economy symbolized by the Banco de España building near the Plaza Cibeles, and ended in front of the Spanish Parliament, a symbol of the democratically-elected government of Republican Spain.[87] With Madrid as the perfect symbolic stage for this spectacle, the parade was the final military event of the war, that much-delayed military conquest of the Republican capital.[88]

Instead of relying merely on the fleeting symbolism of a one-day parade, the Francoist regime also took steps to control the space of the city through a technocratic reconfiguration of the capital – the abstract space of a new regime that hoped to control the populace through a new urban plan. Madrid would be reinstalled as the capital of a new empire, and the organization of the city would reflect the state as a whole.[89] Although the Plan Bigador never fully came to fruition, its vision for Madrid is still worth dwelling on briefly, because it envisioned a new social organization for the city, produced by urban planning. The Plan sought to create a more hierarchical organization of the city's historic center through a formalized process of districting for the old neighborhoods, the use of a green belt to create a natural barrier between the working class and the other residential parts of the city, and a reinvigorated use of the radial highway system to connect Madrid to the periphery.[90] This vision of a hierarchical city organized by class, which also reflected the centralized power structure of the state, was accompanied by an aggressive renaming of the streets and boulevards with references to the National Catholic legacy of Spain. The Falangist regime hoped to impose a new cultural imaginary for the City and the Nation through urban planning and the production of a new lived space for Madrid's inhabitants.

Francoist historiography also canonized the literature of the *Siglo de Oro* as a way to cultivate a connection with imperial Spain, implicitly reasserting Madrid's importance as a cultural center. In this sense, therefore, we might posit that Spanish national identity is closely associated with the cultural legacy derived from the prolific theatrical tradition of *comedias* and *corrales* in which Tirso, Lope, and Calderón de la Barca participated.[91] This argument explains why the cityscape of central Madrid has consistently been inscribed with the cultural legacy of the *Siglo de Oro*. For example, in 1845, when the emerging modern state sought to establish a national theater, it looked to the theater spaces of the *Siglo de Oro*. The actor Juan Lombía, generally given credit for these efforts, used the Corral del Príncipe for this purpose, and eventually established what is still today the Teatro Español.[92] Notably, the facade of this iconic theater space hems in one side of the Plaza Santa Ana – now a prime destination for Madrid's tourists. Other important references to the *Siglo de Oro* include the statue of Calderón de la Barca that sits across the plaza from the Teatro Español;[93] the nearby Plaza Tirso de Molina, named for the important dramatist of the period; the iconic statue of Don Quixote and Cervantes in the Plaza de España, and the statue of the Baroque poet Francisco Quevedo in the Glorieta de Quevedo. It is important to note the convergence in two of these examples of references to the *Siglo de Oro* and a national referent (Teatro Español; Plaza de España). In short, the *Siglo de Oro* in general and the theater in particular sketch themselves across the national imaginary at the level of academic discourse as well as in the material expressions of the urban landscape. In this way, the fascist production of space, like that of the Hapsburgs, relied carefully on the spectacle of urban space to consolidate their power. In addition, the steps taken by the Franco regime to appropriate Madrid point to the historic significance that Madrid had (and continues to have) in the Spanish imaginary. The urban terrain of the capital has consistently been utilized for spectacles that metonymically associate Madrid and the Spanish nation as a whole.

LA PUERTA DE SOL: A SYMBOL OF MODERNITY AND RESISTANCE

While processionals and the theatrical tradition of urban spectacles helped reinforce the spatial myths of the monarchy, and later the Franco regime, the city's central plaza, the Puerta del Sol, functioned as another important stage for the metonymic link between Spain and Madrid. In contrast to the associations with empire, monarchy, and absolutism found in other locations in the city, the Puerta de Sol arose from the socio-spatial contours of the modern state and the increasingly more dominant commercial spectacle of the city. Despite these differences, there remained a centralizing tendency in the way that the spatial imaginary of the city and the national territory overlaid one another, an idea expressed in the city's famous Kilometer Zero marker, literally inscribed into the ground in front of the Puerta del Sol's iconic Real Casa de Correos building (see Figure 1.4). Echoing the imperial project underpinning Rome's famous Millarium Aureum, the marker visually projects Madrid across the terrain of the nation-state. Measuring roughly one meter by one half meter, the marker is at times barely noticed by the steady flow of pedestrians through this busy central plaza in the capital, but it is a powerful illustration of the metaphoric power of urban space. In the center of the semicircular marker, the viewer finds a map of the Iberian Peninsula and the contrasts between red and yellow-hued granite demarcate Spain from its neighbors, Portugal and France. The words "Origin of the Radial Highways" follow the contour along the upper perimeter of the semicircular shape. As if to provide a visual illustration of these words, the image of a sun is emblazoned directly in the center of the map – presumably where one would find Madrid. The six wavy lines that form sunbeams radiate out from the two concentric circles and seem to stretch across Spain.

The Stage of a Nation 51

Figure 1.4 | The Kilometer Zero marker in the Puerta del Sol.

This image of the sun not only visually locates the center of the "universe" in Madrid by alluding to the notion that all roads lead into and out of Madrid. It also reproduces a geographical synecdoche, whereby the part – the Kilometer Zero or the Puerta del Sol – stands in for the entirety of Madrid. The images allude to Lefebvre's suggestion that social spaces "are not things, which have mutually limiting boundaries."[94] Rather, since the same modes of production create the networks of exchange and communication within the local and the global, "scalar structuration," as Neil Brenner calls it, becomes a series of produced spaces that articulate with one another to construct and deconstruct power relations.[95] The Zero marker, the Puerta del Sol, and Madrid overlap as the starting point from which to traverse the territory of the "provinces." Because of the interpenetration of the Puerta del Sol across a range of geographies, it has often served as an urban stage for audiences well beyond the confines of the city.

To better understand this symbolism, we must move backward in time to examine the transformations of urban space that were taking place in Madrid of the middle of the eighteenth century and the rising influence of the modern bureaucratic state. Key to this urban transformation was the construction of the Real Casa de Correos, from 1750 to 1756, along the southern edge of the Puerta del Sol. Built as the key collection and distribution site for the royal mail system, this iconic building marked the Puerta del Sol as a significant node in the bureaucratic network for managing the emerging state. The Real Casa de Correos and its location in the Puerta del Sol would become the principal "stage" from which to demonstrate the state's administrative reach across the national territory of Spain. Alongside this consolidation of national terrain, there was "another city rising up." As Carlos Sambricio describes it, "it is not the city of the Baroque theater anymore but rather an urban domain where the administration holds a new position, where the structure of the state begins to define itself in a new way, and as a consequence, the buildings that are now dedicated to the sacred will be destined for administration."[96] This "new" city came in response to an emerging market economy and the changing flows of capital and credit that altered the character of the elites closely aligned with the crown.[97] The monarchy turned its gaze toward these educated bureaucrats and the rising mercantile class, and in response they developed a new spatial vocabulary to project power throughout the city.[98]

With the Puerta del Sol as the locus of this newly imagined city, the Real Casa de Correos was its centerpiece. It would "secrete" the space of this new society, as Lefebvre describes it,[99] and "represent both the new bureaucracy and the new economic order."[100] The neo-classical facade redefined the ruler's relationship with the inhabitants – one based in the permanent and persistent rationalism of state bureaucracy as opposed to the ephemeral opulence and pageantry of the Baroque city and its periodic displays of royal power in the Plaza Mayor. These changes were material, but also demonstrated new relationships between ruler and ruled and shifting "conceptions of society, sovereignty, and cultural priorities."[101] Relocating the levers of power to the city center marginalized the court and the landed aristocracy on the perimeter of the city in the newly constructed Royal Palace (to the west) and the Palace of the Buen Retiro (to the east). These changes reflected new modes of socialization (i.e., spatial practice) and the new class structures produced by the ascendance of market capitalism.

This transformation of the Puerta del Sol from mere medieval gate at the edge of the city to the bureaucratic center of the Spanish state would see its most profound expression in 1847, when the Real Casa de Correos was designated as the site of the Ministry of Government and became quite literally the bureaucratic center of the state. Beginning in 1866, the clock tower of the Real Casa de Correos became what Queen Isabella II called *el reloj de gobernación* (the government clock). The clock tower broadcast the uniform and rational time of the market across the terrain of the nation-state – the chronometer of "abstract space" spurring an emerging "urbanization of consciousness" in which the "spatio-temporal rhythms of nature would be transformed by social practice."[102] Emanating from the Puerta del Sol, the new symbol of the modern capitalist state, time in Sol becomes time everywhere in Spain.[103]

These administrative changes were accompanied by other reforms in this period that would further rationalize the Puerta del Sol. Demonstrations of technological and industrial advancement offered physical and visual evidence that Madrid possessed "a high quality urban setting, fitting of a modern European capital," as Amalia Castro Rial-Garrone argues.[104] These demonstrations included not only the first public gas lamps in Spain, but also a new fountain in the center of the plaza whose cascading water reminded the public of the recently inaugurated Canal Isabel II, a new source of clean water for the city.[105] The fountain attracted a public ever more focused on consumption, while widened sidewalks encouraged their circulation and access to the enticements found in the kiosks and shop windows that began to sprout up around the plaza: the visual consumption of goods in the stores and on the bodies of passersby accompanied their material consumption.[106] The newly reformed Puerta del Sol was becoming the principal commercial center of the "modern" capital.[107] Writer and intellectual Ramón Gómez de la Serna illustrates this synecdoche in his brief history of the Puerta del Sol from 1920, suggesting it was the "center of Spain and the place of the highest category in Madrid" and that it "[captured] in every way, in its chaos, and in its tumultuousness, the character of Spain."[108] The Puerta de Sol had become a symbol of the state and the nation.

Yet these transformations had another purpose as well, which aligned with the moving of the central government offices to the Puerta del Sol. As Franciso Quirós suggests, the straightening of streets and the widening of the plaza facilitated the ability of the military to intervene against any threats: whether domestic or foreign.[109] Between the Carlist insurgencies that plagued the rule of Isabella II and the spirit of revolution that had been coursing through Europe since 1848, urban space, especially the "center" of Spain, had to communicate administrative power while also allowing the military to easily intervene to suppress rebellion. The Puerta de Sol, then, was a spatial response to the need to assert the "state-territory-sovereignty link."[110] In contrast to the seventeenth century, this violent sovereignty had begun to de-link from the monarchy and become increasingly intertwined in the governmentality of the emerging modern state. The process would culminate some eighty years later, in 1939, when the Franco regime would begin to use the Real Casa de Correos to house its General Security Division. The subsequent sequester and torture of political prisoners would haunt a generation of Spaniards. The polemic surrounding the history of the building is so profoundly tied to the national psyche that, even in the early-twenty-first century, Jerónimo López Mozo would make the rehabilitation of the clocktower of the Real Casa de Correos the focus of his 2001 play *El arquitecto y el relojero* (*The Architect and the Watchmaker*). For López Mozo, the symbolism of the Real Casa de Correos offered the ideal space to explore how struggles over historical memory, urban space, and national identity live in the representational space of the city.[111]

As Susan Larson has so eloquently and effectively articulated in her volume on conflicts over urban space in early-twentieth-century Madrid, the construction of the Gran Vía – another Haussmannization of the city that would connect the affluent neighborhoods of Salamanca and Argüelles – would shift the center of spectacle in the city away from the Puerta del Sol. But this tendency to conflate the Puerta del Sol as both the central plaza of Madrid and its "national" plaza would persist until the present day.[112] These discourses are peppered throughout the book *La Real Casa de Correos, 1756/1998: Sede de la Presidencia de la Comunidad de Madrid* (The Royal House of Mail, 1756/1998: Site of the Presidency of the Autonomous Community of Madrid), published by the Office of Housing and Architecture to commemorate the extensive rehabilitation of the building in 1997. The book offers extensive and useful scholarship on the history of the building and its significance for the Puerta del Sol and the city capital as a whole. It also illustrates very clearly the persistence of these spatial discourses. In his essay from the book, José María Fernández Isla, one of the official architects of Madrid's regional government, attributes the imaginative power of the Puerta del Sol to its iconic clock tower and its "diffusion of that image far and wide across the Spanish state."[113] Yet it is not merely the clock that functions in a national terrain, as another contributor, architect Antonio Bonet Correa, suggests, but rather it is the building itself that functioned like an antenna that "was able to irradiate the extent of the nation."[114] Going further, Bonet Correa argues that, since its designation as the site of the Ministry of Government, the building has been the "angular stone of the Iberian Peninsula."[115] Conceptualized as a "national" space, Bonet Correa conflates Spain with the entirety of the peninsula, even incorporating Portugal into the national terrain through nullification.

This convergence of spatial discourses across a range of scales throws into relief the contention of geographers that scale does not refer simply to "geographical resolution,"[116] but a more complicated matrix that includes "size, level, and relation."[117] Indeed, in the twenty-first century, as in the past, the Real Casa de Correos and the plaza that it adorns become a discursive site for the "articulation" of multiple geographies or scales – a reading that is emphasized by the fact that the building today serves as the home for the regional government of the Autonomous Government of Madrid. This new administrative function connects the urban space of Madrid to the larger regional geopolitical entity of the autonomous community, while the building's persistent presence as an icon of the Spanish New Year maintains its latent national significance.

TENEMOS EL SOL QUEREMOS LA LUNA
(WE HAVE THE SUN, WE WANT THE MOON)

It is perhaps because of these symbolic values that the Puerta del Sol has been, according to Gómez de la Serna, "where repressions have [had] their greatest power, because there was something intrinsic in it where the head of any uprising or revolution was cut off."[118] Gómez de la Serna's words suggest that the potential for spectacle and for the resonance of that spectacle at a range of scales has also been part of the power of the Puerta del Sol – an instrument, as Gómez de la Serna suggests, from which revolution might begin or be snuffed out. As Andrés Antebi and José Sánchez have written, plazas across many cultures and traditions have long been aligned with projections of power, as different groups (government entities, church organizations, police, etc.) "occupied the physical plaza, symbolically demonstrating the who and the how of holding power."[119] And, indeed, the Puerta del Sol has historically served this purpose, often through the plaza's use as a stage to project power.

It was here, on 14 April 1931, that Niceto Alcalá-Zamora proclaimed the establishment of the Second Spanish Republic, an event marked by the unfurling of the Republican tricolor on the facade of the Real Casa de Correos (still the Ministry of Government at the time) – prompting King Alfonso XIII to flee into exile. On the other side of the equation, we recall the aforementioned connotations that the building held as the home of Franco's security apparatus. These shifting uses of the Puerta del Sol evoke Lefebvre's incredulity that there could be any challenge to the power structure "without reading for the places where power resides, without planning to occupy that space and to create a new political morphology."[120] Thus was the power of the Sol Encampment that occupied the Puerta del Sol beginning on 15 May 2011, a counter-spectacle produced by a sea of bodies, tarps, ragtag structures, and stunningly large general assemblies. While this radical use of public space, which would go on to recalibrate Spain's national politics, had little connection with the celebrations of San Isidro taking place that day a few miles to the southwest in Meadow of San Isidro, there was something in the air that day and in the weeks that followed that brought forth – like San Isidro's water-provoking prayers – a wellspring of protest, which rose up and allowed that sense of possibility and hope to be amplified across Spain and beyond.[121]

The encampment known as the Acampada Sol was the result of a series of large protests that had occurred throughout that spring in response to the deepening economic crisis that had begun some years earlier in both Spain and the global economy and its mismanagement by Spanish President José Luis Zapatero's Partido Socialista Obrero Español (PSOE; Spanish Socialist Workers' Party). Convened through online networks like *x.net, Anonymous,* and *No les votes* and given more pronounced focus by the Facebook group *Real Democracia Ya* (Real Democracy Now), the protests took inspiration from grassroots movements that had challenged entrenched political structures, such as those in Iceland in late 2008 and the dramatic events of early 2011 in Tunisia and Egypt that would come to be called the Arab Spring.[122]

With the occupation of Egypt's Tahrir Square in mind, the decentralized network of *Democracia Real Ya* called for protests in fifty-seven Spanish cities on 15 May 2011 as a prelude to the national elections to be held on 22 May 2011. Loosely united by the slogan "no somos mercancía en manos de políticos y banqueros" ("we are not merchandise in the hands of politicians and bankers") the protests channeled frustration at political elites who had not only bailed out the banks, but had ignored the malfeasance of the same banks that created the financial collapse and subsequently stood by as those banks awarded generous bonuses to their executives. Their broad indictment of the cozy relationship between the political class and the financial-services industry called into question a Spanish electoral process that many saw as rigged in favor of economic and political elites that were now foisting neo-liberal economic policies of austerity upon the country, while ignoring the plight of the average citizen.[123]

The protests that saw nearly fifty thousand people in the streets of Madrid, twenty thousand in Barcelona, and similar scenes across cities in Spain were merely the prelude for what would come to be known as the 15-M movement or the *Indignados* (the Outraged). The transformation of a day of protests into a social movement began after the protests of 15 May, when several dozen protesters in Madrid decided to spend the night in the plaza. Through Facebook and Twitter they invited others to join in the conversation. They came, and they brought sleeping bags – proclaiming that they wouldn't leave until they arrived at some consensus "about the meaning of Real Democracy."[124] The following day it is purported that one thousand people in the Puerta del Sol participated in a General Assembly – a non-hierarchical, horizontally organized gathering for making decisions through consensus. Activists in Barcelona quickly followed suit and established their own encampment in the Plaza Catalunya on the night of 16 May. By 20 May, the Puerta del Sol had twenty-eight-thousand *Indignados* participating in the protest, and the small encampment had been transformed into a mini-city, replete with its own radio station and library. In the week that followed, the movement spread to over eight hundred cities throughout the world.

Most notable to the mainstream media desperate for spokespeople was the leaderless and horizontal organization of the encampment, in which decisions were made through consensus in open, participatory assemblies.[125] Also significant were the efforts to pursue *autogestión* (self-management) and provide for the basic needs (shelter, food, water) of the encampment through the ingenuity, cooperation, and drive of the participants. Its seemingly non-ideological character rejected affiliations with the traditional political players – political parties, trade unions, etc. – and attracted people of all ages from across the political spectrum who shared a sense of frustration with the ineptitude of the political system and its response to the economic situation.[126]

The tensions between 15-M's expansive quality, both ideologically and geographically, and its particularities in its spatial strategies (i.e., the fact that it occurred in a concrete and specific location) and rhetorical devices, bring to the fore important notions of space and place.[127] Yi-fu Tuan carefully grapples with this very issue and suggests that, if we think of space as "that which allows movement, then place is pause; each pause in movement makes it possible for location to be transformed into place."[128] Yet, Tuan makes clear that even this distinction between some set of physical coordinates and their emotive qualities is misleading, since they "require each other for definition."[129] In Sol, the "pause" of the encampment had created a sense of place that was, in a sense, like the spatial version of open-code software: it could be joined, co-opted, expanded, and reinterpreted beyond the limits of the encampment itself – and, needless to say, exported via social media technologies across the national terrain and beyond.[130]

In this continual process of spatial production that Harvey would call "creative destruction," the contested meaning of space is deeply embedded in its physical recapitulation. In some sense, this recapitulation is exactly what transpired in the Acampada Sol. In the online how-to manual *How to Cook a Peaceful Revolution*, the anonymous collective of authors write that, during the Acampada, the protesters were "creating from night until morning a mini-city inside the city proper."[131] This mini-city of nearly twenty thousand people, replete with day care, a library, a radio station, health care, and other services, sought to demonstrate the potential for leaderless horizontal organization to build and sustain a community.[132]

Importantly, by reorganizing the spatio-political dynamics of a highly symbolic space, these protests brought attention to the impact of global capitalism on an assemblage of spaces. At the scale of the nation-state, their focus on the sovereign-debt crisis triggered by the broader financial turmoil that had been unfolding since

2008 threw into relief the threat that multinational banks and the global financial system presented to national sovereignty. Protesters also critiqued the related transformation of urban space that had occurred at the metropolitan scale, in the form of both gentrification and a housing crisis that ultimately would become manifest at the scale of the body in the form of *desahucios* (evictions), in which authorities would physically remove inhabitants. Just as capital circulates amongst various geographic scales, the protests were powerful, too, in part because they "articulated" different scales – from the urban scale to the national scale, and, arguably, to the global scale. If the Real Casa de Correos spoke to the way in which "scalar structuration" constructs power relations, then it seems clear that the Acampada Sol (and 15-M more generally) sought to deconstruct power relations across multiple geographic scales

The protests aligned with a broader global movement against despotism and speculative capital – from Iceland and Tahrir Square to Occupy Wall Street and the student movements in Chile and Mexico. Scholars have emphasized the shared values amongst the various protests and the role of social media platforms like Twitter and Facebook in organizing these movements and connecting them to one another.[133] This extensive focus on what Castells calls the "space of flows," prompted some involved in the movement to write that "it [was] not the specific place that [was] the issue, but what happens in it."[134] This assertion only gained more validity over time as the encampments in Sol and other plazas converged with other social movements, such as the Plataforma de Afectados por la Hipoteca (Platform of Those Affected by Mortgages), or PAH, an organization committed to defending Spanish citizens against eviction, and culminated in the electoral success in Madrid and Barcelona of political coalitions that included elements of the 15-M movement.[135] In this sense, the signs from Occupy Wall Street suggesting that you "can't evict an idea" stood the test of time. Nonetheless, as Edward Baker has observed, the Puerta del Sol was the natural location in which to stage these spectacular protests because of the plaza's long history as a locus of the tension between popular and state power.[136] These latent histories imbued the spectacle of the Acampada Sol with rich layers of meaning.

Baker's emphasis on this dialectic between popular resistance and state power in the Puerta del Sol points to a broader tension that characterizes cities and the urban experience. Indeed, going back to

Marx, the struggle to control the working class has always been one of capitalism's many contradictions. Capital needs labor for production and must continually find ways to reproduce the structures that require individuals to sell their labor within the marketplace. Ironically, though, as Susan Larson has observed in her overview of these contradictions, "the manipulation of space is a form of social power for all classes," a statement that highlights the fact that not only is the city a contested space for competing forms of capital (i.e., financial, industrial, etc.), but that labor, too, often has the potential to leverage the control of space to express power.[137] There are always pockets of the city out of control: places where people and communities seek to live outside the logic of capital. Indeed, the diverse assemblage of ideologies that converged during 15-M brought together many voices seeking an escape from the domination of capital on the practice of everyday life: from critiques of Spanish electoral politics and neo-liberal globalization to a diverse range of groups advocating for everything from the ethical treatment of animals to Catalan nationalism. For many, these competing voices distilled a broad desire for a new political vocabulary beyond what has been called the Culture of the Transition.[138] While there have been endless debates about the various ideologies of 15-M and discussion of the ways that it has reconfigured the city through new types of spatial practice, less attention has been paid to the spatial progenitors of 15-M – the spaces of the city where spatial practices and new forms of social organization incubated and developed before spilling out into the plazas.[139] In the case of Madrid, I contend, it is Lavapiés where the dress rehearsal for 15-M occurred.

Much of this influence comes from the important role that previously established alternative social movements played in helping 15-M to coalesce. Within this network of social movements, the *okupa* movement and related efforts at self-management were central, according to Carlos Taibo, a professor of political science who has written extensively about 15-M.[140] In fact, Taibo goes so far as to suggest that, without the work of these movements during the preceding twenty years to construct new modes of organization that emphasized cooperation, horizontality, and assembly-driven decision making, "what happened on the 15th of May and the days following it would have been unthinkable."[141] Indeed, many of the organizational strategies utilized during the Acampada de Sol had gestated in the various Centros Sociales Okupados Autogestionados

(CSOA; Self-managed Squatted Social Centers) around Madrid and other parts of Spain in the previous decades. These strategies would continue to develop in other squatted social centers like the CSOA Patio Maravillas in Malasaña, the CSOA Casablanca in Lavapiés, and the CSA Tabacalera, an important self-managed social center that was not squatted, but rather ceded to neighborhood activists by the Ministry of Culture.[142]

These last two are particularly important because of their physical location near the Puerta del Sol – a factor that made them natural staging areas for the encampment, as well as sites to which activists retreated after police evicted the protesters in the plaza. In the case of the Tabacalera, there was not only an ideological contribution, but also material support. As the Acampada de Sol began to develop and grow during the latter part of May and early June of 2011, there was a need for materials to build the various structures that would make up the encampment. Coincidentally, after the tobacco company La Tabacalera S.A. that owned the building ended production in 2000 and closed down the factory, a huge assortment of tables, chairs, and other pieces of scrap metal and wood filled the basement and other parts of the building. According to Gloria Durán, one of members of the CSA Tabacalera responsible for maintaining contact with the Ministry of Culture (a relationship that will be explained in the following chapter), much of the Acampada de Sol was physically constructed from the detritus of La Tabacalera. La Tabacalera gave body, quite literally, to protests that would eventually sweep the nation and eventually be replicated in Zuccotti Square in New York City in the fall of 2011 in the form of Occupy Wall Street.[143]

Importantly, La Tabacalera's role was not merely reduced to this physical contribution, but also functioned on an imaginary level. In a series of articles that ran in the conservative daily ABC between August 1 and August 8 in 2011, La Tabacalera was described as the "refuge" and "logistical base" where the 15-M movement received its "oxygen."[144] Whether in fact La Tabacalera played such a central role during the Acampada de Sol and its aftermath is somewhat irrelevant, given that it was discursively being constructed as the center of this protest movement.

The role of La Tabacalera beyond Lavapiés would grow even more later in 2011, when the 15-M movement went global. On 15 October 2011, a global day of protest against the role of global finance in politics around the world, which *Democracia Real Ya* had been planning since the summer, took place, but it converged with the height of the Occupy Wall Street movement in New York. The following day, when the Spanish daily *El País* interviewed Jon Aguirre, a spokesperson for *Democracia Real Ya*, the interview took place in the cafeteria of La Tabacalera. The interviewer described La Tabacalera as "one of the neurological points in which the October 15 protest was cooked up."[145] Again, the highly local cultural project of the CSA Tabacalera had come to represent the vestiges of the 15-M movement and had been discursively constructed as one of the sites from which "15-M was exported to the world," as the headline read.

If the encampments of 15-M created new meanings for the Puerta del Sol as a space of national and global protest, this brief genealogy shows that the Acampada Sol fit into a broader network of struggle for space in the city. Within this network the Tabacalera stands out, not merely because of its momentary function as a logistical base for the Acampada Sol, but because, like the Puerta del Sol, the building had its own historical palimpsests as a symbol of popular resistance. Indeed, by calling attention to the Tabacalera, we shift our gaze from the avenues of the imperial city, the theater spaces grappling with new forms of municipal and national identity, and the spectacle of monuments constructed to communicate power. Instead, we turn our attention to the counter-spectacles that always exist at the margins of the city's abstract space. The Tabacalera, like the Puerta del Sol, resonated as a symbol of popular resistance in the press in those months after 15-M because of the building's history as a site of working-class solidarity and of combative politics that have long been associated with the neighborhood in which the Tabacalera is located: Lavapiés.

If much of the spectacle of Madrid has been built on demonstrations of power, it is in Lavapiés that conflicts over urban space and urban spectacle have played out in the street and across the cultural imaginary of different geographies since the late-eighteenth century. From its folkloric *castizo* image of the past to its activist *okupas* of the twenty-first century, the spectacle of Lavapiés has been the site where Madrid's power structures are reinforced and contested at the scale of the neighborhood, the city, and the nation. It is this array of spectacles and counter-spectacles, and their articulations of the neighborhood, the city, and beyond, to which we now turn in the coming chapters.

2

From Lavapiés to Madrid: The Populist Myth of "*Lo Castizo*"

Standing fortress-like on the northern end of the Embajadores traffic circle, the broad facade of the Antigua Fábrica de Tabacos de Embajadores (Old Tobacco Factory of Embajadores), as it is formally known, has served since the late-eighteenth century as a southern gateway of sorts to the iconic neighborhood of Lavapiés. Originally constructed in 1782 as the Royal Factory of Schnapps and Playing Cards, the large behemoth of gray brick would eventually become one of the largest employers in the city of Madrid and one of only a handful of sites around Spain dedicated to the production of tobacco (the others being in Cádiz and Seville). As consumption of tobacco shifted from snuff toward hand-rolled cigarettes, production followed, and female cigar rollers became the principal source of labor, because of their presumed manual dexterity.

Working outside the home made these *cigarreras*, as they were known, anomalous for the period. It was not uncommon for these women to be the sole source of income for their household, particularly given the precarious economic conditions of the lower classes. Nineteenth-century writers and painters in Spain and northern Europe would seize on this independence while creating romanticized visions of Andalusian culture in their representations of Spain. Echoing that classic image of Andalusian femininity associated with French composer Georges Bizet's famous opera *Carmen* from 1875, these artists transformed the working-class laborers of the Tobacco Factories into the coquettish *cigarrera*, an iconic image of Spanish femininity. Bizet's *Carmen* tapped into long-standing tendencies to inscribe Spain within erotic orientalist discourses emphasizing bullfighting and flamenco culture – visions of Spain always tinged with the otherness of the arabesque and the Romani.[1] The famous tasseled silk shawls known as the *mantón de manila* were also tinged with the allure of the exotic. Derived from a related garment in the Philippines (a Spanish colony from 1521 to 1898) and later manufactured in China, the shawls alluded to the "Orient" and its sexualized connotations. This exoticism would continue to be a symbol of Spanish culture into the 1960s, when Francoist marketing campaigns began promoting the idea that "Spain is different" as a way to attract European and American tourists.

While *Carmen* made famous Seville's Tobacco Factory and its *cigarreras*, the Andalusian context also informs the *cigarreras* of Madrid, as many of the women who worked in La Tabacalera were immigrants from Andalusia and other regions of Spain. As critics like Serge Salaün and Carmen del Moral Ruiz have suggested, one of the key features of the *castizo* myth is its assimilation of provincial identities (like the Andalusian *cigarrera* in this case) into a constructed *madrileño* identity.[2] The vestiges of this history are found today in the *manila* shawls and carnations adorning the costumes of women celebrating that most *castizo* of holidays, the feast day of San Isidro. In this context, La Tabacalera evokes this folkloric *castizo* culture and alludes to Lavapiés's important relationship with the urban mythology of authentic Madrid, the topic that forms the focus of this chapter. The *cigarrera* is particularly important to this myth, because it links Lavapiés's present and its past and highlights the neighborhood's important role in Madrid's struggles over culture and urban space, particularly in the cultural imaginary of the city.

FROM *CIGARRERAS* TO *INDIGNADOS*

Behind the romanticized facade of the sexualized *cigarrera* are the combative workers whose strike in 1830 paralyzed tobacco production in the city. Later, in 1885, another strike protested the mechanization of the cigarette-rolling process under the slogan *"¡arriba niñas!"* ("rise up girls!"). By the 1920s, they had become one of the most potent symbols of syndicalism and labor organizing in Madrid,[3] their tactics so successful that they supposedly inspired labor organizer Pablo Iglesias to form his Socialist Workers' Union, the party that would later become the Spanish Socialist Workers' Party (PSOE), one of Spain's largest and most influential political parties of the post-Franco period.[4]

The domestic situation for most of these women reinforced this workplace solidarity. The typical housing for working-class women like the *cigarreras* were the *corralas*, which were constructed from about 1625 to 1868 and have long been a unique aspect of Madrid's urban morphology – spaces in which private space was limited and life was lived in public. These iconic buildings (of which few exist today), characterized by three to five stories of galleried apartments looking onto a central courtyard with a communal water source, allowed for thirty to fifty families to live on one parcel of land.[5] Their development owed much to King Philip IV's construction of a new *cerca* in 1628 and an accompanying order prohibiting the construction of permanent housing beyond the perimeter of this wall. The need to accommodate the city's growing population by privileging verticality and density on the city's historically narrow, but long, lots resulted in these distinctive *corralas* or *casas de corredores* (see Figure 2.1). Each floor would contain eight to ten small apartments – each often less than thirty square meters (three hundred square feet) – for one or more families. The construction of the *corralas* followed generally the emergence of Madrid's industrial manufacturing sector in the city's southern neighborhoods: this included the Royal Tobacco Factory (1781), the Royal Saltpeter Factory (1785), and later the Royal Gas Factory (1848). As in many cities throughout Europe, laborers filled the adjacent neighborhoods, living in tenement conditions in the *corralas*. Even into the middle of the twentieth century, these tenements would typically have only one or two bathrooms per building often without running water. Because of their thin walls and cramped interior spaces, the life in the *corralas* took place in the central patio, on the balconies, or in the nearby street. In other words, life in the *corralas* was highly communal (whether the inhabitants wanted it or not).

The term carried so much resonance into the late-twentieth century that, in the 1970s, the Lavapiés neighborhood association included it in their name, hoping on one hand to evoke this ethos of collectivity while also bringing attention to the need for architectural, historical, and cultural preservation. La Corrala Neighborhood Association regularly drew six-hundred-member general assemblies that by 1977 had swelled to nearly sixteen hundred participants ready to take on issues such as water supply, urban decay, and the displacement of residents by increasing gentrification.[6] The organization deployed other cultural resources in their struggles and adopted the literary

Figure 2.1 | The iconic Corrala de Tribulete, found at the corner of Tribulete and Mesón de Paredes.

stereotype of the *cigarrera* and other folkloric figures from Lavapiés's past to channel this grassroots political activism. They reintegrated the tradition of street parties, or *verbenas*, into the life of the neighborhood, with residents wearing costumes associated with folkloric images of *cigarreras, chulapas,* and *chulaponas* that had been promulgated by Madrid's popular theater in the early-twentieth century (a topic that will be explored in more detail later in this chapter). For a fractured and fading Francoist regime, these protests were a difficult challenge: the citizens of Lavapiés affirmed their right to the city, as well as a sense of shared cultural heritage. More importantly, they reclaimed public space after decades of silence imposed by the oppressive Francoist bureaucracy.[7]

Even in the early-twenty-first century, the *cigarrera* would remain a symbol of neighborhood solidarity and combativity, as activists would appropriate this history during debates that occurred as a result of the factory's closure in 2000. The series of protests, lectures,

Figure 2.2 | Image of a combative *cigarrera* from events during "La Tabacalera a Debate" in 2005.

and activities that took place were significant, in part, because they were the continuation of ongoing efforts to establish an autonomous self-managed space for the community in the neighborhood, with the most recent iteration being the highly influential self-managed social center called the Laboratorio 03.[8] One key event in this process was the project "La Tabacalera a Debate" in 2005, which was created to generate enthusiasm for the endeavor through a series of lectures and street protests that hoped to catalyze community conversations about what would happen to the recently closed factory space. In a poster advertising the event (see Figure 2.2), the gruff *cigarrera* smokes a (presumably) hand-rolled cigar and shouts for "La Tabacalera para el barrio ya" ["The Tobacco Factory for the neighborhood already!"]. The masculine, square-jawed face contrasts the traditional dress and *mantón de manila* that suggest nineteenth-century modesty. With her clenched teeth and her hands on her hips, she projects resolute determination as well as aggression. As the viewer is implored to join with the *barrio de las cigarreras*, or neighborhood of the *cigarreras*, the poster reappropriates the sexualized *cigarrera* of *Carmen* and transforms her into a symbol of the neighborhood's combativity and the possibility for resisting a city devoted to cultural tourists and capital. These reappropriations of the *cigarrera* as a symbol of Lavapiés's contemporary struggles over the right to the city would also occur in a *cigarrera* parade that took the form of a march to urge city officials to cede the Tabacalera to the neighborhood (instead of building a new museum, as was planned). The call to protest offered directions for how to dress like a *cigarrera*, suggesting any long skirt and shawl capped off with a red flower and cigar. It was a modern reincarnation of the nineteenth-century *cigarrera* that attempted to use the neighborhood's cultural patrimony as a tool to recover the buildings and spaces of that very same legacy.

This engagement with the building's past would culminate in a performance called *Cigarreras: Métodos y Tiempos* (*Cigar Rollers: Methods and Times*), an entry in Madrid's eleventh Annual Festival of Contemporary Performance.[9] The performance occurred in the large central nave of La Tabacalera and relied on approximately seven small "sketches" or scenes in which women who had worked at the Tabacalera between 1957 and 1989 pantomimed the various activities related to the production of tobacco.[10] Like an earlier event called *La flor de Lavapiés*, which took place in December 2010, the performance by these female factory workers became "an open day for constructing collectively the memory of La Tabacalera."[11] As a vestige of Lavapiés's mythologized *castizo* past, La Tabacalera recalls deep connections between the neighborhood and the popular theater of the nineteenth and early-twentieth centuries. It alludes to Lavapiés's identity as one of the city's epicenters for grassroots activism and a place that power structures in the city have always struggled to contain. Moreover, the continued resonance of the *cigarrera* brings our attention once again to the role of the theater in constructing the physical and imaginary contours of the city.

While the theater culture of seventeenth-century Madrid negotiated the new spatial and social hierarchies of the emerging modern nation-state, in later centuries it would begin to produce recurring urban types and populist mythologies of urban identity. These myths were less explicitly national in character and fomented a sense of municipal identity based in key working-class neighborhoods, such as Lavapiés and nearby areas like El Rastro and La Latina. Nonetheless, the *costumbrista* tendencies of theatrical traditions like the *sainete* in the late-eighteenth century and the *género chico* in the nineteenth and early-twentieth century would articulate these local identities across the stages of the city and participate in more nationalist discourses occurring at the time.[12] In contrast to the previous chapter, which emphasized urban spectacles aligned with dominant power structures, this chapter looks to a number of counter-spectacles in order to demonstrate not only the way in which Lavapiés has historically been imagined as a site of resistance and popular culture, but also how this counter-culture has been appropriated in order to construct overlapping municipal and national identities. In Lefebvrian terms, the musical theater of the *zarzuela* and its derivative forms helped to produce the representational space that overlaid the physical terrain of the city and imbued it with symbolic meaning.

LO CASTIZO: CASTILE AND MADRID

The *género chico* refers to the hugely popular form of entertainment that emerged in the late- nineteenth century and consisted of small one-act performances of about one hour that combined music, song, and dialogue. Given their tendency to set the action in working-class neighborhoods, the *género chico* has often been lumped together with the more elaborate three-act musical form of the *zarzuela*, sometimes called the *género grande*, or "large-form genre." The two formats both relied on certain "types," or stock characters, whose origins can be found in the short dramatic works called *sainetes* written by Ramón de la Cruz (1731–1794) in the eighteenth century. Although the *zarzuela* is often considered a minor genre within the canon of Spanish literature, with little attention paid to most individual works, it is a genre that is hard to ignore given the persistence with which the *chulapos* and *majos* that populate the urban settings of the *zarzuela* have remained one of the most enduring images of *lo castizo*, a term often translated as "authentically Spanish."[13]

According to the Real Academia Española, the term *castizo* means literally "of good origin or caste." A more nuanced definition, found in the second entry, defines it as "Typical, pure, genuine of any country, region, or locality."[14] What threads these definitions together is their evocation of purity and the idea of the genuine. When used as a descriptor for the lower-class neighborhoods in the southern part of the capital, the term refers not just to any province or region, but specifically to Madrid and sometimes to Castile (the region in which Madrid is located). This evolution from marker of municipal identity to a term with quasi-nationalist associations occurred toward the end of the nineteenth century, when Spanish intellectuals confronted a crisis of Spanish identity in the wake of increasing modernization (and Europeanization) and eventually, in 1898, the loss of key colonial possessions: Cuba, Puerto Rico, and the Philippines. Simultaneously, Spain found itself confronting a resurgence of regional nationalism in Catalonia and the Basque country.[15]

Faced with these challenges and seeking out sources of renewal for Spanish culture, the Spanish writers of the Generation of '98 – as they would come to be known – began to articulate a new sense of Spanish national identity through associations with the central plateau of Castile. This new discursive thread finds one of its clearest articulations in Miguel de Unamuno's collection of essays entitled *En torno al casticismo* (*On Purity*) published first in the periodical *La España Moderna* in 1895 and later compiled as a single volume in 1902. Therein he argues for Castile as the font of "Spanish essence, the most truly essential Spain."[16] Poet Antonio Machado's collection *Campos de castilla* (*Fields of Castile*) (1907) would reinforce this vision of Castile; the region, according to Inman Fox was understood by these writers to be "the true forge of Spanish unity, the nucleus of Spanish nationality."[17] Significantly, despite the clear sense of rural nostalgia here, the role of the urban environment and the theater in forging this relationship between *lo castizo* and national identity should not be overlooked. Ironically, because of the role of rural emigration to the major urban areas during much of the nineteenth century, many of these urban representations are also, paradoxically, embedded with a rural nostalgia. Consistently, however, theatrical representations of the daily urban life of Madrid brought into close association the terms *castizo*, the *barrios bajos* of the capital, and certain working-class types. It is a process that set the stage for the conflation of Spanish national identity in the geographical articulations between Lavapiés, Madrid, and Castile.

PERFORMING LAVAPIÉS: THE *MAJOS* OF RAMÓN DE LA CRUZ

To understand the evolution of the term *castizo*, one must look to its genesis in the eighteenth century and its relationship with the earlier cult identity known as *majismo*. French political and cultural influence on the continent was ascendant during the period, particularly after the death of the last Hapsburg monarch, Charles II (reigned 1665 to 1700), when the control of the Spanish throne was bequeathed to Charles's great-nephew Philip, the Duc d'Anjou. The coronation of Philip V of Spain (reigned 1700 to 1746) as the first Bourbon king brought French influence directly into the political life of Spain. Philip V's efforts to consolidate power in the model of his grandfather Louis XIV's absolutism, and the near-hegemonic influence on the court of French culture in music, fashion, art, and literature, cultivated resentment amongst intellectuals and certain sectors of the nobility.[18] This process would continue through the reign of Ferdinand VI (reigned 1746–59) and Charles III (reigned 1759–88) whose visions of enlightened despotism would drive a wholesale reform of both the Spanish bureaucracy and the city. Echoing the moves of France's Louis XIV (reigned 1643–1715) to consolidate monarchical power, these Bourbon Reforms, as they were known, diminished the influence of the various regional *cortes* and councils that represented the interests of the territories and brought their responsibilities under the control of the crown. The merging of these various bodies into one large Cortes of Castile created a political structure that conflated Spain's central region with its Iberian territories (i.e., Aragon, Catalonia, Valencia, etc.). Within Castile proper, too, the monarchy moved to minimize the influence of the councils that acted as high courts and as consultative bodies. The role and influence of the councils began their gradual shift into what would later become departments or ministries in the nineteenth century – entities that existed beneath the central power of the head of state.

Urban reforms undertaken by both Ferdinand VI and Charles III accompanied these bureaucratic efforts at the national scale and would transform Madrid from a dusty, dirty city into something resembling a modern capital. Under Ferdinand VI, for example, the paving and regular cleaning of the city's main thoroughfares would be a major undertaking, complemented by the official numbering of the buildings and the production of more-accurate city plans using new methods of meticulous measurement. This process would only continue under Charles III – later known as The Mayor King – whose reforms of the city would include the installation of oil lamps along the city's busiest streets at night, the development of a sewer system, and a broad renovation of the periphery of the city, resulting in esplanades full of gardens and fountains.[19] If Philip V broadened the monarchy's ability to control the national territory through administrative reforms, his descendants continued this effort at the urban scale through increased governmentality that made citizens and the city legible through new tools of statistical measurement and detailed maps.[20] Open promenades, better lighting, and the increased policing efforts implemented by the Italian Marquis of Esquilache would make the city and its inhabitants more visible and add another layer of surveillance to complement the newfound statistical legibility of citizens.[21] Perhaps worn down by three years of bad harvests and rising hunger, residents rebelled against the marquis's efforts to enforce city ordinances banning traditional capes and hats with the protests called the Esquilache Riots – an uprising that Richard Herr describes as the "most serious threat to royal authority in Castile since the *comuneros* of 1520."[22]

In the hands of artists and intellectuals such as dramatist Ramón de la Cruz, the traditional capes and hats that prompted this uprising became symbols of what would be known as *majismo*, a type of dress and behavior that would be closely aligned with both national and civic identity.[23] According to Dorothy Noyes, these *majos* were "working-class dandies, male artisans and female fruit and flower vendors from certain 'popular' quarters of Madrid and the Andalusian cities."[24] The typical costume consisted of a "broad-brimmed soft hat, and long cloak" for men and "a black mantilla, a

Figure 2.3 | Franciso de Goya y Lucientes, *La maja y los embozados* [*The Maja and the Cloaked Men*], 1777. Oil on canvas, Museo del Prado.

tight bodice, and a *basquiña* (top petticoat) over a skirt sometimes as high as mid-calf" for women – images immortalized in the paintings of Francisco de Goya (see Figure 2.3).[25] These *majos* and *majas* were contrasted with what were known as *petimetres* and *petimetras*, individuals characterized by a more bourgeois and foreign style of dress and comportment. Within this differential system, the *majo* was understood to be plebian and therefore Spanish, while the *petimetre* equaled bourgeois and foreign.[26]

The appeal of this plebian type was widespread. Jesús Torrecilla, in his work on the construction of "exotic" Spain, suggests that even the aristocracy began to appropriate these symbols of "Spanish" pride as a reaction against French influence, resulting in what might be described as the *aplebeyamiento*, or plebification, of the aristocracy.[27] The nobles began "to define 'Spanishness' by its opposition to that threatening foreign presence: if Frenchness monopolized high culture, 'Spanishness' would be identified with popular culture; if 'Frenchness' is sophisticated and modern, 'Spanishness' should be rude and primitive; if 'Frenchness' is logical, 'Spanishness' could be spontaneous."[28] This reactionary discourse provoked varied forms of cultural production that increasingly focused on the social reality of contemporary society and marked an inward turn for artists and intellectuals toward cultivating an empirically knowable sense of Spain and Spanishness.[29]

As Rebecca Haidt has argued, these constructions of authentic Spanishness were always contradictory, always problematized by the "unsettledness" of urban cosmopolitan life.[30] Often immigrants, many of these residents did not belong to the guilds or commercial enterprises recognized by the state, and thus perpetually lived on the physical and social margins of the city. Living within a subsistence economy, they lacked access to the fiscal and administrative privileges afforded other residents of the city. As such, they were administratively invisible while living in neighborhoods removed from the recently paved and lighted streets of the refurbished Paseo del Prado, their illegibility compounded by a cultural heterogeneity that derived from origins in diverse regions across Spain. Thus, the coherent notions of *majismo* that would come to define *lo castizo* elided the pervasive absences and instabilities produced by the social conflicts taking place in the shadow of the Bourbon city.[31] When Ramón de la Cruz began to produce his short one-act tragicomic pieces, which glorified the "authentically Spanish" by representing characters of Madrid's lower-class neighborhoods like Lavapiés, it was indeed a construction of the city's cultural imaginary: the invisibility offered an opportunity to create a symbol of civic identity, while its lawlessness became an alluring characteristic amidst the rational urban despotism of Ferdinand VI and Charles III.

These one-act dramas rearticulated certain theater traditions of the early-modern period. They appropriated the short forms of the *entremés* and the *sainete* that tended toward more base and bawdy themes and scenarios. Traditionally performed in the breaks between the acts of longer and more elaborate *comedias* focused on nobles traversing far-off lands and elite social spaces (i.e., aristocratic palaces and gardens), the *entremés* and *sainete* put the stories of common people and the practice of everyday life on the seventeenth-century stage. By working within this tradition, Ramón de la Cruz avoided the neoclassical tendencies of contemporary theater of the eighteenth century and its focus on mythology and rigid dramatic structures. Instead, he represented scenes of the city's inhabitants in everyday settings, speaking what the audience would understand as the particular dialect of Madrid's lower classes – Castilian, inflected by the linguistic diversity of rural Castile and other regions of Spain, particularly Andalusia.[32] In doing so, Ramón de la Cruz created some of the most enduring figures of Spanish popular theater and provided the inspiration for the characters and ambience of the popular *zarzuela* tradition.

One of his most important works, *Manolo: Tragedia para reír o sainete para llorar* (1769) (*Manolo: Tragedy for Laughing or Vignette for Crying*), produced the character of the Manolo who would reappear in the nineteenth and twentieth centuries as the typical working-class *madrileño*.[33] The *sainete* links Madrid and Lavapiés explicitly in the opening stage direction by describing the setting as "Madrid in the middle of the broad street of Lavapiés."[34] For Cruz, this section of the calle Lavapiés – likely the area just above the plaza Lavapiés – was "the theater of a public street with a doorway of a Madrid tavern."[35] Eschewing the distant mythology of the ancient Greeks and images of medieval Spain found in so much of Spanish neoclassical drama, Ramón de la Cruz employed the cityscape of Lavapiés as the most appropriate stage for representing the lives and livelihoods of everyday people.[36]

By the time that de la Cruz wrote *Los bandos de Lavapiés* (*The Gangs of Lavapiés*) in 1776, Lavapiés had crystallized as a distinct location in the city – a fact illustrated by the multiple references to Lavapiés on the map of the city made by Tomás López in 1785.[37] The central argument of this *sainete* revolves around the conflict between a suitor from the nearby working-class neighborhood of Barquillo and the inhabitants of Lavapiés. The suitor, Zurdillo, is assaulted while trying to defend the honor of a young girl from Lavapiés. Returning to his neighborhood, beaten and bruised, he stirs his compatriots into a frenzy with his plans for violent revenge. Beginning in Barquillo and ending in Lavapiés, the *sainete* uses the rivalry between these *bandos*, or gangs, to emphasize the territorial boundaries between the two working-class neighborhoods.

The identities of the characters derive from their spatial associations. As Zurdillo riles up his compatriots, they shout "Death to Lavapiés." [38] Zurdillo responds defiantly that "It cannot / die, Lavapiés, you asses."[39] Undeterred, the crowd corrects itself by shouting "Death to those in it."[40] The humorous exchange reveals that the place has become larger than the people that occupy it. Indeed, the inhabitants derive their identity from the immortal neighborhood of Lavapiés that "cannot die." The exchange parallels another that occurs later in the *sainete* when the mob surges into Lavapiés and threatens the residence of Tío Mandinga, the leader of the gang that assaulted Zurdillo. Canillejas, the friend of Zurdillo, cries "Let's kill the house!" and Zurdillo responds" No, / let's kill those inside."[41] The parallel structure of this exchange re-emphasizes one of the themes of the *sainete*: that people are an ephemeral presence in the enduring urban space of the city.

This thematic emphasis continues when Mandinga tries to lure his daughter, Zaina, back by telling her that "Your mother is Lavapiés, / look out for its honor and ours."[42] The sense of place is so strong in this short work that neighborhood affiliation is their progenitor. Mandinga's appeal asks Zaina to consider not only their personal honor, but the honor of the neighborhood. Lavapiés is no informal area of the city, but an identifiable place to which one should pledge allegiance. In the end, Barquillo won't turn Lavapiés "to blood and fire" in vengeance, because Zaina, Zurdillo's lover, lives there, and Zaina will not abandon her compatriots.[43] Significantly, she requires that Zurdillo pardon Lavapiés and then proclaims "Long live Lavapiés triumphantly!" [44] As if recapitulating the absolution granted at the end of Lope de Vega's *Fuente Ovejuna*, the ending implies that the entire neighborhood must be pardoned and not merely the people that live there. This inversion of the dialogues mentioned earlier establishes Lavapiés as a quasi-character in the *sainete*. The identity of the place has superseded any one of its inhabitants. In the twenty-first century, neighborhood activists would use the trope of the *cigarrera* to channel a similar combative spirit as their concept of collective identity and a rooted sense of place called them to action against the possibility that "Lavapiés might die!"[45]

It is also worth pointing out that Ramón de la Cruz relied partly on the prosody of his work to glorify these lower-class characters. Manolo, the main character, speaks in the hendecasyllabic meter that traditionally characterized the dialogue of nobles in the theater of the seventeenth century.[46] The use of these dramatic structures and forms ennobled these lower-class characters, seemingly untainted by the corrupting influences of foreign culture. Ironically, many of Ramón de la Cruz's *sainetes* were almost direct translations of French works or recapitulations of their storylines, but, for spectators, the setting of Lavapiés and Madrid populated by easily recognizable *majos* and *manolos* became a kind of shorthand for the "Spanishness" of the ambience.

The use of recurring types (as opposed to well-developed characters) within the tradition of the *sainete* was also important, because of the interchange they created between the theater, urban space, and national identity. Within the context of the period's xenophobia, the image of the *majo* carried such cultural significance that the act of *aplebeyamiento* (i.e., "slumming" it) consisted of actually dressing like a *majo* or *maja* for the express purpose of making the street into a theater for expressions of identity. Noyes describes how "street and theater mirrored each other" and often people began to dress in ways that directly referenced these theatrical representations and showed their affinity for *majismo*.[47] These costumes allowed the aristocracy to move unnoticed amongst the plebian crowds at popular events like bullfights and outdoor *verbenas*, the popular neighborhood festivals held for favored saints. Costumed as commoners, the nobility benefited from a certain degree of social invisibility and, perhaps, could partake of any range of transgressions outside the view of the gossipy court.

Later, this costume and type would take on nationalistic significance when the inhabitants of Madrid became associated with the popular resistance to French invasion in 1808 – an association made famous by Franciso de Goya in his painting from 1814, *The Third of*

May of 1808. According to Noyes, these events only "strengthened the myth of the *majo* as sole maintainer of the uncorrupted national spirit – warlike, Catholic, patriarchal, not a product of the eighteenth century but a survivor of the Reconquest."[48] In the immediate aftermath of the French invasion, images like Goya's painting only fortified these discourses that celebrated Madrid as a symbol of Spain's character: resilient and defiant in the face of French absolutism

By the middle of the nineteenth century, Spanish writers would continue to look to the crucible of the *barrios bajos* of Madrid as the forge of Spanish identity. This cultivation of the popular would become a dominant part of Spanish letters, as sketches of local life called *cuadros de costumbres* would emerge in the 1830s alongside the growth of daily periodicals and a middle-class reading public.[49] Writers like Ramón Mesonero Romanos (1803–1882), Serafín Estébanez Calderón (1799–1867), and Mariano José de Larra (1809–1837) seized on the images of "authentic" Spanish identity found in paintings, in the theater, and acted out across the streets of the city and reinforced them through journalistic vignettes that offered snapshots of everyday life found in the streets and neighborhoods of Madrid, as well as in the flamenco and bullfighting culture of Andalusia. At times, these two representations coincided, considering that the working-class in Madrid often comprised immigrants from Andalusia.

This surge in immigration was a product of the famine, disease, and economic crisis that had followed Spain's war for independence from Napoleonic rule.[50] Decades after the popular culture of Madrid had been seen as a bulwark against French cultural imperialism, the capital had lost its cachet. As a result, the capital at this time was "more a seat of privilege and bureaucracy than a national symbol of the nation," as Haidt describes it.[51] Ramón Mesonero Romanos began using his short literary sketches of life in Madrid to cultivate an association between Madrid and the essence of the Spanish "nation" for his middle-class readership. The proliferation of illustrated periodicals allowed readers to consume this emerging vision of Madrid as a national capital – a process that did not take place only in the periodicals.[52] Indeed, a particularly significant element of Mesonero's writings during this period were devoted to urban reforms that he believed needed to take place to "bring an authentic yet invisible inheritance of splendor into plain view."[53] Mesonero not only helped to craft the ideological and imaginary space of Madrid through his writing but, by overseeing the completion of these urban reform, he also helped to shape that Lefebvrian "perceived" city, transforming the city's physical appearance and the spatial practice of its inhabitants. Echoing the anxieties and aspirations that would emerge nearly 170 years later in the Urban Plan of 1997, this urban boosterism – as Benjamin Fraser has described it – was aspirational.[54] It would make Madrid more visually appealing to residents and visitors, and perhaps, even more importantly, the urban terrain of Madrid would become, in the words of Haidt, "newly visible as a modern European capital."[55] This shift toward a new kind of spectacle for the city, in which the city might be consumed as a visual product, also could be found in contemporaneous efforts to create a raised hill within the city's Buen Retiro Park, so as to provide an aerial view of the gardens.[56] These efforts to shape the city physically, as well as in the imagination of various publics (i.e., residents, tourists, the periodical-reading public abroad), constructed a myth of Madrid based in a seemingly fixed idea of authenticity, a process that echoed similar explorations by Romantic poets and writers in their quest to recover national myths like *El Cid*, which would reveal the character of Spanish national identity.

Michael Iarocci aligns this awakening of costumbrismo with the nationalist bent of the historical novels of the Spanish Romantics that accompanied their focus on "geographical and cultural specificity." Importantly, he highlights how this nationalism circulated around the conflation of Castilian and Spanish history.[57] The Castile-centered nationalism that emerged from both the historical novel and journalistic costumbrismo inspired a similar search for origins in the other regional nationalisms of Catalonia, Galicia, and the Basque country. While this set of fragmented quests for "national identity" would seem to undermine the notion of a unified Spanish nation, the act of differentiation pursued by these regionalist movements arguably helped fix in place the Spain-Castile synedoche. The Spain-Castile nationalism provided the center against which peripheral nationalisms could form themselves as the non-Castilian other, despite the efforts of the Castilo-philes to blanket the territory of Spain with a hegemonic myth of Castile. The end result is a codification of the very thing they tried to resist.

The explicit tension between the local and the national expressed in the work of Mesonero Romanos very much reproduces these discourses. Indeed, his sketches of Madrid's people and urban spaces are some of the most enduring descriptions of the modernizing capital. While remaining keenly focused on the local character of Madrid, he simultaneously folds a more national thread into his writing. In *Scenes of Madrid* (1842), he purports to share a collection of "sketches that offer scenes of *our nation's* distinct customs, and in particular those of Madrid, which as the court and center of the nation, is the focus in which the distant provinces are reflected."[58] Madrid distills all the regional differences of Spain into some myth of collective identity imbued with both municipal and national associations. Its "customs" are distinct, in that they reflect (simultaneously, it seems) both those of Madrid and those of the nation as a whole.

In her study of ideology, costumbrismo, and the *género chico*, Lucy Harney suggests that these sketches were a tool for crafting an image of popular Spain that was distinct from Europe. They produced easily digestible notions of national identity that would "reconcile the vast regional and socio-economic disparities among Spaniards with the social and economic imperative of aggrandizing the commercial middle class."[59] Later, in the early-twentieth century these ideas would be relocated by Unamuno and others to the more general geographic area of Castile. In both cases, the center of Spain would be projected as a representation of the whole: in other words, as goes Castile, so goes Spain. As the following discussion of the *género chico* will suggest, this synecdoche was reinforced in both the works and the institutions associated with the large-format *zarzuela* tradition.

The images of national identity produced by Mesonero Romanos had a certain currency for his middle-class readership, but the idea of a *castizo* Spain, manifested in the authenticity of the *barrios bajos* of Madrid, would not really find traction until it could overcome the limitations that illiteracy presented for its consumption. Significantly, as the *zarzuela* shifted from its large three-act extravaganza of the mid-nineteenth century to the short one-hour format of the *género chico* that would emerge in the latter half of the nineteenth century and the early-twentieth century, the notion of a *castizo* Madrid and its recapitulation of the *manolos* and *majos* of Ramón de la Cruz would find an efficient vehicle for the disbursement of these images.[60]

LA ZARZUELA AND THE PURSUIT OF A NATIONAL OPERA

There is much debate about how to define the term *zarzuela*, given its long history and its two stages, from roughly 1650 to 1790 and from 1845 to 1965. In the most general terms, the *zarzuela* is, according to Roger Alier, "a variety of Spanish musical theater spoken and sung at the same time."[61] What distinguishes the *zarzuela* from other forms of musical theater is that patrons in general have not looked to the *zarzuela* for a rich literary experience, but rather for capricious entertainment in which a catchy tune, a humorous confrontation, and a certain folkloric familiarity was complemented by virtuoso singers. In general, critics tend to divide the *zarzuela* into two distinct categories, the *zarzuela grande*, or large format, of the mid-nineteenth century, which tended to consist of two or more acts, and the small-genre, or *género chico* (also called the *teatro por horas*, theater by the hour), which would emerge from around 1870 to 1910 and consisted of very short one-hour performances that could be performed multiple times each day.

The roots of the large-format *zarzuela* extend back to the seventeenth century, when Philip IV (1621–1665) would use La Zarzuela palace, located on the grounds of the Real Sitio del Pardo on the outskirts of Madrid, for resting and entertainment. Situated amongst the thorny brambles, or *zarzas*, of this garden palace, the performances took on an associated name: *zarzuela*. Here, performers entertained the king with musical theater heavily influenced by Italian opera.[62] Because of economic pressures and the need to provide actors and singers to the other theaters in Madrid, they began to intersperse spoken parts into these musical performances to alleviate the constant need for singers at one location or the other. As a result, the musicians themselves began to refer to the necessity of travelling to the Zarzuela Palace as having a "*zarzuela*."[63] The name took hold and fixed the association between the *La zarzuela* and a musical theater with spoken parts performed for the royal family. Because of this relationship between the *zarzuela* and the court, the musical form maintained a close association with Madrid.[64] Although the *zarzuela* eventually extended to other cities, Madrid would continue to be the production center for *zarzuelas* throughout the seventeenth century and into the twentieth century.

The rise in influence of French culture and tastes that followed the Bourbon ascent to the Spanish throne in the early-eighteenth century would threaten the *zarzuela*'s influence. In particular, the popularity of the Italian opera amongst the Bourbons and other European tastemakers would come to greatly overshadow Spain's more provincial genre. The rising influence of both Italian opera and other European cultural forms owed much to the patronage of Ferdinand VI and his musically talented wife, Bárbara de Braganza. Following European cultural currents closely, they sought to cultivate these foreign forms of theater in Spain. With the death of the royal couple in the last years of the 1750s, however, this period of dominance by the Italian opera would meet its end and leave an opening for the resurgence of more domestic forms of musical theater. Notably, it was Ramón de la Cruz who sought to bridge the gap between these two competing forms of musical theater and took it upon himself to translate the most popular and famous Italian operas of the day into Spanish. Through its tastes in theater, the court and the nobility in Madrid cultivated a proto-nationalist tendency within the theater culture of the capital. Ironically, while the translations were performed in cities other than Madrid (namely Barcelona, Valencia, and Zaragoza), their rejection in Madrid was firm and absolute. These other cities lacked the xenophobic anxieties of the Madrid theater-going public and found the Castilianized versions of the Italian operas to be unacceptable.[65]

This process can be seen in the emergence of another form of popular theater that served as a direct reaction to the Italianized theater of the time. *Tonadillas* were short musical pieces of lyric theater written with very few lines and requiring just a few players – characteristics that made them easy to produce and disseminate. Because of their popularity, they reduced the market for large-format *zarzuelas* and put more emphasis on the production of short pieces of theater that would reflect the growing market for performances articulating some notion of Spanishness – or, at the minimum, non-Italian or non-Frenchness. Significantly, the *majos* and *majas* from Cruz's *sainetes*, as well as popular *castizo* songs and dances, were an important element of the *tonadillas*, and, like the *sainetes*, were another means by which Spanish composers attempted to react against French and Italian influence and establish their own musical and artistic tradition.[66] In both forms, settings and characters alluding to some *castizo* ambience – at this point loosely defined as pertaining to Madrid – were a distinguishing characteristic.

During the late-eighteenth century, the *zarzuela* underwent a renaissance that would transform its content and result in the forms of the *zarzuela* as they are popularly understood today. Despite the heavy influence of the musical structures and forms of the Italian opera, in particular the Italian comic opera, or *opera buffa*, the renewed *zarzuela* began to look to the works of Ramón de la Cruz for inspiration.[67] There was also an active attempt to move beyond the world of mythology and look to popular customs within the Spanish landscape to represent an idealized notion of Spain.[68] Simultaneously, the more urban, and specifically Madrid-oriented, short *sainetes* of Ramón de la Cruz were flourishing. Both forms combined spoken and musical scenes with representations of popular life in Madrid's neighborhoods.[69]

Alongside these developments on the stage, a formal cultural apparatus began to develop in Madrid that cultivated these connections between Spanish identity and theatrical production. In 1799 the Secretary for Language Interpretation for Charles IV (1788–1808), Leandro Fernández Moratín, prohibited the production of theater performances in languages other than Spanish – first in Madrid, and later in all Spanish cities.[70] While this protectionism sought to support Spanish writers and theater companies, it also led to a proliferation of large-format *zarzuela* productions and translations of Italian operas in an effort to fill the gap left by the suppression of foreign productions.[71] The political situation during the first third of the nineteenth century (namely the invasion of Napoleon in 1808), disrupted this nationalist intervention in theater production. In addition, the subsequent French occupation of Spanish cities saw an infiltration of French comic opera (*Opéras-comiques*). Because of the strong contrast between these whimsical productions and the epics of the Italian opera, the end of the occupation saw a renewed interest in Italian opera, bolstered in part by the marriage of Ferdinand VII (1808 and 1813–1833) to the Neapolitan princess María Cristina, a devoted music aficionado. This conjunction of events left the *zarzuela* by the wayside and seemingly in the dustbin of history.

Ironically, the royal family's fascination with Italian opera led to an increased desire to cultivate Spain's own artistic tradition – an interest that culminated in the creation of the Conservatory of Madrid in 1830. It was founded as a national cultural institution to train young musicians in the art of operatic singing, and its creation calls attention to the efforts to situate Madrid as the cultural beacon of the modern nation by both locating it in the capital and including the name of the city in its title. In this context, the efforts of Spanish musicians and composers to find their own musical voice that was not reliant on the Italian models found fertile ground. There was particular interest in creating operas that would demonstrate the legitimacy of Castilian as a language of high culture that could compete with Italian, German, and French; this *inquietud*, or restlessness, as Alier describes it was most acute in Madrid.[72] Thus began efforts to develop some form of "national" opera in Castilian, a task that was taken up by three professors from the recently established conservatory. These efforts would eventually result in the production in 1839 of *El novio y el concierto*, written, ironically, by an Italian musician living in Madrid. It is significant that this work was advertised as a *comedia-zarzuela*, a double allusion that evoked both the "national" theater tradition of the *Siglo de Oro* as well as the (at that moment) defunct tradition of the *zarzuela*. Given that one of the broader goals of my argument is to consider the relationship between the theater and the construction of the national imaginary, it is important to emphasize that an institution dedicated to the cultivation of a national culture relied on the terms *comedia* and *zarzuela* as the point of departure. Though seemingly insignificant, this choice reflects the cachet that these genres carried; at the minimum, they held meaning for the Spanish musicians charged with constructing a national operatic tradition.

It is at this moment that the *zarzuela* began to re-emerge as a cultural force. In the midst of this resurgence, several Spanish composers established The Spanish Musical Society in 1848. Among its members were Hilarión Eslava, Emilio Arrieta, Francisco Asenjo Barbieri, and others, who would become key figures in the establishment of the modern *zarzuela* tradition. This same year, the stunning success of Cristóbal Oudrid´s *El ensayo de una opera: una zarzuelita en un acto* would add momentum to the influence of this "new" genre on the Madrid scene, and the writers of *El ensayo* were contracted to produce two more *zarzuelas*. In 1851, several composers rented the Teatro del Circo and proposed that each composer promise to produce three *zarzuela*s per year for the space. The success of these various productions attracted other composers to a new theatrical form that was quickly becoming a (lucrative) sensation. Madrid had become the center of this new sensation, and it quickly spread to other cities in Spain.

As the *zarzuela* gained more momentum, there was still a heavy reliance on "Spanish" themes in the form of characters from Spanish literature. More importantly, many writers, still in search of a national opera, employed the folkloric traditions of Spain's regional heritages to perpetuate some sense of the popular. The *zarzuela* often relied on Madrid as the setting for works that included various markers of local (i.e., regional) identity, such as the inflected speech of Andalusia or a traditional folkloric dance from another region, like a Basque *jota* or a Catalonian *sardana*.[73] As a large, bustling city, Madrid had no folkloric tradition of its own to speak of, but by fusing the various regional idiosyncrasies of the historic communities into the urban setting of Madrid, the *zarzuela* "represented the blending of a mosaic of regional music and of the particularized music of Madrid at a archetypical level."[74] This tension between the localized notion of Madrid, the local regional identities, and some sense of national identity would become one of the defining characteristics of the *zarzuela*.

The success of the modern *zarzuela* reached its climax with the opening of the Teatro de la Zarzuela on the calle Jovellanos in 1856. Constructed near the calle Alcalá and the Plaza Cibeles, the theater space aligned with a new modern sensibility coursing through the city. Indeed, it was directly adjacent to the anticipated epicenter of the expanding modern Madrid of the Castro Plan of Expansion.[75] The Teatro de la Zarzuela quite literally straddled the margin between the old imperial city and the modern one under construction. As if to emphasize the significance of the building to both the city and the increasingly modern nation-state, the inauguration of the Teatro de la Zarzuela took place on October 10, the birthday of Queen Isabella II (reigned 1833-1868). It was a national holiday indeed.

Interestingly, one of the most important works to be produced during this period was *El barberillo de Lavapiés* (1874) by Francisco Ansejo Barbieri, featuring a *libretto* by Luis Mariano de Larra. Its enormous success single handedly saved the Teatro de la Zarzuela that was on the verge of backruptcy at the time. It is significant that not only does this work take place in Lavapiés, but it locates the action in the Madrid of Charles III – the historical period during which Ramón de la Cruz was writing his influential *sainetes* and Madrid was undergoing major urban development. Barbieri rearticulated the *manolo*s and *majo*s of Ramón de la Cruz and the eighteenth century and reinforced the associations between Madrid and

Figure 2.4 | Juan Comba y García, *Los teatros y su público/Theatres and Their Audience*, 1883. Woodcut on paper, Museo de Historia de Madrid.

Lavapiés in the imagination of the theatergoing public. Even today, *El barberillo de Lavapiés* remains one of the most widely performed *zarzuelas,* fusing the name Lavapiés in the geographical lexicon of the *zarzuela* tradition.

As a testament to the popularity of the *zarzuela,* the Teatro de la Zarzuela was, at the time, considered the second-best theater in Madrid, next to the Teatro Real, a space dedicated to more traditional operatic performance. The establishment of a permanent physical space for the *zarzuela* legitimized its existence as a formal genre. There was much debate amongst Spanish musicians and intellectuals about the actual validity of this genre, given its reliance on both the Italian opera and the *opéra-comique* for structures and plots. Despite the window dressing of costumbrist elements, many *zarzuela*s were almost directly plagiarized from foreign sources. Nonetheless, the *zarzuela* in the mid-nineteenth century was at its peak, with multiple theaters in Madrid offering performances on a daily basis. A woodcut by Juan Comba from 1883 demonstrates how performances attracted people of all classes – albeit each class attending the theater commensurate with their social status (see Figure 2.4). He includes not only upper-class theaters like the Teatro Real, but also more middle-class spaces like the Teatro Zarzuela and the Teatro Apolo. Notably, he also shows more modest theaters like the Teatro Variedades. As a testament to the collective enthusiasm for these performances, the satirical comment at the bottom of the image refers to the obviously lower-class theatergoers at the Teatro Variedades (located on the edge of Lavapiés on the calle Magdalena) as attending the "Fiesta Nacional."

This period in the mid-nineteenth century would mark the high point for the large-format three-act *zarzuela*. At this time, if it did not meet its desired goal of becoming a national opera, then at least it emerged as one of the most popular forms of entertainment for an increasingly urbanized Madrid. The extensive number of theaters and performances led to a saturated market and made it difficult for both writers and producers to remain economically solvent. In addition, the political and economic instability of the late 1860s, which followed the liberal revolution of 1868 that deposed Queen Isabella II made the high cost of a theater ticket a luxury few Spaniards could or were willing to afford. These factors suppressed attendance and further complicated the precarious economic situation of the theater industry.

CHULAPOS, THE *GÉNERO CHICO*, AND *CASTIZO* MADRID

In the midst of the economic crisis that accompanied the liberal revolution of 1868, the owners of the Teatro de Variedades in Madrid, inspired by the cabarets that they had seen in Paris, developed the ingenious plan to offer many shorter performances for a much lower ticket price. What couldn't be accomplished with the extravagance of the *zarzuela grande* could perhaps be surmounted through sheer volume. This effort led to the creation of what would be called the *teatro por horas*, or theater-by-the-hour. Because these performances were often adaptations of large-format *zarzuelas,* the *teatro por horas* slowly came to be known as the *género chico*, or small genre. This approach brought such success to its purveyors that, from 1870 onwards, the *zarzuela* and the *género chico* would become a "theatrical monopoly" in Madrid and the rest of Spain.[76] Like the *comedias* of the seventeenth century, the *género chico* became not just a trend, but a cultural event.

The popularity of these *sainetes-cómicos* reached their pinnacle between the years of 1890 and 1900, during which time there were some fifteen hundred works performed in fifteen theaters in Madrid devoted to the *género chico*. Some of the most significant and notable theaters included the Teatro Variedades, the Teatro Circo de Paul, later known as the Teatro Lope de Rueda, the Teatro Lara, the Teatro Eslava, and of course the iconic Teatro Apolo. By 1909, 377 of the 411 plays that opened in Madrid were one-act performances.[77] The prolific production and variety of price points (depending on the theater, of course) allowed for the images produced by the *género chico* to permeate the imagination of the theatergoing public. Because of the brevity of the performances, the works of the *género chico* often relied on types in place of characters – a convention that was a holdover from the *comedias* of the Baroque period. Indeed, because of their short nature and their focus on ribald or irreverent themes, these works continued the emphasis on popular life associated with short theater that extended back to the seventeenth century. Madrid's working-class neighborhoods and a certain folkloric representation of its inhabitants became codified in the corpus of the *género chico*. As a result, critics like Pilar Espín Templado often argue that the "the central patio [of the corrala] is the essential *sainetero* setting," a view shared by Carmen del Moral Ruíz, who sees this setting as essential to their mythmaking.[78]

In what is perhaps one of the most iconic works of the *género chico*, the entire action of *La revoltosa* (*The Troublemaker*) takes place in the patio of a *corrala*, with the allure of a folkloric *verbena* providing much of the work's context. Composed by Ruperto Chapí in 1897, with a libretto by José López Silva and Carlos Fernández Shaw, the work garnered such success that its structure and setting were replicated in innumerable other short performances in the years that followed. Central to the *libretto* is a series of love triangles all intersecting in the now-iconic *chulapa* Mari-Pepa, whose playful flirtations with the married men that live in the building generate the play's central conflict. The men all plot to seduce her, while their wives plot to sabotage them. Threaded through the comedy are the authentic affections between Mari-Pepa and the lead, the unattached Felipe. As Lucy Harney notes, Mari-Pepa "emerges as the personification of the alluring, exotic, and quintessentially sensuous other."[79] The exotic quality of Mari-Pepa (and the many similar *chulapa* characters that would follow in her mold) stems, in part, from the efforts to accentuate her Andalusian qualities through cues like the distinct dialect of her speech and her *mantón de manila*. These visual and aural allusions evoke the sexualized Andalusian beauty made famous in *Carmen* and costumbrist sketches by writers like Serafín Estébanez Calderón. Alongside the coquettish and sharp-tongued *chulapa*, there would always be found the proud and strong *chulapo* entranced by her beauty. It is a dynamic that becomes a recurring plot line throughout much of the genre, its appeal likely, in part, from the familiarity that audiences – particularly the male members – had with the red-light activities that typically took place in and around the lower-class neighborhoods. It was in these neighborhoods where men might find poor immigrant women who were more likely to be unattended in public space, and therefore (supposedly) open to advances. The availability of these lower-class women was likely all the more acute at public events like *verbenas*, which attracted many different types of people and allowed for the mingling of different classes.

Indeed, in the über-classic work from 1894 entitled *La verbena de la Paloma* (1894), written by Tomás Bretón with libretto by Ricardo de la Vega, the lecherous pharmacist Don Hilarión describes his amorous adventures in his carriage and spends much of the play seducing Susana and Casta (again lower-class *chulapas*) by offering to bring them to the *verbena* in said carriage. The underlying sexual tension stems in part from the genre's debt to the bawdy humor of the French *opéra comique* and its titillating cancan girls. Despite these salacious undercurrents, the characters ultimately reinforce the long-held emphasis in Spanish society (and drama) on the personal honor (*la honra*) of the main characters. Despite the fact that the play does not take place directly in Lavapiés (it occurs in the adjacent neighborhood of La Latina), the images of *chulapos* and *chulapas* speaking in what would become identified as the inflected speech of Madrid's working class at the turn of the century contributed to the myth of *castizo* Madrid.[80] It is through the works of the *género chico* that Lavapiés and the *barrios bajos* writ large have become synonymous with Madrid's theater tradition and the idea of *lo castizo*.

The neighborhood is not just a site that serves as the setting for the *sainetes* of the *género chico*; it has also often been the actual site where they are performed. For example, as Isabel Gea describes, for many years during the festivals of San Isidro and Madrid's Veranos de la Villa (Summers in the City) celebrations, Lavapiés was the location for open-air performances of *zarzuelas* on a stage built in front of the facade of the iconic *corrala* on the corner of the calle Tribulete and Mesón de Paredes (see Figure 2.1). Notably, because of this legacy and its characteristic morphology, at the base of this building the plaque dedicated to the famous *zarzuela* composer Ruperto Chapi on the seventy-fifth anniversary of his death describes the *corrala* as the "scenario," or stage, on which the *La revoltosa* was born. The urban landscape of Lavapiés continues to be a stage that reproduces the mythologized notions of its own identity – the physical terrain of the city fundamental to the lived or representational space created in the minds of the people.

This conflation in the *género chico* between Madrid and Lavapiés infects the historiography. For example, when Fernando Vela cites the popularity of the *género chico* and its prolific production to argue for the canonization of a "*género chico*" generation that would mirror the recognition afforded to the prolific production of the Generation of '98, Vela demarcates the specific character of these works and makes it clear that "for the authors of the *género chico* the principal source was the *madrileño* life of that time."[81] Given the typical setting of these works, his reference to Madrid in this context suggests that the "authentic" *barrios bajos* serve as the metonymic equivalent of the entire capital.

Significantly, it wasn't just within the works of the *género chico* that Madrid played a role, it was also the center of a whole industry of cultural production.[82] This occurs to such a degree that the principal theaters that produced these short works were absorbed into the sense of nostalgia that permeated them. In her brief history of Madrid, Gea describes Lavapiés as being one of two areas "muy populares y castizas" (very popular and *castizo*) in the Embajadores district of the city (the other is *El Rastro*, an adjacent neighborhood to Lavapiés). She describes how "Lavapiés is the neighborhood of the *sainetes* – Carlos Arniches, Ricardo de la Vega, Ramón de la Cruz – and of the *zarzuelas* – Chapí, Chueca, Bretón, Barbieri – whose center is the *Corrala*, with a capital C because it is the quintessential *corrala*, where each summer *zarzuelas* are presented in the open air in front of its facade."[83]

With Madrid as both a site of production and consumption, the *género chico* greatly influenced the way inhabitants viewed the city and themselves. Moral Ruiz points out that this all occurred at a key moment for the city in which there was a transition from the *ancién regime* to a more modern city. In 1860, the *cerca* of Philip IV was demolished to make way for the architect and engineer Carlos María de Castro's plan for the expansion of Madrid. The expansion of the railroad system accompanied these changes, and the concentrated growth in the city's transportation system transformed the physical and cultural landscapes of the city alongside its increasing industrialization and urbanization. According to census figures from 1857 and 1877, the population of Madrid grew 25 per cent between 1836 and 1857 and subsequently another 77 per cent between 1857 and 1877.[84] Much of this growth was due to rural emigration to the major cities and their developing industrial capacities.[85] As a result of this domestic immigration, the people who populated the working-class neighborhoods of Madrid and formed the backbone of the city's industrialization were often not *madrileño* at all, but rather from various regions of Spain and often from the rural areas of Andalusia and Castile, the countryside surrounding Madrid.

As a result, despite its reliance on the urban landscape and its inhabitants, the *castizo* is also always deeply embedded with a rural nostalgia. Initially, as Deborah Parsons writes, the term "was used by mid-nineteenth century Madrid writers and commentators to describe the popular local color of its lower classes, and in particular the social identity of the southern-lying neighborhoods of

La Latina, Lavapiés, and Embajadores."[86] Later, the writers of the Generation of '98 began to broaden the definition of the term to suggest that it was in the crucible of Castile that the disparate identities of Spain – *la patria chica*, or small-scale homeland – were formed into the *patria grande* (great homeland) of the Spanish nation. Describing this transformation, Parsons asserts that, "redefined by national ideologies, *lo castizo* was naturalized into the 'authentic' expression of Spanish cultural character and lost much of its specific urban context and cadence: multicultural, lower-class Madrid substituted by a fantasized rural Castile."[87] Echoing the xenophobic reactions of the writers of the eighteenth century, this inverting of an urban trope to a rural one reveals the anxieties of many Spanish intellectuals, including, of course, Unamuno, toward the increasing modernization the country was experiencing. Modernization represented Europeanization and a possible diluting of a (at this moment) tenuous Spanish identity. In contrast, the mythological rural type that characterizes Unamuno's text represents an essentialized sense of pre-industrial Spanish identity intimately connected to the physical land: a connection to territory that should persist beyond the surface-level changes brought on by modernization.

Therefore, paradoxically, the *castizo* characters of the *género chico* not only construct an essentialized image of authentic Madrid, but also evoke a rural and provincial nostalgia. This paradox allows for Madrid to serve as the fusing point of Spanish identity, what Jorge Luis Borges in his famous short story calls an *aleph*: a point in space that contains all points. The capital is both unique and distinct, but simultaneously contains all provincial variations of the heterogeneous Spanish nation-state.[88] Castile may be the pastoral source of Spanish identity, but Madrid, as the center of Castile, is the forge where Spanish identity is fused into its modern conception. The *tipos* of *manolos* and *chulapos* that populate the *zarzuela* at the turn of the century, then, are not merely representations of *lo madrileño*, but a "placeholder for a national patriotism."[89] It is in these theatrical forms where a modern mythology of the city is constructed, a representational space in which Madrid and Lavapiés are synecdoches for notions of Spanish identity.

This nationalist discourse underpinning *castizo* culture became an important part of the Falange cultural apparatus, initially as a way of cultivating associations between Madrid and national Castilianist ideology and later as a means of selling Spain abroad. Much of this nationalist discourse circulated around the veneration of Madrid's patron, San Isidro, in preference to more localized street celebrations dedicated to neighborhood saints like La Paloma and San Cayetano – a process whereby celebrations of local identity converted into a veneration of Madrid. The regime co-opted what had been neighborhood expressions of pride increasingly associated with images of urban modernity.[90] In terms of spatial practice and representations of space, this shift moved celebrations out of the individual neighborhoods and into spaces with more national (and imperial) associations (a trajectory that would be reversed by the Citizens' Movement in the 1970s). The celebrations would begin in the Plaza Mayor and culminate in a day trip to the San Isidro Meadow just across the river, where the Palacio Real offered a compelling backdrop. Tellingly, as the work of Parsons illustrates, posters for the San Isidro celebrations during the early years of Francoism "frame Madrid within a closed Christian and romantic past."[91] This new spatial practice of Madrid's *castizo* culture simultaneously used urban settings to transform the celebration of Madrid into a "national" holiday, while also incorporating the rural edges of the city to cultivate a connection with pre-modern Castile – the heartland of the Francoist national geography.

The elision of racial and provincial distinction also contributes to the quasi-national character of *lo castizo*, one fraught with paradox. While the term refers to the purity of Spanish blood, there is of course little purity to be found in a nation whose bloodlines extend back through seven hundred years of Moorish habitation and whose contemporary history is characterized by struggles with a polyglot national identity, a topic that will be addressed more directly in later chapters. Additionally, while the genres of the *sainete*, the *zarzuela*, and the *género chico* perpetuated associations between the working-class neighborhoods of Madrid and pure *casticismo*, these neighborhoods were, and still are, the site of some of the highest concentrations of immigrant populations in Madrid. While in the eighteenth and nineteenth centuries this immigration was domestic, today it is more international. The *castizo* is therefore an ideological construct that arguably has more to do with the landscape than with the individuals that populate it.

That the "purest" neighborhoods of Madrid have always contained a more heterogeneous composition has even led contemporary scholars to glorify Madrid's ability to forge some greater

Spanish identity. José María Gómez Labad falls into just this sort of rhetoric in his book about representations of Madrid in the songs of the *zarzuela* and the *género chico*. In the introduction, Gómez Labad suggests that it is precisely "the *casticismo* ... that has been the product of that mix of the pure *madrileños* and those of the provinces."[92] Even some eighty years after the turn of the century, scholars persist in representing Madrid as some mythical site where the heterogeneity of the modern Spanish nation is fused into some sort of pure Spanish identity.

Moral Ruiz suggests that this myth of Madrid was "forged by the *género chico*,"[93] and describes how "little by little, by the force of repetition, the *madrileño* reality was converted into stereotype. The spectators quit seeking in these pieces the reflection of their problems and dissatisfaction and found in them an image of a fixed city, immobile, in which, without much effort, they could tranquilly recognize themselves while smiling complacently."[94] This dependence on recognized locales and stock characters created, according to Salüan, "a type of consensus or pact that [affected] all the interested parts" and generated "an essential piece of the collective life."[95] In other words, the *zarzuela* strived to emphasize certain national myths and, as a result, issues of class and worker solidarity were superseded by the anodine (albeit appealing) images of flirtatious encounters, catchy songs, and comedic conflicts amongst the lower classes – and the spontaneity and struggle of everyday life slowly but surely converted into a static set piece for bourgeois consumption. In her study of different performances and film versions of *La verbena de la Paloma* at distinct historical moments (1894, 1935, 1963, and 1996), María Teresa Herrera de la Muela demonstrates how these various representations continually create a "metalanguage" that ostensibly traps the working class in a folkloric image that keeps them non-threatening and seemingly celebrated and beloved.[96] In a paradoxical way, the local is used to amplify the national. As a result, the production of theater becomes the stage for a synecdoche in which the urban helps produce the representational space necessary to drape a national imaginary over a particular territory.

Nonetheless, these discourses of *lo castizo* have not merely been for entertainment, but also highly political and tied to the reshaping of urban space in the cultural imaginary. When Madrid's Citizens' Movement began to use open-air festivals and mural paintings as strategic appropriations of public space, these became an important means by which citizens in Madrid began to reassert a popular right to the city that had been functionally denied during Francoism. Later, in the 1980s, the Ayuntamiento and the Autonomous Community of Madrid would deploy these same festivals as a form of civic boosterism that conflated regional, municipal, and neighborhood identities.[97]

Thus, *castizo* culture and its important relationships with popular theater, cultural policies of the state, and the use of urban space are essential to understanding contemporary Lavapiés. It is in this matrix of urban space, everyday life, and the popular theater that one finds the significant conflation of local, municipal, and national geographies. In this sense, Lavapiés functions on a variety of levels: there is the proliferation of physical theater spaces that extends from the seventeenth century on through the twentieth; the employment of these urban landscapes as the backdrop for the theater traditions of the *zarzuela* and the *género chico*; and finally there is the role that urban space has played as a theater for spectacles of power. Today, Lavapiés remains central to the myth of Madrid through its contemporary theater industry and, in particular, the Centro Dramático Nacional Teatro Valle-Inclán. This national theater builds on the tradition of urban spectacle that has been a part of Madrid since the early-modern period. While in the past these spectacles were at the service of the monarchy or industrial capital, now they serve the interests of global financial capital and the production of the twenty-first-century city, a topic to which we now turn our attention.

3

The Global Stage of Madrid: The Teatro Valle-Inclán and the Rehabilitation of Lavapiés

In the closing scene of award-winning playwright Jerónimo López Mozo's play *The Architect and the Watchmaker*, the eponymous Watchmaker offers a sharp critique of "the architecture of glass" that characterizes the rehabilitation of the iconic Real Casa de Correos building in the Puerta del Sol.[1] The conversation reflects the central conflict in the play between the Architect, who has been charged with rehabilitating the building, and the Watchmaker, who maintains the building's famous clock and tries to thwart the Architect's efforts "to clean and sanitize the exterior space."[2] When the Architect reveals the building's new reflective steel-and-glass facade, the Watchmaker expresses a profound anxiety about the transformation of urban space occurring at the turn of the millennium. He suggests that, "when in a facade there appears the reflection of some old building nearby, it has the sensation that the architecture of all periods is integrated into a single one."[3] Yet, the "harmony" of "light and transparency" that this facade is intended to evoke is dubious, because "on occasions, glass is more opaque than steel. It is so attractive that it traps the gaze until it intoxicates the senses."[4] The intoxicating glass architecture "dazzles until it makes invisible the very objects that it illuminates" – translucence transformed into opacity.[5]

Much of López Mozo's concern in this work of "political surrealism," as Magda Ruggeri has described it, addresses historical memory and the need to protect the triumphs and the traumas of the past from the erasures that accompany the physical transformation of the city – in this case the connections between the Real Casa de Correos and state violence during the Franco regime.[6] Yet, the Watchmaker's critique also reflects a broader uneasiness with contemporary architecture, drawing connections to other iconic buildings, like the Louvre and the Reichstag, which have relied on glass as a principal architectural feature for their rehabilitation. The play calls attention to the irony that these glass architectural spectacles, despite their illuminative properties, do not clarify, but rather distract the public and obscure the political struggles reflected in a city's architectural history.

Along with this treatment of contemporary architecture, the play also considers the more generalized spectacle of urban rehabilitation. Early in the play, the building remains covered in tarps, with its changes yet to be revealed. The tarps function like a metaphoric curtain hiding the spectacle of the new building yet to be revealed. Trying to assuage the Watchmaker's fears that rehabilitation will erase the footprints of the past, the Architect assures the Watchmaker that "when the tarp is drawn back, the Real Casa de Correos will still be in its place."[7] As if directly evoking Debord's obfuscating spectacle, this process of construction, as the Watchmaker points out, has transformed the building into "a scene on a stage that does not allow one to see what's behind it."[8] The construction and rehabilitation of this building will alter the facade and undermine the public's ability to "reproduce or interpret the history of Madrid via a series of emblematic buildings."[9] The spectacle of new architecture and the reconstruction of the city distract not only from the unique lived experience of the city's residents, but also from the economic processes at work across the territory of the city and the globe. The use of a globalized architectural vocabulary sanitizes and flattens the discrete narrative of the building and its connections with the city and the national territory. It is a process that assists in the urbanization of capital – global ephemera made material at the urban scale, whether in Lavapiés, in Madrid, or in any number of global cities.

This treatment of contemporary architecture brings attention to the symbolic role that architecture plays in producing meaning in the city and producing different geographies of space and place. While written some years before its construction, the play resonates in significant ways with the Centro Dramático Nacional Teatro Valle-Inclán, which was built in 2003 in Lavapiés as a part of the Urban Plan of 1997. Bounded by the streets Valencia, Argumosa, and Salitre, the Teatro Valle-Inclán occupies a triangular lot adjacent to the Plaza Lavapiés in Madrid's Embajadores district.[10] The dark

Figure 3.1 | Image of the Centro Drámatico Nacional – Teatro Valle-Inclán. Lavapiés, Madrid.

glass of the facade faces the bustling plaza and serves as a bold architectural statement when juxtaposed with the much older buildings nearby, some of them from the nineteenth century (see Figure 3.1).

The previous chapters have illustrated the important historical relationship between urban space, spectacle, and ideology in Madrid and Lavapiés, and their role in the construction of a national imaginary. In the following chapter, I argue that the Teatro Valle-Inclán, as a vehicle for the urban and the cultural policies of the Ayuntamiento of Madrid as well as the central government of Spain, extends these articulations by connecting the local (i.e., the neighborhood), the municipal, the national, and the international. Given its connection with state power and real-estate speculation, the Teatro Valle-Inclán is closely aligned with those spaces of representation or conceived space that Lefebvre calls "abstract space."[11] In short, the architectural spectacle of the Teatro Valle-Inclán illustrates the ways that culture and capital have produced twenty-first-century Lavapiés. The physical architecture, promotional materials, and the programming are all key elements of this discursive production in a new urban space. When these new discourses are considered in the context of Madrid's overall plans for rehabilitation of the city – namely the Urban Plan of 1997 – they reveal how the Teatro Valle-Inclán not only deployed the Madrid-Lavapiés synecdoche, but reframed these interwoven geographies within Madrid and Spain's global aspirations. A theater building is itself an act of cultural production, and the Teatro Valle-Inclán contributed to a broad transformation of urban space across a range of geographies, both in the physical domain and the "representational space" of the urban imaginary.

THE SEARCH FOR A NATIONAL THEATER BUILDING

Using cultural institutions in Madrid as a means for consolidating national identity extends back to the late-eighteenth century. In that period, artists and intellectuals pushed to establish a National Conservatory or National Lyric Theater to help incubate Spanish musicians and writers and protect emerging "Spanish" genres of musical theater (like the *zarzuela*) against the dominance of the Italian opera. Complementing these institutional efforts were the long-standing efforts to create a permanent home for a National Theater. Some of these first efforts to establish a National Theater building began in 1845 with the establishment of the Teatro Español on the site of the old Corral del Príncipe.[12] This event prompted many dramatists, actors, and directors to push for the establishment of a National Theater building that would provoke a more substantial and committed subsidy for the production of Spanish theater. These institutions, as well as the very efforts to establish them, would contribute to what Inman Fox has called "the invention of Spain," a process of ideological construction that mythologized the historical longevity of a Spanish national consciousness through work in historiography, literature, law, and, of course, the theater.[13] The role of the theater industry in the "invention" of Spain would become even more overt as the emerging nation-state of the nineteenth century solidified into its more modern form in the twentieth century. In particular, the strong ideological and administrative state apparatus developed during the dictatorships of Miguel Primo de Rivera (1923–1930) and Francisco Franco (1939–1975) played key roles in perpetuating monolithic notions of national identity and its alignment with a legal and bureaucratic apparatus we might call the state. Under both regimes, the theater was used as an important tool for this process.

During the rule of Primo de Rivera, there had been many intellectuals in the theater community who hoped that the authoritarian regime would intervene and take over the Teatro Español from the control of the bumbling Ayuntamiento whose mismanagement of the building compromised its capacity to truly support theater professionals in the capital.[14] In this context, the death of the famous actress and theater personality María Guerrero in 1928 presented a unique opportunity for the regime and those interested in a national theater project, and momentum built to rename the Teatro de la Princesa in her honor, since she had been the owner and proprietor. Writing in the newspaper ABC in 1928, Rafael Sánchez Mazas lobbied for the national government to intervene, hoping that it would turn the Teatro María Guerrero into the site "of a new Madrid, of a new Spain and the indispensable instrument of an expansion into the world."[15] Not only did Sánchez Mazas understand the importance of culture to the project of building the nation-state, but he sensed the potential for a designated national theater building to reconfigure urban, regional, and national identities. The building was renamed the Teatro María Guerrero in 1931, but it remained in the hands of the Ayuntamiento.

The debate over establishing a national theater building continued during the period of the Second Republic (1931–1939) and focused on the position of the old guard, committed to the notion of a national theater as a "museum" to preserve the classics, and newer voices that hoped to use the state to create a subsidized "laboratory" for the theatrical vanguard.[16] With the Teatro María Guerrero in the midst of rehabilitation, much of the debate focused on the Teatro Español and the Ayuntamiento's reluctance to relinquish control of the building. This bureaucratic impasse was complemented by the national cultural policies of the Second Republic, which pursued "the spread of culture to remote areas devoid of modern notions and conveniences."[17] Under the auspices of the Ministry of Education, the central government devoted more energy and resources to the creation in 1931 of the Pedagogical Missions, projects that included dramatist Alejandro Casona's Theater of the People and Federico García Lorca's La Barraca (The Sideshow), which worked to bring classic Spanish drama to the rural countryside.[18] National theater was to be pedagogical, but brought to people on their terms.

The outbreak of the Spanish Civil War and the overthrow of the Republican government brought an end to these efforts for a national theater building and the commensurate socialist-inspired programming. In the wake of the war, the ideologically committed dictatorship took advantage of a powerful state apparatus to bring the Teatro Español under its management, while also designating the Teatro María Guerrero a national theater building, with the hope of "[recuperating] the national and Christian tradition of Golden Age Theater."[19] Intellectuals like Felipe Lluch Garín saw the need for "absolute control by government institutions and the hierarchical subjugation of the theatrical industry and arts to the political propaganda of the totalitarian state."[20] Naturally it was to Spain's *Siglo de Oro* that the regime turned as a means of creating continuity with Spain's imperial past. As previously discussed, this effort took the form of appropriating the tradition of the *auto sacramental*, one-act plays that have historically been performed since the seventeenth century in honor of Corpus Christi through the allegorizing of the Eucharist. Central to Counter-Reformation propaganda efforts, these plays were not only religious in nature, but also "[instructed] the subject on how to belong appropriately to the Spanish state as well as to the Catholic kingdom of God."[21] As the Nationalists ascended to power and consolidated their rule, the "right-wing regime and its cultural ambassadors reclaimed the *auto sacramental* from their avant-garde predecessors returning the genre to its original position as a didactic tool for a conservative state."[22] While many of these *autos* were performed in public spaces – a recapitulation of the Baroque processional tradition – it was this theoretical perspective that guided the management of the two national theater buildings in Madrid: the Teatro Español and the Teatro María Guerrero. After Franco's death in 1975, the Teatro Español was returned to the Ayuntamiento, while the Teatro María Guerrero remained under the control of the national government.

THE TRANSITION, INDEPENDENT THEATER, AND LAVAPIÉS

Following the death of dictator Francisco Franco in 1975, the theater industry operated within a substantially less-restrictive environment, especially once official theater censorship ended in 1977. Despite the freedom to explore themes of sexuality and morality, the theater industry still found itself, after many years of repression, reluctant to present works with explicit political content.[23] For many involved in the theater industry, the period of the Transition was a time of disillusionment and pessimism about the health of the Spanish theater.[24] The timidity of the commercial theater industry left a void that encouraged the growth of non-commercial independent theater. This theatrical flourishing saw the establishment of many new theater spaces during the Transition, and in this context the small iconic cinema space on the Plaza Lavapiés, known as the Cine Olimpia, was reopened in December 1979 with a specified commitment to independent theater.[25]

When the Socialists finally came to power in the post-Francoist era, they enacted an aggressive policy of subsidies to develop and recover the remains of the repressed Spanish theater industry.[26] From 1978 to 1982, the government's budget to support theater increased 75 per cent, and then tripled yet again in 1983.[27] These subsidies were part of a broader effort by the Socialist government to consolidate a "national" culture during the politically fragmented period after the Transition, when a reconfiguration of the political spectrum was in process. Santos Juliá suggests that these efforts aligned with an interest in Spain to not only cultivate a broader European identity, but also to recover "identity" by "consolidating and extending" the regional nationalisms in Spain.[28] This tension between an outward-looking Europeanization and regionalist isolationism strained the delicate sense of nationhood holding the nascent Spanish state together. According to Juliá, the "government's cultural policy was geared toward favoring the national – the Spanish – by establishing or increasing awards and national prizes in the fields of literature, history, painting, music, etc."[29] Cultural policy was conceived as a kind of glue to hold together a politically and linguistically fragmented nation.

On the other hand, the theater also functioned as a symbol of artistic freedom and offered an important space for the development of a post-Francoist cultural politics for Spain's other linguistic communities. The Constitution of 1978 proposed a decentralized state formed by multiple autonomous communities – something previously anathema to the centralized Castilian state of the Franco regime. Many of these autonomous communities embraced the theater as a vehicle for reclaiming their culture and their language. Money was also invested in decentralized cultural policies in order to bolster these efforts. Valencia, Catalonia, Galicia, and Andalusia, for example, were quick to establish National Centers of Drama and made efforts to provide permanent spaces for the production of theater.[30] This development was due, in part, to the fact that the spoken and public nature of theater made it an ideal format for the literal vocalization of languages and notions of regional-nationalist identity that had been prohibited and/or, at the minimum, barely tolerated for almost forty years.

National and municipal leaders in Madrid also took advantage of this new cultural landscape to reshape the image of the capital during the early 1980s and to distance Madrid from associations with its authoritarian past. The construction of a regional identity through administrative restructuring contributed greatly to these efforts, leading to the creation of an independent municipal administration after 1979, and then later, in 1983, the Autonomous Community of Madrid. As Hamilton Stapell points out, it was the Ayuntamiento's takeover of the Teatro Español that symbolized this shift – a return to the municipal control that had managed the theater since the early-seventeenth century. By appropriating cultural installations at the urban scale, the municipal government began to dissociate Madrid from the nationalist associations produced by the centralizing tendencies of the dictatorship.[31] During the Franco regime, independent theater had served an important political purpose, according to César Oliva, as it represented the "equivalent of struggle, of an alternative situation."[32] As a result of their contrarian and politically charged position, the independent theater companies were well poised to take advantage of the ground-breaking cultural policies of the Socialist Workers' Party that won the post-Franco elections of 1982. The establishment of the National Drama Center, or Centro Dramático Nacional (CDN), in 1978 became one of the central vehicles for this more pluralistic cultural sensibility. In 2009, the CDN described its purpose to be to "disseminate and consolidate the distinct currents and tendencies of contemporary dramatic production, with special attention to current Spanish authors."[33] With these objectives in mind, when the Socialist government added to the network of official cultural bodies in 1984 by establishing the National Center for New Tendencies of the Stage [CNNTE – Centro Nacional de Nuevas Tendencias Escénicas], the Sala Olimpia was the logical choice to house this new bureaucratic arm of the CDN committed to non-traditional theater. After its transformation from cinema to theater in 1979, the space had been managed by the Centro Cultural La Corrala and thus had already become "one of the fundamental options for the development of professional independent theater."[34] Incorporating the Sala Olimpia into the network of cultural institutions in Madrid only further consolidated Lavapiés's position as a center for theatrical production.

A NEW ALTERNATIVE: THE CENTRO DRAMÁTICO NACIONAL TEATRO VALLE-INCLÁN

This history of spectacle and alternative theater was certainly at the forefront when the new Teatro Valle-Inclán was constructed and inaugurated. In a 2006 interview in *El País* just days after the opening of the Teatro Valle Inclán, the director of the Centro Dramático Nacional at the time, Gerardo Vera, claimed that the new site for the Centro Dramático Nacional would be "a reference point of professional rigor and an opening for all types of creative work related to the world of the stage."[35] Vera went on to suggest that, not only would the new site be a center for theatrical enterprise, but that it would be "a center of experimentation that isn't subject to the implacable laws of the market."[36] Freed from the demands of the marketplace, Vera also saw the Teatro as a gestation site for innovative theater productions that could then travel throughout Spain.[37] In Vera's hopeful vision, the Teatro Valle-Inclán would serve as a vehicle for the dissemination of culture "throughout the national territory."[38]

Importantly, at the time of its inauguration, the Teatro Valle-Inclán was not seen as just a site for theater on the national or municipal level. It was also intimately tied to the urban space around it, and, in this context, the notion of the avant-garde served a purpose as well. In the 2002 retrospective *Madrid: Four Years of Management of the General Plan for Urban Ordinance for Madrid 1997*, published by the municipal government's Office of Urbanism, the authors describe the proposed plans for the new location, citing how it had been "during a long time a reference point for the theater lovers of Madrid," emphasizing in particular its role as a "natural stage ... for avant-garde groups of all of Spain."[39] For the city planners, not only was the building's theatrical history important, but specifically its associations with the avant-garde. The imminent rehabilitation of the building would evoke the theater history of the city, but also become a symbol of the nation's modern theater tradition.

It is not only the city planners that had these broad aspirations; the state cultural apparatus had them as well. Gerardo Vera explicitly referenced this more global interest in a 2004 interview with *El Cultural*, the arts supplement to the newspaper daily *El Mundo*, in which he asserted that "the CDN is going to be a center for the promotion of performances that, in collaboration with the Instituto Cervantes, will contribute to the diffusion of contemporary Spanish theater beyond our borders."[40] To this end, the CDN established a department of International Relations at the same time that the new site of the CDN was being constructed.[41] The Teatro Valle-Inclán may have been located in the neighborhood of Lavapiés, but complicity between the cultural institutions of the Spanish state and the urban planners of the Ayuntamiento envisioned the local spectacle of the theater as a global stage for the performance of a national identity.

The very names assigned to the two theater auditoriums in the Lavapiés site of the Centro Dramático Nacional performed a certain ideological work. The principal auditorium, which holds 510 spectators, is named for the iconoclast Galician dramatist of the Generation of 1898 Ramón María de Valle-Inclán (1866–1936), whose expressionist *esperpentos* of the late teens and twenties walked the line between prose and drama and often incorporated the visual possibilities of film. Vera explicitly states that this name was selected to communicate that "Valle-Inclán will be the artistic reference for the CDN."[42] The smaller auditorium, which holds 150 spectators, is named for the stagecraft experimentalist Francisco Nieva (1924–2016). By choosing Valle-Inclán as the namesake, the Ministry of Culture evokes the Generation of 1898 and creates associations with the canon of Spanish letters and its so-called Silver Age, an important historical moment in Spanish letters and the visual arts, which occurred during the first third of the twentieth century.[43] At the same time, both Valle-Inclán and Nieva are closely associated with experimental theater, and therefore the names are suggestive of the non-traditional theater of the avant-garde and its anti-institutional associations.[44] These choices discursively distanced the state cultural apparatus from the building and, in theory, assisted in the cultivation of Lavapiés's image as a bastion of neo-Bohemianism in Madrid.

The promotional materials distributed at the inauguration of the building in 2006 and the architectural innovativeness of the performance space clearly demonstrate this avant-garde vision. The press releases emphasized, for example, that "its modern installations, the flexibility of the interior auditoriums, and its cutting-edge stage equipment [would] make it a standard for the creation of contemporary theater."[45] The emphasis on the theater's scenographic flexibility, its modernity, and its high-tech equipment suggests it was seen as a physical expression of the theatrical vanguard – privileging experimentation and innovation over tradition.

Nonetheless, the programming of the Teatro Valle-Inclán in its early years often did not really live up to this rhetoric of the Teatro Valle-Inclán as an incubator of national avant-garde theater. For example, in the short inaugural season (2005–06), the theater produced one canonical Spanish work (*Divinas Palabras* by Valle-Inclán), two foreign works (one British and one American), and one work in Catalan (performed in the much smaller Nieva performance space). The following season (2006–07) this trend continued, with another production of *Divinas Palabras*, five foreign works (including two international theater festivals), and merely two contemporary Spanish works. The 2007–08 season saw ten total performances, of which four were foreign and six were national works. This seemingly more balanced programming was offset by the fact that three of the six Spanish works were still relegated to the smaller space of the Sala Francisco Nieva. Similarly, in 2008–09, of the six national works that were performed, four utilized the Sala Francisco Nieva. Despite the avant-garde and nationalist rhetoric used to describe the aspirations of the Teatro Valle-Inclán, the list of productions in its first few seasons seemed more suited to the international theater circuit than a "National" theater space.

The design of the performance space itself attempted to bridge this gap between words and actions. Cutting-edge engineering allowed for a wide range of staging possibilities and arrangements of the public. A series of hydraulic lifts, located beneath the principal auditorium, could alter the space to allow for a proscenium configuration (with the stage in front) or more non-conventional approaches to the space, using a black box or thrust-stage theater style. According to Angela García de Paredes, one of the two principal architects from the firm Paredes Pedrosa, which designed the building, the space was from the outset not intended to be "a conventional hall," especially given that, from the beginning, they knew that they would need to create a space "that could be transformed and that would be itself like a stage."[46] Ignacio G. Pedrosa, García de Paredes's partner on the project, described how the principal theater space could change into "a grand container with the imagination as the only limit, from a conventional hall to the most provocative staging."[47] For the architects, this flexibility created a relationship between the performance and the public that was "necessarily open and flexible."[48] Thus, the very engineering of the space was intended to support the sort of relaxing of the fourth wall that has become a hallmark of modern (i.e., avant-garde) theater. The public entering the performance hall would engage in a participatory spectacle communicating the dynamism of the CDN's productions.

According to the architects' own interpretation of their building, the exterior space also relaxes a sort of fourth wall to create a sense of openness and dialogue with the public in the Plaza Lavapiés directly in front of the facade. The footprint of the building is one of the ways that the architects create this effect. In the architects' published descriptions of the building and in an interview with this author, they frequently cited as one of the building's architectural achievements the superimposition of the three rectangular volumes of the building onto a triangular plot – a key feature that produced the building's staggered facade. This technique not only allowed for a more effective use of the interior spaces of the building within the limiting confines of the triangular plot, but also left a portion of the plot open to the adjacent Plaza Lavapiés. For the architects, "this continuous space that extended out in front of the theater entrance, permeable before the plaza ... converted it into an anteroom, a true urban vestibule for entrance to the building and a natural prolongation of the Plaza Lavapiés."[49] The liminal space of this mini-plaza lay on the margin between two spaces, pertaining to both but not exclusively to either – a type of "between" that was both simultaneously public and private, interior and exterior, the plaza outside the theater acting as vestibule or anteroom for the activities inside the building.[50]

This liminality, in theory, is compounded by the facade of the building, whose three square volumes contain "glass fronts [that] ... transform at night into prisms of light that allow the sycamore of the wood-paneled interior walls and the movement of the public in the vestibule to be seen from the exterior."[51] For the architects, there is a visual exchange that occurs between the exterior and interior of the building. At night, the people on the street can see through the glass facade into the well-lit theater. During the day, this liminal quality can be seen in the reflection of the older buildings in the dark

Figure 3.2 | The reflective glass of the Teatro Valle-Inclán.

glass when observed from the "anteroom" of the plaza. The neighborhood appears to be "in" the theater, and, in theory, the theater is firmly entrenched in the neighborhood (see Figure 3.2).

Though Pedrosa and García de Paredes interpret these features of the building as increasing the exchange between the completely public space of the plaza and the fee-for-entrance publicly owned theater, there is another possible interpretation. If one accepts Yi-Fu Tuan's notion that "architecture teaches" by clarifying social roles and relations, one can see that these architectural features communicate outwardly to the viewing public of the plaza (who are very rarely the spectators of the theater).[52] The dark glass of the Teatro Valle-Inclán doesn't necessarily serve to incorporate the neighborhood into the architecture of the building, but rather distances the neighborhood from the interior space of the building, and in turn differentiates the two spaces. As Tuan suggests, "constructed form has the power to heighten the awareness and accentuate, as it were, the difference in emotional temperature between 'inside' and 'outside.'"[53] During the day, the reflective quality of the dark glass functions like panoptic one-way glass in the interrogation room at a police station. The Teatro's dark facade repels the viewer's gaze from the street with its reflective qualities, and permits only the ephemeral image of the Plaza Lavapiés; the simulacrum of the neighborhood's architectural past is fixed as image in the opaque glass of the institutional building. They cannot see inside, but of course can be seen.

This panoptic quality of the building is today complemented by the Special Surveillance program put in place by the Ayuntamiento in January 2008, which called for heavier police presence on the Plaza Lavapiés. Alongside Lavapiés's multicultural milieu was the addition of officers milling about the plaza in their high-visibility yellow jackets, police mounted on horseback, and the use of drug-sniffing dogs.[54] In December 2009, the installation and activation of some forty-eight surveillance cameras reinforced and expanded this disciplining gaze.[55]

At night, the lesson shifts. In *Space and Place*, Tuan spends time describing the use of light in the repetion of history, and describes how Gothic cathedrals used interior light to "produce effects of mystical beauty."[56] The Teatro Valle-Inclán relies on this tradition as well. The contrast between the dark night and the "mystical beauty" of the well-lit lobby maintains the distance between the plaza and the interior from the daytime by transforming the interior space of the theater into an illuminated fishbowl. The spectators milling around inside the building become "extras" in the urban spectacle of the Teatro Valle-Inclán; their ethnicity and class likely form a visual contrast to the multicultural plaza, while the quiet space of the interior contrasts with the bustle and noise on the plaza at night. The spectacle of the Teatro Valle-Inclán is not found merely within the confines of the performance hall, but also in the plaza outside the building where the architectural rhetoric of the building's facade communicates its message. In this interpretation, the Teatro Valle-Inclán, turning to Debord, "presents itself as something enormously positive, indisputable and inaccessible."[57] Just as the performance within the Teatro Valle-Inclán is echoed by the spectacle of the building itself, the building contributes to the urban spectacle around it.

The theater straddles an invisible line in the neighborhood between the streetscape to the west and the street life found to the east along the calle Argumosa. According to a 2004 article in the Properties section of *El País*, when one leaves behind "the plaza of

Lavapiés and continues East towards the Glorieta del Emperador Carlos V, the appearance of the Embajadores neighborhood changes radically. From the variegated multiracial environment that is found to the West ... one passes into a much less noisy space ... A space emerges where residential use predominates, with higher quality and much-better-preserved dwellings."[58] Here, the terraces are full of a much more homogenous population, which Gómez describes as the "newbie" neighbors: "a new population of relatively young middle-class citizens – around thirty or forty years old – more or less socially and politically progressive, bohemian to various degrees, possibly artistic as well."[59] They are the pioneering gentrifiers of Richard Florida's "creative class," and have even been referred to by one city council member as "the new colonists."[60] The square black volumes of the Teatro building, then, also serve as a gateway of sorts to the tree-lined and terrace-dotted cale Argumosa, which runs in almost a direct line between the expanded Museo Reina Sofía and – as it was described in *El País* in 2004 – one of the new architectural icons of Madrid, the Centro Dramático Teatro Valle-Inclán.[61]

This spot between the gentrified calle Argumosa and the bustling and diverse streets to the west is almost directly in the center of what the Urban Plan of 1997 designated as Sector I of Lavapiés as a part of the Integral Rehabilitation Plan of Lavapiés, an area of about 50 square blocks (32.5 hectares), since 1997 the focus of a major rehabilitation effort for the Centro district of the city. The city planned to combat the problem of *infravivienda* (sub-standard housing) by rehabilitating 2,500 housing units in the neighborhood at the cost of nearly 24.6 million euros (35.3 million dollars).[62] Ironically, this same set of city blocks was also characterized by some of the highest real-estate prices per square meter in the city, and by 2002 it wasn't uncommon to find a difference of 2,404 euros (3,450 dollars) per square meter in Lavapiés between buildings right next to one another.[63] In 2003, the price had risen to 3,500 euros per square meter for rehabilitated housing units.

For those critical of this process, the investment in Lavapiés and the transformation of the housing stock was never about the improvement of the lives of its inhabitants. Rather, it was always about real-estate speculation. The rising cost of housing and its suspected connection to the city's investment in the neighborhood led one local activist, Jordi Claramonte, to complain in June 2003 that the urban change occurring was "the conversion of a degraded neighborhood into a hip neighborhood, and later into an expensive neighborhood."[64] At the same time these complaints were being voiced by residents about the gentrification occurring in Lavapiés, the dean of the Official College of Architects of Madrid, Ricardo Aroca, lamented to *El País* that "during the last decade the municipal Administration and the speculators have been indistinguishable."[65] This suspected relationship between speculative interests and the Ayuntamiento implicated the Teatro Valle-Inclán in this broader plan for the redevelopment of Lavapiés in the minds of many activists. The investment in the cultural resources of the neighborhood and the improvement of the housing stock would change the economics of the neighborhood and displace the "undesirables" (i.e., people without acquisitive power). These dynamics led activists like Carlos Vidania and others to describe the Teatro Valle-Inclán as a "cultural bunker" and a "cultural bulldozer."[66]

The morphology of the Teatro Valle-Inclán, with its impenetrable dark glass looming above the plaza, evokes this idea of the "cultural bunker." Likewise, the flat facade of the building stands poised as a metaphoric bulldozer blade, ready to roll through the plaza, leaving a gleaming, gentrified neighborhood in its wake. But as a symbol of the gentrification to come, the building was merely one showpiece in an urban spectacle with connections to global flows of capital and Spain's interest in increasing Madrid's international profile: a relationship made clear in the writings of urban planners in their retrospectives of the Urban Plan of 1997.

A NEW IMAGE OF THE CENTER: IMAGINING LAVAPIÉS
IN THE URBAN PLAN OF 1997

The retrospective book *Madrid: Four Years of Management of the PGOUM 1997*, published in 2002 by the Office of Urban Management of Madrid, summarizes in less technical language the goals for the Urban Plan of 1997 and the steps taken to implement those goals. Significantly, a careful reading of the language used by the writers illustrates how many of the dynamics of scale, cultural production, and urban change that converged in Lavapiés were very much intentional.

Before moving on to the urban-planning texts, it is useful to see how the documents produced by the CDN itself situated the Teatro Valle-Inclán in the discourse of urban redevelopment. In particular, the press materials distributed upon the inauguration of the theater explicitly stated that the theater "[responded] to various objectives of a urbanistic, architectural, and cultural character shared by the agencies involved; on one hand, the effort [embedded] in the process of revitalization of the center of the city (specifically in the neighborhood of Lavapiés), and, on the other, it [proposed] the creation of a completely new public theater in Madrid, specifically constructed and conceived for producing and exhibiting dramatic performances."[67]

The building was to be both a cultural resource for the residents of Madrid, while also contributing to the urban transformation of Lavapiés and the Centro district of Madrid. The Teatro Valle-Inclán would be "a new urban reference point in the itineraries of the historic zones of Madrid, taking advantage of its proximity to the National Museum of Art Reina Sofía, the axis of museums of the Paseo del Prado, and other important centers of cultural activity in the center of Madrid."[68] Not merely an important site in Lavapiés, the Teatro Valle-Inclán contributed to a broader spectacle of urban change taking place across the city.

One indication of the building's engagement with different geographic scales is that the building's management relied on the convergence of local and national entities. At the urban scale, Madrid's Ayuntamiento paid for the construction of the building, the preliminary urban planning and architectural studies, the purchase of the property, and the execution of the project. At the national scale, the (former) National Ministry of Culture and its National Institute for Music and Performing Arts covered the costs of the interior of the building, including the stage and its technical components, as well as the office space and interior corridors.[69] This administrative layering of the local and national continues today, as the Ayuntamiento owns the property, while the central government manages the facility through the Ministry of Culture and Sport.

The collaboration between urban planners and the national cultural apparatus illustrates the expansive role that government plays in the production of space. For Lefebvre, these relationships are a given, since the modes of production aligned with "abstract space" always imply a top-down conceptualizing of the city. When it comes to spatial production necessary for the accumulation of capital, it is not merely to be found in the factories of industrialization or the gleaming office towers of global finance. There is a need for the social reproduction of values, desires, interests. The very notion of the "urban" must be produced.

Lefebvre explores this idea of the "urban" in his influential monograph from 1968, entitled *The Right to the City*. While seeking to define what he calls the "urban problematic," Lefebvre insists on the intricate and intrinsic relationship with "the process of industrialization."[70] This relationship creates "a *double process* ... industrialization and urbanization, growth and development, production and social life."[71] This social life, or *urban society*, is made up of an *urban fabric*, a "phenomenon of another order, that of social and 'cultural' life."[72] For Lefebvre, this "cultural life" becomes manifest in the process of socialization produced by urban space and "carried by the urban fabric ... [to penetrate] the countryside."[73] In other words, the urban society created by industrialization results in not only architectural and demographic transformations, but also in a series of cultural transformations (basically consumer culture) that project across the entire territory, whether that be the urban space of Madrid, or the national territory of Spain.[74]

Although Lefebvre wrote in the context of late-twentieth-century industrial capitalism, his concept of the *urban fabric* applies quite aptly to the post-industrial context as well. The advanced-services economy and its correlative consumer culture is one that must produce its own space. Essential to the production of this space is the establishment of a new bureaucratic system of power. Interestingly, Lefebvre seems to anticipate these new systems of economic production and suggests that this system of power recreates the urban core as a "high quality consumption product for foreigners, tourists, people from the outskirts and suburbanites."[75] This consumer product, the new urban entity, is not merely produced physically, but within the discourses of academic disciplines like History, Economics, and Sociology.[76] The result of these converging academic discourses is a social practice called urban planning, which, according to Lefebvre, sees the urban environment in terms of a series of particularities and generalities.

In a theoretical move that has been important for culture critics, Lefebvre aligns these concepts to the concepts of performance/competence used by structural linguistics, seeing the activities within particular cities and those of particular individuals as speech acts (*parole*) within a more generalized system of language (*langue*). In other words, individual cities might be organized in a particular way or rely on certain cultural practices that are distinct, but this seemingly unique *parole* or "speech" act, always functions within the general *langue* (language) that defines all cities. Similarly, within a particular city's system of discourse (*langue*), individuals perform it in particular ways (*parole*). The *langue* of the city is the urban fabric or abstract space produced by planners and projected over the city. In the case of Lavapiés and the Teatro Valle-Inclán, that *langue* can be seen explicitly in the aforementioned retrospective *Madrid: Four Years of Management of the Urban Plan of 1997*.

The preface to the book by then-Mayor José María Álvarez del Manzano (1991–2003) warns that, in "an era of political, economic, and cultural globalization, a city like Madrid should not examine itself from a local perspective."[77] For this reason, the Urban Plan of 1997 – as he describes it – sought to develop "instruments for confronting the challenges of a modern capital integrated into the European Union that takes advantage of the opportunities afforded by its privileged geographic situation as the potential head of the Mediterranean arc and a bridge to Africa and the Americas."[78] Both in 1997 when the plan was developed and in 2002 when the retrospective book was published, the planning establishment in Madrid saw the rehabilitation of urban space in Madrid as a means of integrating the city into the supranational body of the European Union, while positioning it as a leading city in a variety of transnational global networks.

The vice-mayor of Madrid and the head of the Division of Urbanism, Infrastructure, and Housing, Ignacio del Río García de Sola, also emphasizes this discourse of globalization in the Introduction to the book. He hopes quite explicitly that Madrid might be transformed "into the great financial center of Southern Europe, as well as an Olympic city," achievements that would situate Madrid amongst the "great capitals of the world."[79] The mayor's preface also emphasizes the Madrid's Olympic candidacy, and suggests quite emphatically that it would be "the reference point for centralizing [the] efforts towards a better future."[80] Although we could naively believe that the attraction of hosting the 2012 Olympic Games derived from interest in the feelings of goodwill associated with this global event, the purpose was likely more pragmatic. For the city leaders, the Olympic Games would put Madrid onto a global stage, jumpstarting its marketability for investment and tourism.[81]

This goal had, and continues to have, a strong precedent. Ferrán Brunet, a researcher for the Center of Olympic Studies and a professor at the Autonomous University of Barcelona, supported this assertion in his comments to *El País* in November 2009 regarding the 2016 Summer Games in Rio de Janeiro. He suggested that, in general, "it isn't only the derivatives of the athletic event and the investments that are put on the table to attract it, but rather the foreign investment that one can attract before the event itself and for years afterwards." For example, Brunet calculated that the 2000 Sydney games generated over three billion dollars in economic activity in Australia. Likewise, the 2008 games in Beijing generated nearly twenty-three billion dollars in economic impact.[82] The increased visibility and infrastructure investment that would accompany the games was presumed to be a financial shot in the arm for any municipality. Of course, Spain had already seen these benefits first-hand after hosting the 1992 games in Barcelona. According to Christopher Hill's political history of the Olympic Games, "even if accurate figures are difficult, perhaps impossible to produce, Barcelona has been put on the map as a city of world importance; more hotels have been built, and the city attracts more visitors and conferences than ever."[83] The Olympic Games for Madrid and other cities were seen as a fast track to global visibility and a means of attracting foreign capital.

While articulating the process for accomplishing these goals, Álvarez del Manzano, intentionally or not, echoes the vision of Richard Florida's notion of the "Creative City."[84] The mayor suggests that Madrid must be "like an active stage in which citizens can freely develop their professional, social, and cultural activities in an environment of respect and tolerance."[85] Draped in the language of tolerance and cosmopolitanism, Álvarez del Manzano's description in the preface points to the plan's neo-liberal quality. The notion of "freely developing" one's interests hints at the free-market agenda that accompanied the Popular Party into power in 1995 and implicitly informs the assumptions of the Urban Plan of 1997. This neo-liberal agenda can be intuited if we accept geographer Neil Smith's assertion that "urban real-estate development – gentrification writ large – has now become a central motive force of urban economic expansion, a pivotal sector in the new urban economies."[86] Behind the utopic platitudes lay an interest in developing a global financial capital and the subsequent economic expansion this would create.

This situation prompted the then-president of the Catalan Socialist Party and former mayor of Barcelona (1992–1997), Pasqual Maragall, to suggest in 2003 that, despite the Spanish constitution's picture of a pluralistic democracy, there seemed to be the belief in

Madrid that the unsettled political situation required "a firm hand in the center for dominating its demons; although now a hand as much economic as political, as much 'liberal' as dictatorial before."[87] The power of the new centrist state run by the free-market boosters of the Popular Party would leverage its economic power, with Madrid serving as the principal "stage" for attracting foreign investment.[88]

This neo-liberal discourse can also be found in the retrospective book's language describing the "recuperation of the historic city center." [89] In theory, this recuperation would result "in the maintenance of the [Center's] traditional population and the renovation of the real-estate offerings without historic-artistic interest." [90] Bolstering the real-estate market is a key piece of the Urban Plan of 1997, as a means of addressing the pressing problem of housing in the city.[91] The lack of land and the cost of housing had created a crisis that was expelling "new families to the metropolitan periphery." [92] With the middle class on the periphery of the city, the city center had lost one of the key features of a consumer society: consumers.

It was hoped that the infrastructure improvements resulting from the Urban Plan of 1997 (increased access to housing, sidewalks, limits on the use of buildings) would not only maintain the current population, but make the center more appealing to people of different ages – hopefully enough to shift demographic trends.[93] The physical transformation of the city would socially transform the urban environment. Central to these plans was the neighborhood of Lavapiés because, as Gómez points out, the logic of monopolistic capitalism that was driving these redevelopment plans "couldn't tolerate that the central zones of the city – attractive for their historic urban design and for their cultural attractions, both historic and modern – were occupied by the most humble classes living in old buildings and impeding the speculation of the land."[94] The physical modification of the neighborhood, though discursively articulated in terms of improving the lives of its inhabitants, was arguably merely prepping the neighborhood for real-estate speculation. The very fact that so much money was directed at a national theater building meant to attract spectators from across the city, instead of new health centers, social centers, or sports installations that would directly impact the lives of the residents, is one illustration of this fact.[95]

The Ayuntamiento's assessment of the Urban Plan of 1997 quite explicitly called attention to these objectives for the social transformation of the Center. The authors of *Madrid: Four Years of*

Management of the Urban Plan of 1997 emphasized that "revitalizing and recuperating the historic center of Madrid, especially the *Casco Antiguo* [old quarter], [was] one of the greatest challenges assumed by the Urban Plan of 1997, problematized, moreover, by the major scale of this operation with its emblematic character and strong social component."[96] The plan's interest in the neighborhood's "emblematic character" and the project's "social component" was an unsubtle xenophobic allusion to the problematic social situation in the center of the city.

According to Antonio Zárate Martín's study of the changes in Spanish urban centers in the last fifty years, the number of foreign residents in Madrid went from 32,120 in 1986 to over 500,000 in 2005, over 16 per cent of the population. Significantly, most of this presence was found in the central part of the city, in the districts of Sol (35 per cent), Embajadores (34.5 per cent), and Universidad (30 per cent).[97] A large elderly population complemented this multicultural presence, and in 2005 it represented nearly 21 per cent of the population of the Centro district.[98] In total, immigrants and the elderly made up nearly 40 per cent of the overall population in the early part of the 2000s. These numbers do not correspond to Florida's image of a city full of young, youthful tech-savvy workers prepared to meet the challenges of a global financial capital in the new century. With this context in mind, it is important to note how the authors of the retrospective emphasize not only the "social component" of the plan, but also its "emblematic character." The Urban Plan of 1997 was designed to create an urban symbol, a spectacle that would appeal to the International Olympic Committee, as well as companies looking to invest internationally. Madrid was a city in pursuit of becoming a global capital.

Key to this spectacle was, of course, the neighborhood of Lavapiés, discussed at length in the retrospective book.[99] Lavapiés was seen as the "*stage* of action" for the "final touch" of the plan.[100] Central to this urban "spectacle" was the image that would be consumed by the pedestrian spectators passing through the "performance stage." To accomplish this objective, the Urban Plan of 1997 established several administrative tools, including the "Commission on Urban Aesthetics, whose function [consisted] of defining the principle directives related to the protection, maintenance, and improvement of the fundamental values of the urban landscape."[101] This new bureaucratic arm of the Ayuntamiento would be charged with closely guarding the "image" of the city of Madrid.[102] One of the key provisions was the power of "executive substitution" (i.e., eminent domain), a tool intended not only for "the maintenance of constructed patrimony, nor only distinct monuments, but rather the city as a whole."[103]

Echoing the desire of the monarchy in the seventeenth century to convert the city into "an immense and integrated décor," the Commission on Urban Aesthetics was charged with requiring property owners to maintain buildings to address both issues of safety and aesthetics.[104] These codes would revive the visual landscape of the city. As an example of the success of this program, the Ayuntamiento celebrated the rehabilitation of seventeen buildings in and around the Plaza de la Paja. There, in the heart of Hapsburg Madrid, these "residential buildings of the eighteenth and nineteenth centuries, and their facades were recuperated utilizing traditional techniques, returning them to their original colors and textures. As a result, the red, yellow, white, or indigo tones of the plaster facades lent a polychromatic richness to the landscape."[105] Not only does this "polychromatic richness" literally renew an image from the past, but it also reasserts the streetscape as a place where power and capital can express their influence. If Baroque architecture functioned as urban spectacle to instruct the spectator on the splendor and power of the sovereign, then the bright colors of the refurbished historic city center would communicate the control of urban space by the modern-day municipal sovereign, the Ayuntamiento. Though pleasant to consume visually, this rehabilitated urban space was designed to attract certain inhabitants and visitors (i.e., young professionals and tourists), while displacing others (the working and lower-working classes) to the periphery.

This interest in using image as a means of controlling urban space can also be seen in the criteria for construction laid out in the retrospective book. The document describes the city "as a conjunction of elements within the urban fabric that configures the space of the city from the perspective of the environment and landscape."[106] This criterion is possible because the city's visual landscape is conceived as "a singular element thanks to its architectural, morphological, and typological quality."[107] Gentrification and urban change function as the result of economic processes, but they also rely on visual cues in the form of decor and ambience (coffee shops and hip bars, for example) to transform the symbolic and exchange value of a particular neighborhood. In the case of Madrid, this symbolic value was constructed by means of an aesthetic code that attempted to integrate the entire city into one cohesive visual experience. Another way of altering this system of exchange value was through the use of cultural capital. In a post-Fordist context, cities need to compete to attract the new workers of the contemporary service economy. The dominant paradigm, to which Florida has contributed so heavily, suggests that these workers of the new economy require "places that offer abundant economic opportunity, [and an] exciting cultural and social environment."[108] This cultural discourse pervaded the Urban Plan of 1997, particularly in its interest in the "maintenance and fomenting of institutional sites and facilities that allow for the development of the symbolic and emblematic character of the center without interfering in its residential purpose."[109] In line with my overall argument here, institutional cultural sites would play a key role for establishing the symbolic value of the city center. Via these cultural resources and this symbolic work of the city center, Madrid would improve its image as a global capital and leverage the position of the nation-state of Spain amongst various global financial networks (namely the Mediterranean arc and the European–Latin American exchange).

But both the issues of geographic scale found throughout the Urban Plan of 1997, as well as the plan's focus on the city's cultural resources, have another important element. Specifically, the neighborhood of Lavapiés was seen as a key site for the overall redevelopment of the city. It was also seen as a model for urban change throughout all of Madrid and the entire territory of Spain. *Madrid: Four Years of Management of the Urban Plan of 1997* emphasized that Lavapiés "[had been] converted into the point of reference, and the focus of the new rehabilitation policy of *Spain and Madrid*."[110] Significantly, this process required the involvement of bureaucratic entities across various administrative scales, from central, autonomous, and local administrations, to the European Union in the form of subsidies from the Cohesion Funds.[111] The confluence of these funds contributed to the monies used in the designation of the neighborhood as an Area of Integrated Rehabilitation.[112]

In *Madrid: Four Years of Management of the Urban Plan of 1997,* these sites are defined as "those in which there has been detected a great necessity for public investment, because of the poor state of the neighborhood, a condition defined by the limited economic power of its inhabitants, and overall social and environmental degradation.[113] Of these projects, the "ongoing operations in Malasaña and Lavapiés are, perhaps, the most relevant examples."[114] In addition to the references to the physical rehabilitation of the neighborhoods, these Integrated Rehabilitation Zones also had "a social dimension of great importance," an aspect of reform that would be addressed through cultural projects like the "Plan for the Theaters and Cinemas Route" that would connect that the various Rehabilitation Areas.[115] The cultural resources of the city formed the connective tissue by which the Urban Plan of 1997 actively sought to subsidize and foster change at both the scale of the neighborhood and the city at large.

In particular, the work being done in Lavapiés was to be a preliminary step in the expansion of the tourist corridor of Recoletos-Prado: home to two of the most important museums in Madrid, the Museo del Prado and the Museo Thyssen-Bornemisza, and the central node for the tourist itineraries of Madrid. The writers of *Madrid: Four Years of Management of the Urban Plan of 1997* stated this interest explicitly and described the work of what they called Operation Lavapiés as essential to "the expansion of influence to the West along the Rondas until their intersection with the calle Bailén and the environs of the Royal Palace."[116] They would go on to emphasize that, "in this context, the new cultural enclaves related to the rehabilitation of Sector 1 of Lavapiés (Sala Olimpia, Circo Estable), together with the imminent expansion of the Centro de Arte Reina Sofía, constitute the first movement in this direction."[117] Finally, the city planners saw the Tabacalera as the "definitive impulse for the consolidation of the new cultural axis."[118]

Looking at a map of the area, one sees that this "cultural axis" begins at the Museo del Prado and extends in a curving line to the south and west through the Museo Reina Sofía and Teatro Valle-Inclán (see Figure 0.3). It would include the planned Museum of Visual Arts in the old Tabacalera. Turning toward the northwest, it would extend up through the important tourist site of the Rastro neighborhood, where the famous Sunday flea market is held, and move through the steadily gentrifying neighborhoods of La Latina and the historic neighborhoods of Hapsburg Madrid to arrive at the Palacio Real. Along the northern perimeter, this axis would include the Plaza Mayor, the Puerta de Sol, and the Plaza Santa Ana. This series of tourist destinations and cultural sites would form a touristic and cultural belt around the neighborhood of Lavapiés. The aforementioned "cultural bunker" would consist not only of the Teatro Valle-Inclán, but the "network of urban landmarks" that form a virtual ring around the highly desirable real estate of this iconic neighborhood – a cultural besiegement dazzling visitors with its architectural innovation, while speculative capital would work to alter the "social fabric" of the neighborhood.

But it wasn't just the activists who cynically believed in this outcome. The city planners, too, clearly saw the establishment of new cultural facilities as central to the renovation of the neighborhood. The cultural loop replete with new cultural sites would generate "attractive focal points of urban activity that would break the traditional isolation of Lavapiés with respect to the rest of the city".[119] This increased connection to the other touristic parts of the city center would help to improve "its urban image" by recuperating the vitality of a key neighborhood of the historic center.[120] Finally, the improvement of the cultural resources in Lavapiés would increase "in value the cultural character of the city center in *its entirety*."[121] Indeed, the planners predicated their plans on "the capacity of architecture to serve as a motor for the rehabilitation of the old quarter of a city."[122] The most significant "motor," they believed, would come from making "the Sala Olimpia a cultural landmark worthy of its prestige."[123] The symbolic capital generated by this new architectural icon would work in conjunction with the other projects proposed in the Urban Plan of 1997, "a network of urban landmarks," as they put it.[124]

Importantly, the writers juxtaposed their discussion of integrating Lavapiés into Madrid's cultural offerings with commentary on the extensive problems facing the neighborhood: the deficient state of the neighborhood's basic infrastructure; the lack of green public space; the lack of cultural and athletic facilities; the poorly maintained buildings; the lack of economic activity, with 24 per cent of commercial space closed or in disuse; an aging population; and high levels of undocumented immigrants.[125] In basic terms, the neighborhood's capacity to function as a productive space was limited by its social and physical situation. This list, presented as a sidebar in the book, also included the curious comment that one of the problems with Lavapiés was "the inadequate use of the public patrimony."[126]

This ambiguous comment alluded to Lavapiés's character as a mythic place, a myth that Gómez describes as "a manner of living, a style, a history – a legend."[127] She goes on in her description to emphasize that this emblematic character is an unmistakable personality constructed and accepted by the collective imaginary of a whole city and, possibly, of an entire country."[128] While Gómez is quick to point out the ephemeral quality of these categories and spends much of her article deconstructing these received notions of identity regarding Lavapiés, her characterization does speak to the role of Lavapiés in the cultural imaginary of the city and the nation. This mythic character dances between Lavapiés's *castizo* legacy and its contemporary associations with a unique blend of neo-bohemianism and multiculturalism.

This image isn't just a subtext, but one that the Ayuntamiento has actively sought to cultivate in recent years, and in doing so has used the perception of Lavapiés as a crucible of Madrid's diversity as another component of its urban spectacle. A number of cultural events in the neighborhood have illustrated these efforts. For example, in May 2009 the city hosted an event entitled Tangopiés: A Festival of Urban Tango in Madrid. It took place over two days and saw booths selling Argentinian empanadas and other delicacies, accompanied by the offering of free tango lessons on the Plaza Lavapiés. In the evening, the events moved two blocks to the nearby Plaza Agustín Larra for a series of concerts and dance performances.[129] In a more direct appropriation of the neighborhood's multicultural character, the neighborhood for several years has been the site of the city's annual BollyMadrid Festival, an event devoted to the profusion of Bollywood and Indian culture that has included films, food, and a market of clothes and goods. According to the now-defunct home page of the event, "the streets of the *castizo* neighborhood of Lavapiés [would] be filled again with the sounds, the colors, the flavors, and the beauty of Indian culture in a jovial ambience of coexistence."[130] The description captures aptly the way the city had intertwined the neighborhood's *castizo* past and its diverse present into the unique modern urban spectacle of Lavapiés. This connection with the past and its flavor of a globalized future clearly appealed to the Ayuntamiento, whose writers devoted sixteen of the 256 pages contained in their retrospective to a section of the city that only officially exists as a metro stop, a street name, and the name of a plaza. Despite this fact that the neighborhood of Lavapiés does not even exist in any official way, the Ayuntamiento entitles the section about Lavapiés "the new image of the center."[131] Converting Lavapiés into a spectacle to promote the city as a whole alludes to the way that the urban development in Madrid in the early 2000s was profoundly embedded at a range of geographic scales: the neighborhood, the metropolitan, and the global.

GLOBAL CAPITAL FOR THE CULTURAL CAPITAL

The retrospective book *Madrid: Four Years of Management of the Urban Plan of 1997* illustrates how Lavapiés was redeveloped as yet another entertainment district in the city. City leaders and urban planners hoped to leverage the various vectors of its symbolic capital: its multiculturalism, its *castizo* myth, its political counterculture, and its reputation as a locus of independent theater. Richard Lloyd and Terry Clark have described this urban-development strategy as an "entertainment machine," by which cultural offerings at the urban scale are implicitly linked to the broader flows of people and capital occurring at the global scale.[132] Diego Timón Barrado builds off this work in his study of Madrid as a post-industrial tourist city and highlights how these strategies reduce the city to a series of "archipelagos" spread across the city that one should hope to visit.[133] For David Harvey, these spectacles of urban space are part of a broader shift in city governance, from management to entrepreneurialism, with cities increasingly more focused on competing with one another in the global arena and attracting tourist and investment dollars. Consistent in the scholarly approaches to this subject is the clear emphasis on the ways in which these processes articulate various geographic scales.

Barrado Timón offers a compelling way to understand these tensions between the process of concentration occurring at the neighborhood or urban scale and the outward metropolitan diffusion that occurs as cities integrate more fully into the global flows of advanced capitalism. He describes the centripetal force toward the exterior of the city (both economically and physically) that tends to accompany a city's incorporation into the advanced service economy. Evidence of this centripetal force can be seen in the office buildings and skyscrapers that emerged in the AZCA complex in the north end of the city, which, since the late 1970s, formed the heart of the city's financial district.[134] More contemporary examples would be the Four Towers Business complex (named for the city's four tallest skyscrapers) that anchors a network of conference centers on the perimeter of the city.[135] As Barrado Timón emphasizes, this expansion of the city is made possible by the deep investment in transportation infrastructure that has allowed for greater movement of people within the city and, perhaps more importantly, out of the city – the most significant example being the construction of longer runways and a new terminal at the Barajas airport, which opened in 2006 and greatly expanded the airport's capacity. By 2008, Madrid had become one of the top ten sites in the world for business conferences.[136]

These developments successfully repositioned Madrid as an important node in the global economy in the first decade of the 2000s. Eduardo Santiago Rodríguez sees this repositioning as a process that began in the 1960s and has continued into the 2000s as Spain slowly and surely emerged from being a European backwater to join "the select club of rich countries that control the global circuits of accumulation and plunder."[137] This shift has occurred principally by "reorienting itself to the activities of the financial, decisional, informational economy and of control and management of flows of materials that feed the system."[138] According to the study *Global Urban Analysis*, produced by an international consortium of scholars, these efforts to position Madrid in the global economy were highly successful. By 2011, Madrid ranked number ten in their Business Command Index, just behind Beijing but ahead of Los Angeles and Stockholm.[139] Likewise, Madrid ranked in or near the top ten in other metrics such as Gross Connectivity, which measured how well a city was integrated into the world city network of advanced services producers (i.e., high-value services like financial consulting, insurance, accounting, etc.). The sectors of financial connectivity and management consultancy (ten and nine respectively) were also particularly strong for Madrid, along with its ranking in the top twenty for sectors like law, connectivity, and advertising (sixteen and twenty respectively).[140]

When put in a more regional context of European cities, Madrid's competitiveness is even more apparent, as it consistently began to appear in the top five rankings for these various categories, with a particularly strong presence in Global Network Connectivity (fourth behind London, Paris, and Milan) and Financial Services Network Connectivity (third behind London and Paris).[141] By the second decade of the 2000s, Madrid had effectively repositioned itself as the relational node between Spain and the global economy. In addition to articulating the national and global economies, Madrid had become a gateway city for global flows of capital and information between Latin American and Europe, a fact that allowed Madrid to become, as Santiago Rodríguez describes it, a "global hyper-connector node."[142]

The growth in Madrid's economic clout during the late nineties and early 2000s (until hitting the financial wall in the global financial crisis of 2008), occurred despite the size of the city's population as well as its corresponding region (the Autonomous Community of Madrid). Despite representing only 2 per cent of the national territory in the 1990s, and then merely 13.5 per cent by 2007, the Autonomous Community of Madrid was responsible for 17.5 per cent of the Gross Domestic Product.[143] Much of this economic influence came as a result of Madrid's ability to develop the most strategic service sectors. From 1993 to 2004 (the period during which the Urban Plan of 1997 was developed, published, and implemented), Madrid saw employment in business services, financial brokerage firms, and real estate grow by 116 per cent.[144] By 2009, over 65 per cent of businesses in Madrid were associated with the distribution of goods and services. Indeed, the managing of the movement of people, commodities, capital, and information intermediation (also called intermediation) began to outpace production in terms of number of employees.[145] Madrid's integration into the knowledge economy, as Ricardo Méndez Gutiérrez, Jésus Tébar Arjona, and Luis Daniel Abad Aragón suggest, demonstrated a certain dematerialization of the economy and a reinforcing of its position as a central node in the material and immaterial flows that connected the city to the national and international economy.[146] It highlights, yet again, how urban changes transforming Madrid during this period occurred along multiple axes: at the urban scale in the form of rehabilitation projects focused on increased cultural offerings, renewed building facades, and the renovation of public spaces, and simultaneously at the metropolitan scale through the expansion of the city in the form of new housing developments and transportation infrastructure.

These changes occurring at the metropolitan/urban scales were also closely linked to the broader internationalization of Madrid's economy. From the 1970s to the early 2000s, Madrid saw a shift from a small number of national financial institutions and banks to the majority of these institutions maintaining a site in the capital.[147] In the broader European context, the trend is the same, with every foreign bank in Spain having a site in Madrid, a situation that has facilitated Madrid's ability to secure extensive foreign investment.[148] The role of Madrid as a central node in the circulation of foreign capital contributed significantly to the development of what Emmanuel Rodríguez and Isidro López describe as the "Spanish Model." This "model" carried out by the Popular Party after their ascent to power in 1996 was predicated in part on the privatization of strategic sectors in Spain, such as the phone company Telefónica, the gas company Repsol, and others.

The transformation of the economy in Spain converged with similar privatization efforts by the International Monetary Fund in Latin America. As Rodríguez and López point out in their postmortem on the economic crash that began in 2008, there were suddenly "significant opportunities for internationalization for leading Spanish firms," and banks like BBVA and Banco Santander began to dominate the Latin American market, while other firms like Telefónica and Madrid-based electric companies grew to similar prominence in other sectors.[149] Rounding out Madrid's command-and-control function in the global economy was its growth as a logistics center. At the end of the first decade of the 2000s, it had become the fifth-largest logistics market in Europe – a sector that grew by 25 per cent from 1993 to 2001 and 17 per cent from 2003 to 2004.[150] While Madrid may not have been able to compete with London, Tokyo, or New York to become an alpha "Global City," there is a preponderance of evidence to demonstrate that it had solidified its position as a key beta city. It played a significant role in the flow of goods, people, and capital in the global economy, with over 70 per cent of foreign capital flowing through Madrid, and nearly 80 per cent of Spanish investment flowing out of the city.[151]

These changes had an inevitable impact on the other economic regions of the country. In particular, they reoriented the traditional rivalry between Madrid and Barcelona "clearly in favor of the capital."[152] In a 2001 article, "Madrid Is Leaving," Pasqual Maragall describes this shift, pointing out that "before, Madrid was the political capital and Barcelona and Bilbao, and later Valencia, the industrial and economic capitals. Now it appears to be the reverse. Now Madrid is the economic capital, the capital of innovation and of the new economy, while the political power has been decentralized."[153] By 2006, this image of Madrid's economic power had been actualized, with the capital city accounting for twenty-one of the twenty-nine businesses located in Spain that were included in the Forbes 2000 (detailing the 2000 most important corporations in the world). Similarly, of the nine businesses located in Spain that were recognized in the Fortune Global 500, seven made their home in Madrid and its corresponding region.[154] By July of 2009, these developments had vaulted Madrid to seventh place among cities with Global 500 companies, and had placed Spain in tenth place among countries with the presence of these large corporations.

During this time that Madrid was consolidating its position as global node in the advanced-services economy, the Spanish economy was experiencing one of its most productive periods in history. From 1995 to 2007, Spain became one of the darlings of the global economy. The "Spanish Miracle," as it came to be known in the international financial press, saw the creation of nearly seven million jobs and an economy that grew at a rate of nearly 4 per cent.[155] Much of this growth came not from increasing wages or public spending, but rather through the financialization of household economies, a product of years of domestic housing policy, liberalized credit markets, and the securitization of mortgages. As in the United States, this process inflated the value of household financial and property assets and subsequently fueled the consumer economy. In Spain, though, the scope and scale of this model was substantially greater. In 2007, home ownership stood at nearly 87 per cent, compared to rates in the United States and the United Kingdom that never rose above 70 per cent during the same period.[156] Because of this disparity, López and Rodríguez suggest that Spain was like an international laboratory for this new model of economic growth, an economic model that follows closely what David Harvey has called the secondary circuit of capital accumulation. Capital, its value under threat from over-accumulation, switches from the "primary accumulation circuit" (i.e., increasing production output) to the secondary accumulation circuit of fixed assets found in the built environment, like public works or housing.[157]

As urban-studies scholars like Fernando Roch Peña and Eva García Pérez, and multiple publications by the Observatorio Metropolitano research collective, have demonstrated, the state "played a crucial role in lubricating the different parts of the property circuit to maintain a permanently increasing housing supply."[158] These state interventions included policy changes, such as 1998's Land Act (Ley de Suelo), also known as the build-anywhere law, which turned over huge tracts of land to developers and expanded the metropolitan footprint of the city. Municipal and state investments in transportation infrastructure supplemented these legal reforms by opening up large areas of land for urbanization. The financial–property-development circuit was sealed through reforms of the regulatory frameworks surrounding the securitization of debt. Because buyers had access to easy money, housing prices soared by nearly 220 per cent. Thus, alongside the immateriality of the knowledge economy that was emerging in Spain and Madrid was a parallel transformation of the built environment.

Of course, despite reaching all these benchmarks as a global financial capital, Spain was one of the hardest-hit countries after the global financial meltdown of 2007–08. At the time, the editors of the *Economist* described how "the housing bust at home, as much as the financial turmoil abroad, [sent] Spain skidding towards recession."[159] By April 2010, Spain's unemployment rate reached 20 per cent, nearly double the 10 per cent rate of the Euro Zone in general, with some 4.5 million Spaniards out of work – the product of six straight quarters of economic contraction that followed the collapse of its credit-driven economic-growth model.[160] The dual facades of the financial-service sector and a highly inflated housing bubble eventually undermined Madrid's ascension to global prominence. "After the fiesta" as the *Economist* described the crash, Spain, with Madrid as its financial figurehead, found itself classified with the other "PIGS" (Portugal, Italy, Greece, Spain) of the European Union whose financial problems threatened to spread the contagion of economic collapse across Europe.[161]

In the midst of Madrid's ascension, the presence of global capital had had implications for the cultural life of the city as well. One of the key nodes in the previously mentioned "bunker cultural" was the Casa Encendida, a cultural center that opened in December of 2002. Since its opening, the Casa Encendida has been a place for cultural offerings from "the most avant-garde artistic expressions, to courses and workshops about areas like the environment or solidarity."[162] It was established as a new locale in the neighborhood of Lavapiés for the "scenic arts, cinema, exhibitions, and other manifestations of contemporary creativity."[163] Importantly though, this project was and is an initiative of the private foundation and social programs of Caja Madrid (one of the largest financial institutions in Spain). The space was a direct expression of global capital into the cultural scene of Madrid and of Lavapiés. As a result, this cultural center, despite the generally high quality of its artistic offerings, was built, arguably, on the coattails of the newly refurbished Reina Sofía museum just a few blocks away. In other words, its public was not the neighborhood of Lavapiés but rather the international tourists that made the Reina Sofía an essential part of their visit to Madrid. It was the clearest example of the links between global capital, the production of culture, and the transformation of Lavapiés into a twenty-first-century urban spectacle.

Ironically, in February 2002, it was the adjacent building around the corner at Amparo 103 that local activists chose to *okupar* in order to establish the third manifestation of the Laboratory Self-Managed Squatted Social Center (Centro Social Okupado Autogestionado El Laboratorio 03). This self-managed social center sought to create its own spectacle of Lavapiés that would call into question the program of real-estate speculation and gentrification being carried out by the Ayuntamiento in collusion with the interests of capital across the city. In contrast to the urban life imagined in the Urban Plan of 1997 and manifest in the Teatro Valle-Inclán, the Labo 03 imagined a different neighborhood and a different city, albeit still enmeshed in the complicated geographies produced in the spectacle of contemporary Lavapiés.

4

Resisting the Spectacle:
The Practiced City of the Laboratorio 03

On 21 February 2006, Madrid's city leaders and other dignitaries inaugurated the Centro Dramático Nacional Teatro Valle-Inclán with much fanfare and celebration. More than just another new theater venue for Madrid, it figured prominently in the Ayuntamiento's plans to rehabilitate the long-neglected Lavapiés neighborhood, while continuing to consolidate a circuit of cultural attractions throughout the capital's Centro district. Many local activists, like the Surrealist Group of Madrid, a Situationist actors' group working in Lavapiés and Madrid, saw the facade of glass and concrete as a "an imitation of a bunker, of a trench, of the West Bank wall, the monolithic materialization in physical space of despotic power and of the social relations that it creates."[1] Rather than celebrating the presence of a new cultural asset, the group imagined it in militarized terms, a cultural bunker protecting the advance of speculative capital into the neighborhood.

Others in the neighborhood shared this view and organized protests on the day of the building's inauguration. As several important city leaders, including the mayor of Madrid, Alberto Ruiz-Gallardón, arrived for the event, a local activist situated himself in a window high above the plaza with a bullhorn.[2] From there his catcalls and mocking slogans rained down on the plaza. The protester's shiny red clown's nose lent his actions an air of theatricality, a frivolity shared by his compatriots on the ground, who carried banners and signs and wore, of course, their own shiny red clown noses. With slogans like "dead from so much culture without a health center," the protesters' signs emphasized the absurdity of investment in such a luxurious cultural facility while basic neighborhood services remained absent.[3] Similarly,

Figure 4.1 | Protest of Teatro Valle-Inclán inauguration, 21 February 2006. Lavapiés, Madrid.

protesters wondered why, after so much money (nearly twenty million euros invested by the Ayuntamiento and the Ministry of Culture), the neighborhood remained devoid of cultural space to call its own. For many, the brand-new Teatro Valle-Inclán did not represent a contribution to the neighborhood, but rather was the product of a policy dedicated to, as one sign described it, "Everything for the beautiful people, so the ugly folks get out." Another sign read "This bunker is declared inaugurated," an allusion to the sense that this shiny cultural institution served an almost-martial function, besieging the territory for the sake of monied interests.[4]

Yet the protests during the inauguration of the Teatro Valle-Inclán were not merely about the theater building itself, as signs from the protesters also asked "Is this the new social center?"[5] (See Figure 4.1.) Their question alluded not to any social center but rather to one that would fill the void left by the eviction in July 2003 of the self-managed occupied social center called the Laboratorio 03, a reference made explicit in the distinctive encircled lightning bolt found on the sign – a typical symbol of *okupas* across Europe.[6] Other signs, like one that read "Three years without the Laboratorio, A social center in the Tabacalera already!"[7] juxtaposed more explicitly the new national theater building with the grassroots efforts under way to negotiate the cession of the old tobacco factory nearby into a community resource to replace the Laboratorio.[8] The juxtaposition of these two spaces – one self-managed and anti-institutional and the other funded and administered by layers of national and municipal bureaucracies – revealed that the confrontation over the Teatro Valle-Inclán was merely another chapter in a broader narrative of contested urban space in Lavapiés.

If the Teatro Valle-Inclán was the material representation of the city promulgated by the Urban Plan of 1997, the Laboratorio became what Guy Debord might have called a counter-spectacle, intended to be an antidote to the city of spectacle. Just as the Teatro Valle-Inclán and the Urban Plan of 1997 put forth Lavapiés as a space for articulating the scales of the local, metropolitan, and the global, the Laboratorio also performed a similar function. While the former produced these spatial articulations around the mobility of capital, the Laboratorio sought to deconstruct the power relations that imagined the city as reified commodity. In its very presence, as well as in its activities, the Laboratorio helped the "streets become the stage and ... [a site] for the construction of new participatory situations."[9] According to Stephen Vilaseca, this theatrical, performative, and participatory aspect of squatted social centers derives from their indebtedness in one aspect of their genealogy to the guerrilla theater of the Diggers in late 1960s San Francisco. The Diggers channeled the tactics of the Situationists into the American frame and used happenings and other types of street performances (including a Free Store) to build a new culture around economies of sharing that eschewed money.[10] The theater in this context, as Peter Berg wrote at the time, was "about becoming something new together."[11] Likewise participation in the "theater" of the Laboratorio would help the neighborhood and the city to "secrete" alternatives to the model of the postmodern mercantile city.[12] It is this spectacle of resistance that the present chapter will explore in more detail. To contemplate the eighteen months during which the Laboratorio 03 existed, however, it is necessary to move further back in time and situate this spectacle of urban resistance in its historical context.

WHAT IS AN *OKUPA*?

To *ocupar* (or *okupar*), or "squat," can allude to a wide range of activities, almost all of which call attention to the issues of ownership and private property. Squatting can range from an act of political resistance, like workers occupying a workplace or a student "sit-in," to other actions with a more explicit economic character, like rural tenants appropriating arable land or the mere habitation of a domicile out of necessity. In the Internet age, squatting might even refer to more tertiary activities, like buying a domain name or other intellectual property (such as a patent), generally with the intention of monetizing it. Here, I use the term "*okupar*" to refer to a particular phenomenon in which a building is inhabited by a group of individuals as an act of civil disobedience to critique social norms and/or put in practice certain ideas of social organization, usually those aligned with horizontality, autonomy, and self-management. This use of the term *okupar/okupa* distinguishes it from the more generalized practice of squatting that is often a product of necessity.[13] In Madrid, what might loosely be called the *okupa* movement has always been an extremely heterogenous movement made up of a diverse set of collectives dedicated to different causes: from antifascism and feminism to antiglobalization and alternative media.[14] Always ideologically ephemeral, *okupas* challenge whether the term "movement" applies at all.[15] Fundamentally, the act of *okupar* calls into question issues of private property, an aspect that is all the more salient when the *okupas* actively make their presence known (as will be shown later in the case of the Laboratorios). For this reason, the use of squatting in its various manifestations has been utilized as a form of direct-action political resistance throughout Western Europe for some time.

Establishing a finite starting point chronologically or geographically for this multivalent social movement is difficult – particularly because politically motivated squatterism is not something limited to the Spanish context.[16] Rather, this direct-action technique has its roots in movements that emerged across Europe in the economic turmoil of the postwar period in England, Holland, Germany, and Italy. In each of these cases, the sixties and seventies were seminal periods in the development of squatterism, as the economic needs of large swaths of the urban population – particularly around issues of housing – converged with a more general radicalization of the Left that allowed for squatting to grow into a loosely affiliated social movement.

In England, the relationship between economic necessity and the more general political context was particularly notable. There, self-managed social centers emerged from the government-sponsored community hostels established to accommodate the extensive homeless population of the postwar period. Over time, the mismanagement of these spaces and the intervention of anarchist activists transformed many of them into highly visible examples of direct-action politics. Individuals occupying buildings in search of housing gave way to a more dynamic process in which the squatters used occupied buildings to demonstrate and practice "self-managed alternatives ... to the problems of housing."[17] These first "squats" consolidated ideological tendencies like autonomy, self-management, and horizontality with concrete practices that included assembly-driven decision making and the creation of common services. They became sites for establishing new spaces of community outside of the dominant discourses on social services offered by the state or the market.

Another important influence on the Spanish *okupa* movement was the *kraaker* movement that took place in Holland during the 1980s and 1990s, in part because of the sheer numbers of squatters believed to have been involved: an estimated twenty thousand individual squatters in Amsterdam alone in the mid-1980s.[18] The case of Holland was an inspiring model for many activists in Spain, not only because of these sheer numbers, but also because the social-center model that had become paradigmatic also included many that had successfully negotiated a legal existence with municipal governments.[19] These social centers were so embedded into the urban fabric of some Dutch cities that, in many cases, the municipal governments would send homeless people to the collectives so the squatters could use their extensive knowledge of abandoned buildings in the city to find them housing.[20]

In Italy, ambitious anarchist and communist political activists established social centers that would become models for those that would develop in Spain. Unlike the squatter movements in England and Germany (another notable example mentioned by Martínez López), the squatter movement in Italy gained momentum as the nineties began and the punk, DIY (Do-It-Yourself) aesthetic of the eighties began to subside (cultural strains that were important in Holland and England).[21] The Italian squatters tapped new sources of political energy associated with the burgeoning anti-globalization movement as well as the new ecological activism emerging in the 1990s. Alongside its spatial interventions, the Italian models actively deployed new technological and tactical approaches, such as the use of free radio and Internet servers. This more cyberpunk/hacker orientation made the Italian models particularly "modern" (or postmodern if you choose).[22] Spanish squatters would adapt and replicate these techniques for broadening their influence and expanding their visibility.

OKUPAS IN SPAIN

In Spain, as in the other countries of Western Europe, the first strains of the *okupa* movement occurred in the late 1970s, with scattered instances of communal living and social centers found in both rural and urban contexts – projects often influenced by the countercultural visions of utopia emerging out of the hippie movement. Frustration with the lack of state services and an overall deterioration of the lived space of everyday citizens prompted efforts to make cities work for residents and would ultimately lead to the emergence of the Citizens' Movement in Madrid and other cities.[23] These groups were committed to protesting the problems of collective consumption: housing (*chabolismo*, or shanty towns), the lack of health centers and green spaces, and the general deterioration of public installations in neighborhoods throughout Spain. Together, the *okupas* and the Citizens' Movement were some of the clearest examples of urban movements with a progressive character.[24]

During this period of the late 1970s and early 1980s, squatted social centers appeared with more and more frequency in urban centers throughout Spain. In most cases these early strands of the *okupa* movement transpired in the urban triad of Bilbao, Barcelona, and, of course, Madrid, and they built on the established networks and activism of the anarcho-syndicalist traditions in these places. This radical left inherited the urban activism of the 1970s, but began to construct new space – both literally and politically – that would distance them from both the parliamentary left and the more radical Leninist organizations of the hard left.[25] In other words, squatted social centers became spaces in which non-institutionalized political discourse could incubate and develop. It was in the Basque country where the greatest proliferation of squatting occurred, particularly those established by youth collectives.[26] These *gaztetxes*, or youth houses, were some of the first CSOAs (Self-Managed Squatted Social Centers) to come onto the Spanish scene that endured more than a few weeks or a few months.[27]

Table 4.1 | Brief chronology of occupied social centers and spaces of self-management (*autogestión*) in or near Lavapiés.

Amparo 83	November 1985 (10 days)
Ronda de Atocha	April 1987 (13 days)
CSA La Eskalera Karakol	Embajadores 52 (November 1996 – Present)
Laboratorio 01	Embajadores 68 (April 1997 – December 1998)
Laboratorio 02	Plaza Cabestreros (6 January 1999 – 28 August 2001)
Laboratorio 03	Amparo103 (9 February 2002 – 9 June 92003)
Laboratorio 04	Ministriles11 (9 June 2003 – 23 July 2003)
El Solar	Olivar 48 (2003 – March 2010)
Solarpiés	Valencia 8 (2012 – 2015)
Esta es una plaza	Doctor Forquet 24 (2008 – Present)
CSOA Casablanca	Santa Isabel 21 – 23 (April 2010 – 19 September 2012)
Campo de Cebada	Plaza de la Cebada (2010 – 2017)
CSA La Tabacalera	Embajadores 53 (2012 – Present)

The first *okupación* occurred in Madrid in this period in the mid-1980s when activists established a social center in Lavapiés at the calle Amparo 83 in the offices of an old hydroelectric company. Just a block and a half from where the Laboratorio 03 would be located some eighteen years later, this was one of the first sites to function as both a social center and a space for housing. This combination earned the experiment the support of neighborhood associations, the Department of Youth for the Autonomous Community of Madrid, and lots of attention from the media. Nonetheless, it was shut down after only ten days.[28] This early *okupación* and subsequent ones on the calle Argumosa and the calle La Madera all took place in Lavapiés, foreshadowing the important role that the neighborhood would play as a center of counter-cultural activity in the city center (see Table 4.1). Established by a loose conglomeration of punks, leftists from the anarcho-syndicalist party of the CNT (the National Workers' Federation), and the network of radical social movements known as Lucha Autónoma, or Autonmous Struggle, the *casas okupadas* in these locations did not last long (the site at the calle Argumosa, like the Amparo site, lasted only thirteen days).[29] Nonetheless, the calle Amparo 83 squat existed long enough to allow for the first Squatter Assembly of Madrid to convene, a key moment for the sharing of techniques, the refining of ideology, and the development of a sense of identity emphasizing what would become recurrent themes for the early squats: prisons, antimilitarism, and repression.[30]

Much of this ideological framework also resulted from visits made by activists to Hamburg, Germany, where they encountered the iconic CSOA Haffenstrasse, a squat that became a reference point for the consolidation of "the new urban autonomy: total confrontation with the State, international solidarity, anti-prison resistance, community life."[31] In the 1990s, the *okupa* movement in Spain, and in Europe more generally, would begin to lose its scattershot quality and begin to develop as centers of resistance, not only against the state, but also against the rising tide of globalization. The catalyst for this process was a 1991 meeting of CSOAs held in Venice, which would be highly influential for the Spanish participants. In contrast to the more underground tendencies of the squatter movements in England and Germany, the visible activity of the Italian model and its direct engagement with localities and neighborhoods inspired the activists, who would begin to establish squats in Madrid.[32] They saw how the Italian model of squatting was "totally rooted in the territorial, in their urban context, participating in political conflict and in daily life, including health services, the factories and other productive experiences. Lucha autónoma would assume in Madrid the task of bringing the political project of the social centers to the neighborhoods, to the territory, just as was already occurring in the Basque Country with the *gaztetxes*."[33] Despite a lack of focus and refinement in their techniques, the movement began to consolidate a distinct identity and approach, in part due to the social and economic circumstances of this period.

In the late 1980s and early 1990s, high rates of speculative growth (in particular, in the real-estate market) led to a financial crisis. The transformation of the Spanish economy toward advanced services left many young people behind (for lack of skills) and without access to housing (because of the speculative boom in the real-estate market). The combination of these two factors altered the character of many working-class neighborhoods as local factories begin to be abandoned.[34] In 1996, a key shift in the legal context coincided with significant growth in the sheer number and quality of the *casas okupadas* across Spain. The penal code was amended in 1996 to make squatting a crime. That same year there were forty-two *okupaciones* and subsequent evictions across Spain. By 2000, this number would grow to nearly two hundred across Spain (again with most of this activity occurring in Catalonia, the Basque country, and Madrid.)[35] Because squatting became a punishable crime, several of the evictions became spectacles for the expression of state authority. For example, some two hundred anti-riot police, twenty-five police vans, several fire engines, as well as helicopters participated in the eviction at the Cine Princesa in 1996 in Barcelona. Nearly sixty people were arrested, and subsequent protests saw fifteen hundred to three thousand people in the streets.[36]

Similarly, the next year in Madrid, the eviction at La Guindalera saw 160 people (some reports say two hundred) arrested. The large number of arrests and the sheer size and cultural importance of this iconic social center transformed this eviction into one of the seminal moments in the history of the *okupas* in Madrid. The building held nearly three thousand people and, as a result, had become a key focal point for the underground music scene, with concerts and performances filling the building to capacity.[37] La Guindalera's important role in the cultural life of Madrid, and the intensity of the confrontation with the authorities during the eviction, provoked a protest in which, according to some estimates, five thousand people took to the streets in defense of the 160 *okupas* arrested. It was the largest protest associated with a *casa okupada* in the history of Madrid. According to participant and journalist Jacobo Rivero, La Guindalera was "like the Seattle of the anti-globalization movement" – a watershed moment, due to the convergence of media attention and the authoritarian response that had transformed the very act of *okupación* and *desalojo* [eviction] into a theatrical display of resistance with urban space as its stage.[38]

Resisting the Spectacle 139

Instead of deterring the *okupas*, the authorities' aggressive tactics emboldened and inspired them. In the wake of the events of La Guindalera, an assembly of *okupas* took place in Madrid and resulted in a commitment to stage another squat in the city center.[39] They chose Lavapiés for this strategic and symbolic move and, in April of 1997, activists occupied number 68 on the calle Embajadores, the old site of the National Institute of Agricultural Research. They called the social center El Laboratorio, or The Laboratory, an allusion to both the building's history and to the experiment in self-management and autonomy that the center symbolized.[40]

LOS LABORATORIOS:
IDEOLOGY AND PERFORMANCE

The turn of the twenty-first century became particularly important for the *okupa* movement in Madrid, and in Lavapiés in particular. The change in the penal code not only prompted spectacular police responses to squatting, but ironically also increased the visibility of social centers by attracting media attention. Squatting would become an alternative spectacle to the steel and glass that was beginning to rise in the north of the city. As Stephen Vilaseca highlights in his work on *okupas* in Barcelona, these conditions also spurred squatters to view the city in terms of the *procomún*, or commons: "a desire to foment social relations and exchanges other than and distinct from those that occur within the market ... [Where] people are brought together to share informal knowledge, creativity, and culture."[41] This is precisely the process that took place in the Laboratorio 03 during its eighteen-month tenure at the calle Amparo 103.[42]

Lavapiés offered the perfect urban stage for this counter-spectacle. There were several reasons for this choice, according to Jacobo Rivero, who participated actively in all the iterations of the Laboratorios. The historical significance of Lavapiés figured prominently, as many identified the neighborhood as the birthplace of the squatter movement in Madrid.[43] In addition to its importance to the history of the *okupa* movement in Madrid, Lavapiés had appeal because it was "a very metropolitan space ... [and] everything that happens in Madrid has something to do with, or occurs in some way or another, in Lavapiés."[44] Yet, just as a dramatist might carefully consider the setting of a work for its potential symbolic value, the location of a social center might be imbued with layers of meaning based on its setting. Thus, the social diversity and economic marginality of Lavapiés also made it appealing.[45] Despite its iconic associations, Lavapiés was an administrative void, characterized by its large immigrant population and the poor condition of the housing stock. The spectacle of this symbolic *okupación* would lay bare the tensions between the conceived space of the globalizing city and the lived experience of everyday life.

In describing this new social center's foundational period, Rivero alludes to this spectacular quality. He describes how the *okupas* of Madrid, as diffuse as they were, consciously sought to "*okupar* again in the center of Madrid and create a very large and extensive site that [would generate] all kinds of activities ... political, social, cultural."[46] Activist and participant Carlos Vidania likewise described the founding of the Laboratorio as a "symbolic response and experimental proposal." [47] By bringing together a heterogeneous network that included social movements along with artistic and cultural groups, the founders hoped to establish "a small experimental city of social movements."[48] From its diverse composition to its symbolic location in the center of the city, the hope was that the Laboratorio would be "an experimental space, heterodoxical, open, and complex in which the real diversity of social languages [could] express itself with liberty until it [would] generate a new, always changing, constitution of space itself, with its feet in the local and a projection into the global."[49] The space would allow for the convergence of different interests, uses, and visions of the city – particularly those that exist outside the mercantilist logic of the post-Fordist city. In doing so, these new spatial practices could manifest Lefebvre's vision of the urban as living creature, one that he describes as having "shaped its shell, building and rebuilding it, modifying it, again and again according to its needs."[50] By "secreting" this new structure, the *okupas* hoped to articulate a differentiated vision of the city that would stand in contrast to an abstract vision that sees no difference of lived experience, or of background, but only the productive value of inhabitants as consumers of urban space.

For this reason, it was hoped that the size of the new site would attract attention. Indeed, by becoming an important locus of cultural and political activity in the city, the Laboratorio would be a "radically public space because all the people that entered would implicate themselves in the crime of *okupar*."[51] Thus the size of the social center – both spatially and in its inclusivity – would allow the next step in the *okupa* movement in Madrid to "amplify to the maximum just what *okupación* was" through an act of civil disobedience that was "very very visible ... [and] very focused on changing the modes of life of the city."[52] The spectacle figured centrally in the ability of the Laboratorio to encourage these new spatial practices to alter the social dynamics of the neighborhood, the city, and possibly beyond.

Somewhat ironically, these discourses of visibility and inclusivity that seem to indicate an audience well beyond the ephemeral boundaries of the neighborhood contrast with the hope that this new site would be a "social center from, for, and by the neighborhood and not foreign to the neighborhood."[53] Other documents produced during each of the Laboratorios reveal this tension between various geographic scales and a commitment to the production of an alternative urban space outside the logic of the market. These discourses will be discussed shortly, but it is important to step away from the documents for a moment to emphasize that fundamental to the *okupa* movement and any struggle over urban space in Spain is the paradox written into the Spanish Constitution of 1978, which puts the right to private property in conflict with more progressive provisions protecting the right of individuals to have access to decent housing.

Article 33 establishes "the right to private property and inheritance," but at the same time suggests that one may be deprived of "goods and rights ... for justified cause of public utility or social interest."[54] Article 47 similarly not only proclaims that "all Spaniards have the right to enjoy dignified and adequate housing," but entrusts "the public power" with the responsibility of promoting "the necessary conditions ... for making effective this right, regulating the utilization of the land according to the general interest in order to impede speculation."[55] In short, the state's responsibility for an individual's right of access to decent housing conflicts with a market regime that encourages real-estate speculation. The acts of *okupación* threw into relief not only the contradictions embedded in these commitments to fair housing and the combating of speculation, but also the articulations of scale as they are expressed across the urban terrain.

On a local level, the high numbers of abandoned buildings and the problem of *chabolismo vertical* (vertical shantytowns) made Lavapiés a prime target for *okupas* to assert their vision of a new city and highlighted the consequences of speculation and the lack of housing. Yet their concerns extended beyond merely protecting Lavapiés. In their "Report on the Activities of the Laboratorio Squatted Social

Center," written during the *okupación* of the Laboratorio 01, they describe how their activities "not only denounce the difficulty of affordable housing, but also through direct appropriation question directly the ruling economic, political, and social system."[56] There is no mention of Lavapiés, or of any concrete location at all for that matter. Rather, the writers focus on changing the system, and in doing so seem to abide by Lefebvre's assertion that a shift in the production of space requires a shift in the modes of production, a process implicitly embedded in the local, the national, and certainly the global scale.

In the same document, the authors define the term "*okupa*" in similarly systemic terms that emphasize their opposition to "the high cost of housing and the authoritarian and bureaucratic management of social resources ... [and] flagrant cases of speculation."[57] While these activists were engaged with fighting speculation in a specific locale (Lavapiés), their actions were also intended to combat the more generalized extraction of profits that come from the process that Neil Smith calls "uneven development." In Smith's formulation, capital moves back and forth between global containers (i.e., different state economies), while simultaneously shifting amongst various parts of the city and squeezing profits out of the changing land values. Notably, the crux point of this uneven development occurs, according to Smith, "where capital is the most mobile – that is at the urban scale."[58] The rent-gap, as he calls it, in essence, is at work globally, just as it is at work at the scale of the city. Likewise, the *okupas* are occupying urban space at the neighborhood scale, but are resisting a globalized process of monopoly rents.

During the Laboratorio 02, resistance became more focused on the scale of the neighborhood. In the "Manifesto in Defense of the *Okupación* of Self-Managed Spaces," the authors describe the reappropriation of a particular building: a recently occupied building on the Plaza Cabestreros that had been vacant for twenty years.[59] For the *okupas*, this vacant building's mere exchange value as a commodity in a speculative real-estate market could be converted back to "its use value."[60] This use value derived from continuing the project of the first Laboratorio and creating "public, non-institutional, autonomous and self-managed spaces – the so-called occupied social centers."[61] Despite more attention to the particular locale of Lavapiés, the discourse remained in the abstract, positioning their acts of subversion against "the tendency of making cities uninhabitable."[62] The lack of a definite article and the use of the plural form broadens their complaint into a critique of modern Spanish urban planning in general and not the concrete problems of Lavapiés. Despite being "radically separated from the norms of consumption and the market" and providing "wealth for the territory and for the social network," the *okupas* remained entrenched in a broad-based struggle against the state and the free-market system regulating urban space across Spain.[63]

This tension between the local reclaiming of urban space and the more diffuse struggle against processes at work at other geographic scales is not just a subtle component of the *okupa* discourse. In another document produced during the time of the first two Laboratorios, "Spatial Stories" ("Maxims about *Okupación*"), the writer, Juan Gelman, says that he hopes that to "talk about squatting here – in Lavapiex [sic] – would be to talk about squatting here – in Madrid – and that would be to talk of squatting there – in whatever city on the globe or in the galaxy."[64] But this scalar discourse also resists a totalizing view of the project in Lavapiés when Gelman writes that "necessarily, nonetheless, it will not be the same thing to squat in Lavapiex than La Guinda or in Barna or the Basque Country or in Cádiz, without those who squat being neither equals nor the same."[65] The act of *okupar* is both distinctly local as well as differentiated by geography. The practices are different, because they respond to local circumstances while simultaneously forming a conglomerate capable of enacting a broad-based movement of social resistance.

One of the key ways that *okupas* maintain a connection to their locality is through the important principle of *autogestión*, or self-management. This key "organizational practice" of self-managed social centers presumes that "the collective that is affected by the decision can and should be the author of said decision."[66] Thus each social center relies on its own General Assembly, and "the basis for making decisions is the consensus produced by the general assembly, a consensus not imposed by a majority or a minority, but rather one that has the collective as a reference point, and individual and collective autonomy as a constructive axis of differences."[67] In other words, just as the establishment of an occupied social center engages both with the locality and with the broader geographies and social systems, the process of *autogestión* is similarly imbued with a tension between the authority of the collective (i.e., the Assembly) and that of individual. The consensus requirement paradoxically asks that the entire collective of individuals act as one body to prevent any one individual's autonomy from being compromised by the majority or the minority. The individual's interests are subsumed by the interests of the collective, and the tension between the local and global, the micro and macro, functions as a fractal pattern that gets replicated throughout the urban spectacle of squatting.

The documents describing the cultural activities in the Laboratorios also reveal this tension between the local and the global. For example, the cultural projects in these squatted social centers are described as "a socializing instrument of values, attitudes, and motivations."[68] The writers of this particular manifesto go on to describe how this effort to socialize individuals was predicated on the idea that "the forms of social relations and cultural constructions (roles, customs) serve as an ideological foundation for economic, political, and social models."[69] These documents also demonstrate a deep skepticism of institutionalized cultural production because of pervasive privatization and the obstacles created by excessive bureaucracy, such as increased costs and scheduling issues. The Laboratorio was not merely a response to these issues (i.e., an alternative or secondary space), but rather a space where individuals (and therefore also the community) could "unlearn attitudes and limitations that would allow for other experiences of sexuality, love, and work."[70]

The activities available for this objective ranged from leisure activities (yoga, tai chi, cooking, etc.) and from alternative modes of consumption based in cooperative living to politically activated uses of technology (i.e., Hacktivism) and the written word. Through these "webs of cooperation," as they called it, the social center might transcend the need for a permanent site to occupy.[71] For this reason, one of the *okupa* slogans (both in Lavapiés and more generally) is that "houses can be evicted, but ideas cannot."[72] The hope was that these acts of *okupación* would be simultaneously site-specific but also ephemeral: engaging with multiple publics and communities across geographic scales. It was in the Laboratorio 03 where these possibilities came to fruition in their most visible way.

RESISTANCE AND SPECTACLE IN LAVAPIÉS: EL LABORATORIO 03

The manifestos and documents discussed up to this point offer an overview of the political and ideological orientation that informed the development of the first two Laboratorios. When activists established the Laboratorio 03 in 2002, their objectives remained the same. Yet this third iteration would become much more visible and influential, perhaps due to the accelerating transformation of Lavapiés – a process symbolized by the construction of the Teatro Valle-Inclán. In this sense, the protests that marked the inauguration of this national theater building were the culmination of efforts over the preceding months to convert the city itself into a stage that would assert citizens' right to the city. To better understand the details, tactics, and contours of this counter-spectacle most fully, we turn now to the 2007 documentary *Laboratorio 03: Ocupando el vacío*, produced by Kinowo Media, and the series of texts included as an insert in the 2003 book of photographs edited by Julien Charlon and entitled "A (Guided) Stroll through Lavapiés: Compiled Texts."[73]

Before engaging fully with the activities of the Laboratorio 03, it is worth briefly dwelling on the way in which earlier iterations of the Labo set the stage for the impact of the Laboratorio 03. As mentioned earlier, spectacle was key to establishing the profile and visibility of the project. This was a lesson learned at the first location on the calle Embajadores, an old industrial space with nearly twenty thousand square feet (contained in three buildings), whose size and openness allowed for large concerts and other public events.[74] The idealism and functionality that characterized the Labo 01 (April 1997 to December 1998) gave way to a more complicated situation in the Labo 02 (6 January 1999 to 28 August 2001) located several blocks to the north in the Plaza Cabestreros, where the layout of the vacant apartment building used for the purpose compromised many of the social functions of the Labo. Despite these limitations, the Labo 02 developed activity vectors that would play a role in later iterations. In particular, the occupation of this space coincided with the movement to support and protect the rights of immigrants, and various collectives in the neighborhood that were working with the undocumented used the Labo 02 as a meeting space. Community meals, organized each week, provided opportunities for networking and the development of stronger connections amongst the activists and groups engaged with these issues in the community.

According to Rivero, while this period was much more one "of reflection and of theoretical construction than of intervention," the spatial limitations of the building led activists to turn to the public space of the streets to produce art, theater, and performances.[75] These activities on the street increased the visibility of Labo 02 and proved instructional during the time of the Laboratorio 03. When activists occupied the old printing-press building on the calle Amparo on 9 February 2002, the experiences of these earlier iterations laid the groundwork for a much more ambitious project, which was not only more deeply embedded in the social networks of Lavapiés and the city more generally, but also had developed a rich compendium of tactical knowledge.

The building itself fostered these qualities, as it contained many large spaces for meetings, concerts, communal meals, theater performances, exercise workshops, and such. The combination of the space, the visibility of the project, and the robust connections that had been developed with the local community positioned the Laboratorio 03 as an incubation space in which broad alliances emerged among political activists and those connected to the city's cultural apparatus: architects, urbanists, well-known theater groups, painters, etc.[76] The Laboratorio became not only a neighborhood center for arts and culture, but a space enmeshed with the modes of cultural production across the city. Notably, the cultural activities in the social center became key to integrating the space more fully into the neighborhood and the broader metropolis.

In the longest text that appears in the Charlon book, the anonymous collective of authors highlights both the power of cultural production and the extent of those efforts.[77] In particular, the writers assert that, in the Laboratorio, "[they] are not, nor do [they] want to be mere spectators. [They] are actors, artists, magicians, witches, who, affected by urban and global transformations, transform [their] lives."[78] The mere physical presence of bodies in urban space utilizing cooperative social practices was envisioned as a means to establish new social codes and forms of resistance to dominant modes of production and reproduction. They recognized both the danger and the power of spatial practice and write that it is in "bodies ... where the mechanisms of control are inserted and connected until converting them into tools of power, [and] are at the same time ... the most powerful instruments of transformation."[79] It is through this tension between the "body" as a tool of resistance and cultural production as another that the Laboratorio might become, in their view, an "artifact for the production of a collective intelligence,"[80] a place where any activity, from a theater performance to a community meal, is transgressive and potentially an opportunity for "constructing ... participative, creative, and living social webs, spaces of liberty and of experimentation, of cooperation and mutual support."[81] The very act of being and doing was understood to be necessary for creating the new spatial practices that might produce a new kind of space in the city.

As an artifact in and of itself, therefore, one of the main spectacles produced by the Laboratorio 03 was the building itself. Two features call attention to this spectacle. The first is illustrated early in the documentary *Laboratorio 03: Ocupando el vacío*, when the actual occupation is filmed. Notably, this event takes place under the cover of night. Though part of the reason for this timing is due to the illegality of the activity, it also points to the fact that the actual taking of the building was not the important act of *okupar*. Rather, it was the actual *being* in the place, and then, later, the eviction, which would generate the most spectacular outcome. As a result, one of the very first acts that the activists carry out as they enter the building is to spray paint the *okupa* symbol of the encircled lightning bolt onto the front of the building: the facade of the building transforms from a nondescript vacant building into a proclamation of *okupación*. In later images that show the social center well established, the word "Labo" adorns the doorway in large carefully painted letters (see Fig 4.2). There is no hiding the Laboratorio 03, because this act of civil disobedience, as Rivero pointed out, was intended to be extremely visible. The very presence of an occupied building contrasted with the spectacle of the gentrifying cafés and art spaces that would come to characterize the calle Argumosa corridor just a few blocks away leading to the Reina Sofía museum.

This spectacle of "being" was complemented by the actual spectacles that took place in the Laboratorio. According to the activists in the documentary, "the first thing that was important in and of itself was the cinema that spurred on other things. That was the first big thing that we did."[82] These "other things," seen in short clips throughout the documentary, demonstrate the diverse activities occurring in the center: a jazz performance, a flamenco performance, a communal meal, the opening of a café space, and the performance of classical theater.[83] The space of the Laboratorio became "a space for everyone wanting to do something, if they [wanted] to set up a workshop, if they [wanted] a meeting space ... it [was] there."[84] In contrast to the national theater building under construction at this time, all of these

Figure 4.2 | Entrance to the Laboratorio 03 Calle Amparo 103.

activities were generated by individuals as opposed to institutions. They occurred outside the mercantilist models of cultural consumption that were being used to create a new identity for Lavapiés.

Significantly, one important form of cultural production that occurred in the Laboratorio 03 pertained to theatrical performance, as the Laboratorio served as both an incubation space for theater professionals throughout Madrid, as well as a key tool for direct political action when the eviction of the site became imminent. According to local theater activists Laura Corcuera and Belén Rubira, the Laboratorio 03 offered meeting and rehearsal space for members of the theater community in Lavapiés and Madrid and "was like a hotbed of activity during this time."[85] It was here that these two were able to join with others to form Cedepalo, a small theater collective committed to "investigating and bringing into action a common spirit of political and artistic inconformity."[86] Corcuera and Rubira were not the only ones to avail themselves of the Laboratorio, and indeed "there were many different types of theater and many different theater groups, some of which did nothing more than use the Laboratorio to rehearse."[87] Significantly, these groups came from "many parts of Madrid ... with the need to present their work, to merely rehearse, or to offer courses, also."[88] By merely offering free self-managed space, the Laboratorio 03 provided an outlet for artists throughout the city.

While large cultural institutions like the Teatro Valle-Inclán often focused their attention on participating in a more global network of theater productions and festivals, the Laboratorio 03 filled a void for the broader theater community across the city. Simultaneously, the alternative theaters, most of which were located in Lavapiés, offered their own obstacles to theater production. Corcuera and Rubira describe how, even in the independent theater spaces, "you [had] to go through a series of bureaucratic steps ... sending a dossier, a video, and who knows what, etc."[89] In the Laboratorio, artists could find the freedom and space to develop their craft without having to rent a space or negotiate the bureaucracy associated with the formal theater spaces in the community, a situation that formed a stark contrast to the austere monolithic cultural production of the "national" theater building under construction.

In the midst of these more city-wide connections, there were important local connections as well. Given that the theater performances were staged for free, many local residents from the Senegalese and Moroccan communities would attend.[90] In the view of Corcuera and Rubira, the theater brought together the diverse population of the neighborhood, because without it "there were probably lots of people of many different cultures from the neighborhood that wouldn't come by the Laboratorio."[91] As a result, these cultural connections complemented the Laboratorio's function as a meeting space for a multitude of neighborhood groups. These groups developed a collective voice through their affiliation with one another in the informal Lavapiés Network (La Red de Lavapiés) that brought together some twenty-nine collectives associated with different interest groups in the neighborhood. These included the Association of Moroccan Immigrants in Spain, the Bangladeshi Immigrant Association, the Senegalese Immigration Association, the neighborhood association La Corrala, the feminist group Eskalera Karakola, and Civil Service International. It was a diverse and tumultuous group, but the availability of free meeting space allowed these disparate voices to coalesce

Figure 4.3 | Protest symbolically closing the Office of Municipal Rehabilitation, Lavapiés, Madrid.

around shared concerns regarding the lack of services and the disproportionate investment in the cultural facilities of the neighborhood that seemed to come at the expense of more basic needs.

The politically engaged theater techniques of groups like Cedepalo influenced the Lavapiés Network by encouraging theatrical street protests throughout the neighborhood. In one notable protest organized by the Lavapiés Network, the "performers" dressed as bricklayers, replete with full coveralls and protective facemasks, and literally bricked closed the entrance to the Municipal Office of Rehabilitation, the bureaucratic entity overseeing the infrastructure improvements laid out in the Urban Plan of 1997.[92] Lit by torches at night, the bricklayers moved silently and methodically as they subverted the constructive work of laying bricks – an everyday occurrence in the neighborhood's ongoing rehabilitation – into a direct challenge of the bureaucratic authority managing this transformation of urban space (see Figure 4.3).

The Revistas Kaminadas, or Walking Revues, were another important example of this technique, which occurred during various points during the spring of 2003.[93] These short performances of music, theater, video, and public readings relied on the movement of spectators from location to location throughout key sites in the neighborhood and the Centro district to weave the "audience" into a spatial narrative of resistance – each performance offering another "page" of the "magazine" (an alternative translation of "Revista"). The web page of the Alternative Information News Agency lists the themes and types of performances included in the Revista Kaminada organized to celebrate the one-year anniversary of the Laboratorio 03. In the announcement, the organizers described themselves as "social movements, collectives, citizens," and indicate the inclusive nature of the proceedings by describing the protagonists of the upcoming drama as "Ustedes vosotr@s" (you all).[94] Amongst the distinct "pages" – as they are described in the document – included in the itinerary was a performance of rap and hip-hop in the Plaza Callao near the flagship store of the iconic Corte Inglés department store. There was also a "Page against the War [in Iraq]" in the Puerta del Sol. In another significant location, the Plaza Mayor, there were "Pages of Housing, Responsible Consumptions, and Education." Interestingly, as the path of the Revista wound its way toward Lavapiés, the themes became more pertinent to the locality of Lavapiés. In the adjacent Plaza Tirso de Molina, the Revista exhibited a "Page of Women: A Vision of Gender and Immigration," an extremely significant topic in the multicultural context of Lavapiés.

Finally, this wandering *dérive* through the urban space of Madrid culminated in the heart of Lavapiés in the Plaza Cabestreros (now called the Plaza Nelson Mandela), with a page dedicated appropriately to "Neighborhood, Housing, and Speculation." Just as the location of the Labo 03 in Lavapiés functioned as part of its spectacle, the setting for each "page" of the Revista sought to attract the broadest audience possible by appropriating locations dedicated to tourism (Plaza Mayor, Puerta de Sol) and consumption (Plaza Callao). Importantly, in the midst of this engagement with these more globalized spaces in the city, the Revista and the urban spectacle of the Laboratorio returned to the local space of Lavapiés to address the pertinent issue of gentrification and real-estate speculation. Just as capital leverages the local to move at the global scale, the *okupas* and the activists of Lavapiés intertwined their local confrontations with development with the seemingly more global processes of consumption, speculation, immigration, and war.

This overlay of the global and the local also characterized one of the most important protest performances associated with the Laboratorio 03. In June 2002, while facing a serious threat of eviction, the *okupas* of the Laboratorio 03 locked themselves in the building and transformed the eviction process into something more akin to a performance that relied on an orchestrated series of events. These events included a cultural forum with film actors, directors, and musicians to debate the eviction; panels on urbanism; music concerts; guided tours of Lavapiés, highlighting alternative uses for abandoned buildings; and various other workshops.[95] One of the key moments during the "lock in" was the "drama" that took place on the facade of the building at Amparo 103.[96] It featured so prominently in the documentary *Laboratorio 03: Ocupando el vacío* that a still from these scenes serves as the cover image for the DVD case.

In this performance, as before, the building itself served as the stage, as the "actor-vists" appearing in various windows of the facade dressed as seemingly everyday people: a housewife, a child, a working man shaving in his bathrobe (see Figure 4.4). Their nondescript clothing suggested a lack of status and alluded to their identity as the "neighbors" of Lavapiés. The performance opened with two inhabitants gossiping back and forth between the windows of the building, as in a *zarzuela* scene from a bygone era. In this case, though, the topic was not the flirtations of Mari Pepa, the *chulapona*, but rather their imminent eviction, a point that is made clear when one of the residents shouted, "They want to evict us."[97] Their everyday appearance made their identities ambiguous and thereby conflated the eviction of the Laboratorio with the more general displacement of the inhabitants of Lavapiés. In a sense, this conflation echoed discourses that had characterized the Laboratorio project as early as 2001, when, for example, the conservative daily *ABC* described the Laboratorio 02 as a "symbol in the neighborhood of Lavapiés."[98] By 2002, when the Laboratorio 03 was firmly established, these associations between Lavapiés and the social center had become so strong that an article in the newspaper *El Mundo* from 26 June 2002 suggested that the *okupas* of the Laboratorio had become an integral part of the neighborhood, enjoying the support of the majority of its inhabitants.[99] An amusing moment

Figure 4.4 | Protesting the eviction of the Labo 03. The Facade Performance.

in the documentary reflected this breadth of support when Sara, an elderly resident of the neighborhood and one of the members of the collective "Mothers against Drugs," declared that "if taking what is there, what's yours, and something that's being denied to you, for questions of housing or for making a place to organize activities ... if that's being an *okupa*, well, I'm an *okupa*."[100]

Yet during the performance other elements indicated the overlay of other geographies beyond merely the neighborhood or the city. For example, during the climax of the performance, the "shaving man," replete with red clown nose (a trope that readers should recall would reappear in the Teatro Valle-Inclán protests), turned to the crowd below and shouted, "I am not going," followed by the slogan "The Laboratorio Stays in Lavapiés."[101] At this moment, he opened his robe to reveal the *okupa* lightning bolt symbol painted onto his chest, a move that highlighted the Laboratorio's connections with the broader Spanish *okupa* movement. Likewise, a large banner hanging on the facade during the performance read "No to War: Another World Is Possible, Another Madrid," alluding to the Labo's engagement with local, municipal, and global conflicts: from real-estate speculation in the neighborhood to opposition to the invasion of Iraq by the United States. Their attention to this topic of international concern had national implications as well, given Spanish President José María Aznar's close allegiance to the president of the United States at the time, George W. Bush, and the strong support (both material and ideological) Aznar provided for American policy in Iraq.

The Laboratorio's connections with the anti-war movement were also expressed in more concrete ways beyond merely hanging banners on a building. In February 2003, the Laboratorio 03 established a center for independent media against the war and, as a result, became a "meeting point" for different initiatives protesting the invasion of Iraq.[102] Significantly, a high-profile performance by the theater group Animalario in April 2003 bolstered the visibility of the Laboratorio as an important space for opposition against the policies of the Spanish state, and, more specifically, the cronyism and lavishness of the presidency of then-Spanish President José María Aznar (1996–2004).

"AS IF FOR US THE THEATER AND THE STREET WERE DIFFERENT": ALEJANDRO AND ANA: BEHIND THE SCENES AT THE WEDDING BANQUET OF THE DAUGHTER OF THE PRESIDENT

As has been detailed, for the activists of the Laboratorio, the street functioned as an important performance space for direct-action political theatrics like the Revista Caminada and the eviction performance on the facade of the building. While these performances reflected efforts to reclaim urban space politically and artistically and create a new social space to challenge and redefine the relationship between citizens and the city, the social center gained new levels of visibility after it became the venue for one of the most compelling dramas produced in Madrid at this time: *Alejandro and Ana: Behind the Scenes at the Wedding Banquet of the Daughter of the President*, a work co-written by dramatists Juan Mayorga and Juan Cavestany in collaboration with the theater group Animalario and directed by Andrés Lima.[103]

The high-profile nature of the play and the fame of those involved (both the dramatists and the actors) added cultural cachet to the activities of the Laboratorio; the project could no longer be dismissed as merely a collection of miscreants violating the law, and the Labo began to garner national media attention. The intertwining of this play with the story of the Laboratorio is important for two reasons. First, it points to the way that the Laboratorio incubated cultural projects, direct-action political tactics, and even political discourses that would emerge during the 15-M movement and that would continue to resonate across the Spanish political landscape into the 2020s. Secondly, the play merits a detailed analysis because of the way it reflects the emerging preoccupation with the corruption of political elites and their distance from the lives of average citizens themes that are explored through the work's very intentional use of urban space.

The theater group Animalario was founded in 1996 when the actors Willy Toledo, Alberto San Juan, Nathalie Poza, and Ernesto Alterio, from the company Ración de la oreja, met Andrés Lima while performing the work entitled *Animalario*. In 1997, they collaborated on the performance *What Do You Care That I Love You?* adopted the name Animalario, and later debuted *The End of Dreams*. *Alejandro y Ana* continued their characteristic collaborative approach. As if evoking the spirit of collectivity and horizontality found in the squatted social center, the work defied traditional definitions of authorship. While the dramatists Juan Mayorga (b. 1965) and Juan Cavestany (b. 1967) are credited with writing the play, Mayorga himself described writing it "always in dialogue with Andrés [Lima] and with the four actors that would represent the hundreds of characters in the work."[104]

As a result, despite the authorial heft of the principal dramatists, the play should not be understood solely as the product of two well-established writers from Madrid's theater scene. In 2005, when *Alejandro y Ana* appeared in an anthology of plays performed by Animalario, the book credits Juan Cavestany and Juan Mayorga with writing three of the six works. In two of those works, the writer/actor/director Alberto San Juan and the writer/director Andrés Lima (mentioned above) are also credited as writing the plays. The other works are credited individually to either San Juan or Lima. Notably, since this period in the early 2000s, this network of dramatists and actors has continued to be fundamental to both Madrid and Spain's national drama scene, not only in the Centro Dramático Nacional, but also in influential alternative theaters like the Teatro del Barrio, which not only descends directly from Animalario, but, as Scott Boehm has argued, has played a key role in the post–15-M cultural landscape.[105]

Both writers were well established at the time when they worked on the play, but have also gone on to achieve even greater success. For Cavestany, his theatrical successes beyond *Alejandro y Ana* came with the work *Urtain* (2008), a play that was co-produced by the Centro Dramático Nacional and Animalario. The work garnered him the Premio Max Best Theatrical Author in Castilian in 2010. His other notable works include *El traje* (*The Suit*) (2012) and *Tres en coma* (*Three in a Coma*) (2014). Since that time, Cavestany has focused mainly on writing for the cinema and television, achieving several film credits and awards.[106]

Juan Mayorga's trajectory has stayed more narrowly focused on the theater, and he has developed into one of the most famous – if not the most famous – and decorated contemporary dramatists in Spain, a status exemplified by his induction into the Real Academia Española in 2018.[107] He has also won a number of awards nationally and internationally, including the National Theater Prize (2007), the National Dramatic Literature Prize (2013), and the Max Award for best author in 2006, 2008, and 2009.[108] Mayorga's success within the Spanish theater establishment has provided him with a range of opportunities to have his original plays and adaptations performed at a number of prominent theaters in Madrid. In recent years, he has become a fixture at the Teatro Valle-Inclán, where both his original works and adaptations perpetually appear on the stage.

One of the key features of Animalario's dramas, according to Julio Vélez-Sainz, is that they are "openly political works, that establish a theatrical model that oscillates between the ideological and the documentary."[109] The persistent use of real or quasi-real material to build their dramatic world contributes to this documentary quality. For Vélez-Sainz, this tendency situates their theatrical project firmly within the tradition of what has been called Verbatim Theater, the Theater of the Real, or Testimonial Theater, an aesthetic and political approach typically associated with the dramatist Peter Weiss and his best-known work, *Trotsky in Exile*, from the 1960s. Within this tradition, the dramatist or dramatists take actual historical documents (transcripts, video footage, speeches, interviews, statistical tables, etc.) and structure them in a particular way to achieve an ideological coherence and communicate a specific political theme.[110] While *Alejandro y Ana* does not derive from concrete documents per se, both its overall aesthetic and its scenography create a documentary quality that resonates with the post-reality of a media landscape informed by the pervasiveness of docudramas and reality television. These associations with Documentary Theater have only become more compelling in recent years, particularly after the founding of a new co-operative theater space in Lavapiés called the Teatro del Barrio in 2013 by Animalario member Alberto San Juan. There, San Juan helped to produce works like *Ruz/Bárcenas* from 2014, a recreation of the 2013 cross-examination of Luis Bárcenas by Judge Pablo Ruz about Bárcenas's work as treasurer for the conservative Popular Party and the corruption scandals that rocked the party in recent years. This work, along with others, like *El rey (The King)* from 2015, have continued a trajectory that began with *Alejandro y Ana*. While *Ruz/Bárcenas* relied quite concretely on actual historical documents (the transcripts of the cross-examination) for its documentary material, *Alejandro y Ana* sought to represent an actual event, albeit based on the descriptions of this event found in the celebrity gossip magazine *Hola*. The play in this sense sought to "recycle reality," as Carol Martin has described this kind of theater, and call attention to the corruption behind the media spectacle.[111]

In the case of *Alejandro y Ana*, the documentary event was the wedding that took place in the Monastery San Lorenzo del Escorial on the outskirts of Madrid between Ana Aznar Botella (daughter of Spanish President José María Aznar) and Alejandro Agag, a financier and longtime operative of the Popular Party. While the debut of the performance occurred on 18 February 2003, the world had a prelude to the drama some two weeks earlier, on the evening of 1 February, when the members of Animalario (Alberto San Juan, Willie Toledo, Roberto Álamo, and Javier Gutiérrez) hosted the Spanish-film-award program, the Goyas. With Gutiérrez comprising the role of José María Aznar, the group performed a series of satirical sketches throughout the night that would later be developed into the full-length work *Alejandro y Ana*, which would have its theatrical debut later in the month as a part of the alternative-theater-spaces programming of the Contemporary Scene Theater Festival.

The performance at the Goyas was significant for two reasons. First, it put Animalario on Spanish National Television [RTVE] during a highly publicized event with a large audience. While Willie Toledo and Alberto San Juan had both achieved substantial visibility and popularity as film actors, it was the first time that the ensemble appeared collectively on the national stage. The Goyas became a teaser for Mayorga and Cavestany's dramatic performance later in the month, and perhaps contributed to the longevity of the show and the breadth of its geographical reach: nearly 350 performances across Spain, including in San Sebastian, Zaragoza, Barcelona, and other cities. Secondly, the gala occurred just one month prior to the invasion of Iraq, an invasion in which Spain's participation seemed likely.[112] The lead-up to the war had mobilized many coalitions on the Left, groups that had already been engaged in a national movement to protest the devastating Prestige Oil Tanker spill off the coast of Galicia in November 2002, one of the worst environmental disasters in Spain's history. The convergence of these two events transformed the Goyas into a sharply pointed attack on the national government, with many award recipients and other participants (including Animalario) proclaiming "No to War" and "Nunca máis" ("Never Again"), a key slogan from the Prestige protest movement.[113] This preliminary performance at the Goyas firmly situated *Alejandro y Ana* within this national protest discourse and created an unprecedented level of interest for a dramatic performance.

The drama, organized into eighteen discrete scenes performed consecutively, had a very simple premise: a behind-the-scenes view of the post-wedding banquet celebrating the nuptials of Botella and Alejandro Agag. Relying on a combination of Cavestany's more media-oriented sensibilities and Mayorga's philosophical preoccupations, the play made a pointed critique of what Catalonian writer Manuel Vázquez Montalbán called *aznarismo* near the end of its ascendance: an ideology characterized by a "neo-liberal version of Spanish Catholicism and ... bellicose atlanticism."[114] For Germán Labrador Méndez, *aznarisimo* was characterized not only by these ideological contours, but by a "telepolitics attempting to produce consensus through the media."[115]

In a retrospective interview from 2014 in the digital newspaper *El confidencial*, the authors emphasized the play's political context: the conservative Popular Party had achieved an absolute majority in parliament and seemed poised to go to war in Iraq, despite extremely intense opposition from the Spanish public. Perhaps because of this political climate, Animalario describes the play on its website as "a documentary, not a dramatic work," despite its comedic qualities.[116] They rejected any characterization of the work as a parody and insisted on its inspiration in the tradition of the *Teatro de urgencia,* or Emergency Theater of the early 1930s in Spain: brief, highly ideological theater pieces intended to provoke political action. As the authors explained on a number of occasions, including in that retrospective interview in 2014, what they attempted to document was: "How does the Right think? Why is the 'absolute majority' of Spain, or at least one half plus, aligned with the Right? Why is someone of the Right? Deep down, am I of the Right? And most definitely, who is that beautiful woman accompanying Flavio Briatore?"[117] On a technical level, the work was also notable for its use of different kinds of media and of everyday locales as theatrical spaces. While recent scholarship has studied the urban in the work of Mayorga, these approaches typically limit themselves to examining the symbolic nature of urban spaces *within* the works – for example, the map of Varsovia in *el Cartógrafo: Varsovia: 1:4000.000* or the significance of the city of Reykjavik in the eponymous drama.[118] It is my contention that *Alejandro y Ana* is innovative in the oeuvre of Mayorga for the way it actually *used* urban space: where, when, and how it was performed lent additional resonance to the play's social critique.

Meandering through eighteen snapshot scenes of various wedding guests in dialogue with one another, the work offers a sarcastic and biting takedown of Spain's elite – what José María Aznar described at the time as the "caste." The four actors represent some forty different characters throughout the work, including the bride's mother; the presidential candidates poised to succeed Aznar; an Italian arms and pharmaceutical dealer; the "most important chauffeur in the world"; household servants; and even Aznar himself – all without costume changes. The original wedding was covered with great aplomb by the Spanish media, and the Spanish celebrity gossip magazine *Hola* even dedicated a special issue to the event – an issue that provided part of the inspiration for the play and its "documentary" material. Indeed, it was after looking over this special issue that Mayorga and Lima "decided to do something."[119] The result was a piece of political satire in which the guests were revealed to be egotistical and out of touch, with a hyper-inflated sense of the national.

This attitude was very much in line with Mayorga's "Prologue" to the anthology in which the text version of the play appears. Therein Mayorga emphasized his belief in theater's implicitly critical component. He suggested that "the men that govern us believe themselves to be gods and as gods they demand our silence. They forget that the theater was born precisely to interrogate the gods."[120] For Mayorga, the relationship between theater and urban space was essential to this interrogation, because these modern-day gods act "as if for us the theater and the street were different."[121] More explicitly, he argued that it was "only in the meeting of actors with the city, only then does theater take place."[122] It is no surprise then that embedding the work into the urban fabric of the city made the satire of *aznarismo* found in *Alejandro y Ana* so compelling.

From the outset, space formed one of the key rhetorical techniques for conveying the play's humor. The play debuted in the Lady Ana banquet hall in the Prosperidad neighborhood in the northeast of Madrid. The selection of the space was intentional and, according to Mayorga, was intended to undermine the declaration made by the mother of the bride that they were just a normal family. For Veléz-Saenz, the banquet hall used for the debut and other performances around Spain lent an air of verisimilitude that contributed to its documentary feel. At the same time, these locations also called attention, as Mayorga notes, to the great difference between an average wedding hall on the edge of the city and El Escorial.[123] In so doing, the theatrical space created a kind of Brechtian distance from the work that allowed one to reflect on the absurdity of this quasi-royal event in a modern democracy. There was a certain irony in being a "guest" at the Aznar wedding, since it was unlikely that anyone attending any of these performances would ever find themselves in a position to actually see what happened that night.

The opening voice-over reinforced this ironic tone through hyperbole, describing the silhouetted figure sitting with his back to the audience as not only "the most prestigious statesman of Spain" but "perhaps of Europe."[124] The stage directions identify the voice-over and the music that accompany it as "No-Do Music" – an allusion to the documentary films produced during the Franco regime, a quality that reinforces the work's pseudo-documentary quality. The serious tone of the voice-over made the commentary even more ironic and humorous. The audience, one might presume, well aware of Spain's true position in the pecking order of Europe, would have understood this hyperbolic description as a jab at Aznar's inflated sense of importance. The hyperbole struck a different note later in this voice-over description by pointing out that, at this profound moment, "besides the man of State, we find ourselves with the human being, with the husband, with the father."[125] The juxtaposition of these descriptions – the greatest of statesman and the most humble of human beings – presented a caricature of the president that undermined both his credibility as a statesman and as a human being.

The play's use of irony continued after this introduction, as the voice-over began to describe the wedding guests as they left the ceremony. As the actors sashayed back and forth through the "theater" (i.e., the banquet hall) as if on the red carpet or a fashion catwalk, the voice-over called out the names of a who's who in politics, in finance, and in celebrity culture. It was a list of the elite not only from Spain, but also from around the globe: from Italian Prime Minister Silvio Berlusconi and British Prime Minister Tony Blair to media baron Rupert Murdoch and the president of the Corte Inglés Department store, Isidoro Álvarez. A number of prominent politicians from the Transition, such as Adolfo Suárez, were also mentioned, as were members of the Francoist old guard, like Manuel Fraga. In short, the wedding was a congregation of the rich and famous and hardly an event of "normal" people, nor an event for a modest banquet hall located in a nondescript neighborhood in Madrid, Barcelona, or one of the other locations where it was performed.

Alejandro y Ana didn't just focus its critique on the elite, but also took shots at the "new" Spanish citizen: the global consumer that had emerged in the boom years of *aznarismo*. The most pointed critique appeared in the vignette entitled "Secret Service." During the course of a conversation between two secret servicemen about the invasion of Iraq, "Number one" spoke to "Number two," describing how "one of them comes to me and says 'No war.'"[126] He continued: "They say: peace, dialogue, negotiation, solidarity, they say that, in the bar on the corner, you know what I am saying? They say that and they are out drinking beers with their parents' money."[127] This judgement of armchair activists became more pointed later, when the Secret Service agent suggested that this imaginary pacifist should "quit buying clothes on sale at the Corte Inglés, because that's how it is, yes, when there are sales everyone's off to buy themselves four pairs of Ray-bans, but then: solidarity, poverty in the world, oh what pity, what a pity."[128] In other words, the telepolitics of *aznarismo*, with its emphasis on spectacle and facade, extended across the political spectrum, as the easy money of these boom years made any resistance to the bellicose policies of the Bush-Blair-Aznar-Berlusconi alliance into hollow words.

In this way *Alejandro y Ana* offers one of the more poignant assessments of the socio-political context during which it was produced. The world of *Alejandro y Ana* is one in which everything is for sale behind the facade. In three vignettes, entitled respectively "Innocence" 1, 2, and 3, the character Volpone sells everything from "Scuds from the Gulf war" and Leopard A4 fighter planes to pharmaceuticals, Asian women, and Rolex watches.[129] In "Innocence 2," Volpone approaches one of the other guests about his pharmaceutical offerings. When the guest responds that "'Pharmacy' is table 15. This table is Combustibles,"[130] Volpone shrugs it off by pointing out that "these days, as we know, with globalization, everything is mixed with everything. Go out for wheat and you return with aircraft carriers."[131] The recurrent presence of Volpone throughout the play suggests how the spectacle of the wedding was not only a celebration of Aznar's daughter's marriage, but a celebration of the politics of the Right in general. The original wedding was, in the opinion of the play's first director, Andrés Lima, "more like José María's wedding."[132] According to the dramatists, this "wedding" like any other wedding, was a "theatrical event *par excellence*," but in this case the spectacle contained "all of the strata of the Right."[133]

By converting traditionally non-theater spaces into spaces for performance, the dramatists, the director, and the theater group Animalario highlighted the spectacle of the original wedding, a media event designed to benefit the image and influence of José María Aznar and his Popular Party. The intentionality of this choice by the theater group is clearly illustrated in the film version of the play produced by Animalario, particularly the opening, which consciously directs attention to the urban setting of the performance.[134] As the film opens, a mid-shot focuses on the entrance to the Prosperidad metro station. The camera tilts downward to capture a woman ascending the stairs. She fills the frame and moves past the camera as a tracking shot follows her through the city, a voice-over interview revealing that she works "for the play."[135] A handheld shot accompanies her into a local market, where she buys shrimp, before finally arriving at the banquet hall. A jump cut reveals the woman in her work uniform sweeping the floor. This meta-theatrical opening not only calls attention to the context of the city, but also to the space itself being prepared for the upcoming spectacle, and to her labor cleaning it. Her modest socio-economic status stands in stark contrast to the opulence of the event that the play satirizes, an event produced in part by the labor of women and men like her.

Also important is the way that the opening simulates, to some degree, the route that many of the patrons of the performance would take. They would pass through the working-class streets of the Prosperidad neighborhood – like the working-class cleaning woman – only to be transported to the elite world of *aznarismo* and its aspirations for global recognition. The local space of the city serves as a counterpoint to the world of the global elite represented there. Its appearance online has also allowed it to reach a broader audience (36,774 views as of May 2021). That first night in the Lady Ana Salon, on the heels of the Goya Gala, *Alejandro y Ana* was a performance for not only an audience in Madrid, but a national one. In a theater market ever more controlled by government subsidies and the private market, these dramatists and actors have found a variety of different spaces for their political spectacle exactly at the convergence of the local, the national, and the global.

When, some weeks later, *Alejandro y Ana* made its debut within the central meeting space of the Laboratorio 03, these themes carried even more weight. Stephen Vilaseca has argued that *okupas* are an "entanglement," as he puts it, of "word, art, body, and built environment" that challenge capitalism's commodification of language, thinking, and writing.[136] It is a process that Jonathan Snyder, in his work on the 15-M movement, has described as "oppositional literacy," which makes use of collective action and participatory cultural practices like those found in the Acampada Sol or squatted social centers to make "legible" the strategies of accumulation.[137] If the modest banquet hall threw into relief the contrast between the average citizen and the global elites, then the performance in the now-highly-visible squatted social center – a locus for anti-war organization and other national protest movements – brought to bear the material consequences of the Popular Party's neo-liberal agenda: disparities in housing, in social services, in access to political representation. Indeed, the themes of *Alejandro y Ana* would resonate all the more fully in the context of the practiced city promoted by the Laboratorio 03.

FROM SOCIAL CENTER TO POLITICAL CENTER

The spectacles of the Laboratorio transformed it into a symbol of leftist politics and a place for local and regional politicians to enact their own spectacles in support of their candidacies. By the spring of 2003, the local and regional candidates from the United Left party, such as Fausto Fernández and Inés Sabanés (candidates for the presidency of the Autonomous Community of Madrid and the mayor's office respectively), declared their support for the Laboratorio 03 and participated in the protests against its eviction. Later, the Spanish Socialist Workers' Party threw in their support, and together the two parties voiced public opposition to the eviction and a hope of working toward a "public and self-managed use for the site."[138]

The role of technology and the use of the Internet was also one of the keys ways that the local, national, and global intertwined. In an interview with Emisora Libre Orcasitas, Santi Jartos and Iñaki Correcaminos asserted the local emphasis of the Laboratorio because they could not imagine "the Laboratorio outside of Lavapiés nor Lavapiés outside of the Laboratorio."[139] Simultaneously, they suggested that "in Madrid it is notable that there [didn't] exist a movement of *okupación* as such, but rather an anti-capitalist movement uniting a number of things."[140] It is in this union of a "number of things" that the Laboratorio's identity as a site for merely neighborhood or municipal activism is most compromised. Indeed, through its associations with the "anti-capitalist movement," the Labo 03 became a site for both anti-globalization and national political activism.

The extensive use of the Internet and other forms of "hack-tivism" helped to broaden the impact of the Labo beyond the local scale. For example, the Laboratorio 03 was the site of the third "Hack-meeting" that occurred in Spain, which brought together anti-capitalist hackers from across the country. In their study of the Internet and the *okupa* movement, Igor Sábada Rodriguez and Gustavo Roig Domínguez describe how the interpersonal contacts made at these meetings led to the establishment of a whole series of hack-labs across Spain. Importantly, this network facilitated the emergence of "an independent, horizontal, and democratic media, whose massive and global mobilizing capacity, had no immediate referent in the history of communication and contemporary technical development."[141] In the years after the Labo's eviction, as technology would play an ever larger role in organizing protest movements, the tactics and infrastructure developed in the Laboratorio was likely instrumental.

In 2011, when the Indignados of the Acampada Sol began broadcasting their own radio station online and leveraging a technical knowhow under ad hoc conditions, it is logical to conclude that many of these individuals had either developed these skills in the hack-labs of a squatted social center or had been taught by someone who had. The *okupas* in the Laboratorio 03 used and continued to use the Internet to articulate their local resistant practices into a global frame. Similarly, the participants in the Laboratorio 03 also actively supported the free-software movement and anti-copyright activity – two important anti-capitalist movements that would converge in opposition to Spain's controversial hardline Ley Sinde, or Sinde Law, from 2011, which was intended to crack down on copyright infringements in media and software. These resistant forms of cultural production would not remain neatly contained in their "nested" locality, but rather used the local as a way to reinscribe the scale of the municipal, the national, and the global. In other words, the space of the Laboratorio became a launching pad for an online spectacle whose public was most decidedly local – but it found spectators around the world.[142]

On 9 June 2003, police in full riot gear smashed through the door to evict the eight or ten *okupas* who had decided to remain in the building in defiance of the court order of eviction. Naturally the eviction was filmed, and it appears in the documentary about the Labo 03. During these last moments, the spectacle of the Labo 03 continued. One lone *okupa* sat in a plastic lawn chair attached to the facade of the building via rope and carabiners. As the police and firemen arrived, they were turned into participants in the performance as they detached him from the wall and physically carried his passive body away from the building. The Laboratorio 04 was occupied that same day, but lasted only fourteen days. Nonetheless, the Laboratorio continued to live online at websites like sindominio. net and other anarchist and *okupa* websites. In subsequent years, other spaces in the neighborhood would be occupied with the spirit of self-management that incubated in the Laboratorio. For example, the vacant lot at 48 Olivar Street was home to the project called El Solar from 2003 to 2009, and many of the activists from the Labos participated. It was a space for the free distribution and sharing of culture, with one notable example being the sixth annual Festival de Cine de Lavapiés that took place in early June 2009. The project in El Solar would continue to apply pressure on government officials to provide a space for grassroots cultural development. Their efforts would ultimately culminate in the cession of the iconic Tabacalera in the Plaza Embajadores to activists in the neighborhood and the establishment of the Centro Social Autogestionado La Tabacalera. It would become an essential space from which the Acampada Sol was launched and in which members of the 15-M movement took refuge after the dismantling of their encampment in June 2011.[143]

In a manifesto written in response to the eviction and posted online at sindominio.net, the *okupas* recognized the expansiveness and ephemeral quality of the Laboratorio: "the Laboratorio ceased to exist: for now there hasn't been a Laboratorio 05, but its experience resonates in a multitude of other social initiatives, inside and outside of Lavapiés, in new practices of action and critical thought, in the obstinacy of independent art and culture, in the modes of life and disobedient and rebellious social attitudes."[144]

Like a traditional drama that can be read and performed in a multitude of physical settings, the resistant spectacle of the Laboratorio was converted into a "political practice between reality and fiction that invents other worlds."[145] Its urban spectacle sought to "secrete" that new kind of space and new modes of production across a range of geographies. Yet it was not only in the Labo 03 where we find the spectacle of Lavapiés, and we turn now from spatial practice to explore the overlapping geographies found in the representational space of dramas about the iconic *barrio bajo* of Lavapiés.

5

The Representational Space of the City: Lavapiés in the Theater

In the middle of the nineteenth century, Madrid began a process of modernization and industrialization that would transform the city into a modern, bustling urban capital. No longer merely the administrative center of the state and a site for activities of the court, the city was in flux, a place of constant change, full of new sounds, new smells, and new rhythms of life emerging from the city's growing consumer economy. In the midst of these changes, writers like Román Mesonero Romanos were busy crafting sketches of the people and places of daily life in Madrid and helping to consolidate the city's mythical *castizo* character.

In the essay "Madrid by Moonlight" from the collection *Scenes and People of Madrid* (1842), Mesonero Romanos describes Madrid as "an immense book, an animated theater where each day I encounter new pages to read, and new and curious scenes to observe."[1] This "animated theater" alludes to a city that exists not as inert text to be read by one reader, but rather one shaped and reshaped by people's use of the city. Seeing the city as a social space presages the approaches to the urban experience that scholars of the twentieth century, like Henri Lefebvre, would begin to put forth. The city, like a literary text, is not merely read passively and observed, but rather constantly recapitulated and resignified by different readers at different times. The way cities are used and imagined leads to the perpetual construction and destruction of its material makeup: the concrete, bricks, and mortar always responding dialectically to imagination. Mesonero Romano's allusion to an animated theater is even more apt, as the city, like a theater, provides a spectacle that is always experienced – on some level – collectively with a public;

it is always a social experience imagined in connection with others, a situation that contrasts the exchange between the writer and the solitary reader that characterizes the encounter with a book.

As earlier chapters of this book have argued, this description suits Madrid all the more appropriately because the city not only gave birth to Spain's commercial theater industry, but also to various other types of urban spectacles: from royal processions and the architectural rhetoric of the Hapsburgs to the popular theater genres of the *zarzuela* and the *género chico* that would consolidate the *castizo* myth of Madrilenian authenticity. As I have suggested throughout this book, Madrid has long been a space (both literal and imaginary) where unique tensions between the city and the nation's geographies have been laid bare.

In the recent collection of essays, *Cartographies of Madrid*, Edward Baker suggests that an asymmetry and later a tension between Madrid's identity as *Villa* and *Corte* – or city and state – not only was a key factor in its founding, but would later come to define the city. When Philip II established Madrid as the site of the royal court in 1561 it was, according to Baker, the very fact that the *villa* of Madrid was so weak and inconsequential that made it attractive.[2] As a settlement with little economic power and physically removed from the influence of the powerful Archbishop in Toledo (the previous site of the royal court), the locale could easily be molded into a center for royal administration – the weak city easily subjugated to the power and demands of the state. This tension between Madrid's identity as a city and the center of an emerging state apparatus would continue to define its culture for centuries. It has been my contention that these same tensions and asymmetries have been expressed historically in Madrid's theater industry and in spectacular uses of urban space. During most of its history, these tensions, overlaps, and fault lines have occurred along Baker's state/city formulation, but as Chapter 2 explored, the rise of the *castizo* myth of Madrid added a third layer to this dynamic in the conflation of the neighborhood of Lavapiés with a popular identity for the city – albeit one tinged with nationalist flavors.

Over the course of the twentieth century and the early-twenty-first century, as David Harvey has argued, the production of space in cities would shift from one focused on urban planning to reshape the physical terrain of the city and improve the lives of inhabitants to an emphasis on urban design.[3] Malcolm Compitello, building on

Harvey's work, demonstrates how the Urban Plan of 1985 was a hinge point in this process for Madrid (in general) during the 1980s and then Lavapiés (in particular) from the early 1990s until the early 2000s.[4] In his view, it is in the later years of the 1980s and into the early 1990s that city leaders abandoned their interest in defending the "right to the city" for all citizens and instead focused on boosting Madrid's image – investing heavily in the city's cultural infrastructure as a means of cultivating the symbolic capital of key neighborhoods. Following Harvey, Compitello describes this process as the means by which "art becomes the art of rent."[5] It was less important how the city functioned in practical terms and more important what it looked and "sold" like – a shift from use value to exchange value that would benefit speculative capital. As has been detailed in Chapters 3 and 4, many of these trends came to a head in the neighborhood of Lavapiés, which figured so prominently in the Urban Plan of 1997, a fact illustrated by the reaction of activists in squatted social centers like the Laboratorio 03. What is important about this shift is that, in an age of global competition amongst cities and the transformation of the culture of cities into an economic driver and a means for spatial reconfiguration (i.e., "selling place"), Madrid's asymmetries or tensions have shifted from merely including the city, the state, and the neighborhood, to geographies always overlaid by globalization.

These geographies include transnational flows of capital and people; the influence of multinational corporations and financial institutions; and the emergence of supranational governmental bodies (i.e., the European Union, the International Monetary Fund, The World Trade Organization, etc.). Lavapiés has been a stage on which the various tensions regarding how to understand and build the twenty-first-century city have played out. Given the neighborhood's iconic status since the late-nineteenth century, it is no surprise that Lavapiés has continued to act as a kind of urban synecdoche for Madrid in the early-twenty-first century. This dynamic is perhaps seen most clearly in the underlying discourse of the Urban Plan of 1997, which seemed to suggest that, as Lavapiés goes, so goes Madrid. As a result, Madrid has relied on its often-metonymic relationship with this iconic *barrio bajo* to project new meanings across the stage of the capital.

Like any literary text, a theatrical work offers a series of interconnected metaphors and symbols that attempt to recapitulate and resignify the reality of the viewing public. For this reason, Lavapiés might be considered an urban spectacle in which the urban landscape functions as a metaphoric theater space, where technocrats, playwrights, and *okupas* have attempted to re-articulate the meaning of the neighborhood and its function as a synecdoche of Madrid and the nation. This chapter continues to explore the theater of Madrid, but moves beyond thinking merely about theatrical uses of city space to consider the ways in which theater texts have been a vehicle for imagining the neighborhood and reflect the tensions between the local, metropolitan, and global geographies that form the focus of this book.

IMAGINING THE LIVED SPACE OF THE CITY

In this intersection between the material and the metaphoric, contemporary chroniclers have attempted to resignify and recapitulate the urban space of Lavapiés. Like a modern-day Mesonero Romanos, Julien Charlon has used both his self-described multimedia Participatory Book and DVD, entitled *Mundo Lavapiés*, and his book-length photographic essay on the Laboratorio 03 to try to give meaning to the "new and curious scenes" that the "enlivened theater" of Lavapiés's urban landscape offers.[6] One of the poems from this collection, Juanjo Martín Escriche's "Teatro de kif," illustrates this intersection between the material and the metaphoric.

Central to the poem is the transformation of the Teatro Valle-Inclán building into a metaphor for the physical and social changes occurring in the neighborhood. The nostalgia that tinges the poem when the speaker pines for "that other one / with the pink wall" that the speaker "loved," alludes to the tone of lament within the poem.[7] The title's use of the term "kif" is an allusion to the Valle-Inclán poem "La pipa de kif" – a poem recited multiple times by the character of el Chivo in César López Llera's play *Un Chivo en la Corte del botellón o Valle-Inclán en Lavapiés* (2005), one of the dramas that forms the focus of this chapter. This subtle reference and the more explicit statement later in the poem, "thus your name: Valle-Inclán," makes it clear that the "Teatro" of the title is the recently inaugurated Centro Dramático Nacional: the Teatro Valle-Inclán.[8] For the speaker, the building is quite literally an abomination, whose "outline is so monstrous" that the "horizon departs," while at its "feet concrete paving stones" serve only to "twist ankles."[9]

The speaker's use of the possessive pronoun "your" and the reference to the building's "feet" personify the building and conflate the writer Valle-Inclán (referenced in the title) and the national theater building itself. This architectural monstrosity called Valle-Inclán is like a deformed reflection of the bearded Galician poet and his work, and therefore is "the very latest recognition of the grotesque."[10] Here again, the material and the metaphoric converge, as the building becomes a representation of the *esperpento* – the literary genre of the grotesque made famous by Valle-Inclán. As the speaker wonders in the subsequent lines whether this deformation of urban space will be appealing "to the oh so perfect gentleman," the frame of the poem broadens from being mere critique of the building to a contemplation of the social changes occurring in Lavapiés.[11] In this reading, the "perfect gentleman" is an allusion to what Mayte Gómez describes as the newbie neighbors, or *novísimos vecinos*: attractive, tidy professionals that will fulfill the Ayuntamiento's hopes to change the "social component" of Lavapiés.[12] This image endures even today in 2020, as the neighborhood becomes one of the "coolest neighborhoods" in the world, according to the global media company Time Out.[13]

The poem uses the specific site of the Teatro Valle-Inclán as a means to critique the neighborhood as a whole. The figurative power of language converts the building into a metaphor, while emphasizing its physicality, its immensity, and its presence as monstrosity. Thus, the material merges with metaphor and reflects the fractal nature of urban space – the building as metaphor folds into the neighborhood as metaphor, which likewise metonymically folds into the city's symbolic vocabulary. Lastly, this series of synecdoches represents the aspirations of the nation-state (at least, as understood in terms of administrators' aspirations for international status and influence). These synecdoches of urban space are the point at which the written word and our understanding of place intersect.

Early chapters in this book have emphasized two key components of Henri Lefebvre's triad of spatial production. The discussion of the Teatro Valle-Inclán and the Urban Plan of 1997 illustrated how the *conceived* space of Lavapiés relied on articulations between global and local discourses to produce the "abstract space" of Lavapiés – that space associated with technocrats, urban planners, architects, and the dominant discourses of power and capital. The previous chapter broadened this discussion of urban space in Lavapiés by considering how the *perceived space* of Lavapiés also situated itself at the intersection of multiple geographical scales. Lefebvre associates this *perceived space* with the terrain of the body in space and spatial practice. He argues that *perceived space* is not necessarily complicit in the productive use of space associated with the dominant modes of production, but is nevertheless essential to the social reproduction of space; as the body moves through space, it reproduces the social codes of that space. Benjamin Fraser, in his incredibly useful overview of Lefebvre's key concepts in *Henri Lefebvre and the Spanish Urban Experience*, calls this tension between *perceived* and *conceived* space a "juxtaposition of the 'planned city' with the 'practiced city.'"[14] For Lefebvre, as Fraser articulates it, "the modern city ... was intimately connected with the capitalist mode of production, but also a necessary part of radical social change."[15] It is precisely this conflict over urban space that the dueling images of the Teatro Valle-Inclán and the Laboratorio reveal. As I have repeatedly argued throughout this book, this conflict not only played out in competing urban spectacles, but these spectacles were simultaneously immersed in local, metropolitan, and global discourses.

In these formulations of the city, Lefebvre's triad is often distilled into a more traditional Hegelian Marxist dialectic: mode of production vs. revolution; urban planners vs. the practice of everyday life. It often appears that these discussions of urban life ignore the tripartite nature of Lefebvre's triad of spatial production and skirt the third axis of Lefebvrian spatial production: *lived space*. This third aspect, what he also calls *representational space*, occurs not in urban-planning offices, nor in the way inhabitants use the city, but rather in the cultural imaginary that binds the two together.

Manuel Delgado put forth his own consideration of urban life in *El Animal Público*, questioning the validity of using the theater to understand life on the street.[16] Echoing Richard Sennett in *The Fall of Public Man*, Delgado suggests that the chaos and serendipity of street life undermine any coherent "plot" that might tie together this drama and argues that "the spontaneity of the passerby has nothing to do with theatrical delivery."[17] Indeed, to imagine the life of the city as guided by some overarching plot disregards the agency of individuals to create the city, and may be problematic. What I hope to do in this chapter is to reverse this formulation. Instead of attempting to deduce the "plot" of the participants, I set out to extend Delgado's call for "floating observation" of the city. Except, rather than gathering together a series of vignettes of public life, I look to what Lefebvre calls the "representational spaces" of the city to uncover how the spectacle of Lavapiés and contemporary Madrid is imagined as a space of metaphor and metonym.[18]

This chapter analyzes two plays. The first, David Planell's *Bazar* (*Bazaar*)(1997), engages with issues of immigration, assimilation, and national identity in contemporary Spain. In the second play, César López Llera offers readers a modern urban *auto sacramental* entitled *Un chivo en la Corte del botellón o Valle-Inclán en Lavapiés* (2003). I chose these works not only because they describe a particular moment in Lavapiés, but they are, to my knowledge, the only plays from this period that take place in Lavapiés and that make the setting a prominent context for the works. These contemporary plays not only reveal much about current struggles over the meaning and uses of urban space in contemporary Madrid, but also allude to important trends in dramaturgy in general in Spain at the beginning of the twenty-first century.

THEATER AND TECHNOLOGY IN CONTEMPORARY SPAIN

In the years surrounding the development of the Urban Plan of 1997 and the establishment of the first iteration of the Laboratorio in Lavapiés, theater in Spain was in a transitional and difficult situation, confronting a multi-headed hydra of challenges. César Oliva suggests that an over-reliance on state subsidies for survival and increasing doubts about the sustainability of this situation were compounded by the excessive expense of the public theater network and the decline of private theater businesses. These economic concerns, he suggests, were complicated by the disappearance of the dramatic arts from the mass media and a virtual vanishing of the remains of the independent theater movement of the 1970s.[19]

Of particular interest in this diagnosis is the relationship between the media and the theater industry, because it reflects a broader issue in Spanish letters during the first decade of the twenty-first century. In the introduction to *New Spain, New Literatures*, Luis Martín-Estudillo and Nicholas Spadaccini highlight an important element of Spain's new cultural and artistic landscape during this period: its transformation into a "democratic, plurinational, and multicultural society ... marked by a thriving cultural production, which highlights 'difference' as a major asset."[20] For the authors, this focus on "difference" led not only to a "redefinition of nationhood," but also, significantly, to an incorporation of "global commercial and cultural trends on local symbolic systems."[21] In essence, the process of cultural production in Spain has had to assimilate a more fluid notion of the Spanish nation than the seemingly fixed monolithic image that dominated official Spanish discourse during the Francoist period. Simultaneously, as Spain has become a more consumer-driven society, logically the access to mass media has become more widespread. As a result, Spain's writers and artists have also found their cultural production more integrated into – and ever more influenced by – new technologies, such as film, television and the Internet.

As a visual medium, the theater, perhaps more than any other literary art, is susceptible to these influences. The relationship between the new media and the theater has been a preoccupation of critics and intellectuals during much of the twentieth century, with many enthusiastically predicting a natural fusion.[22] Despite the enthusiasm of these predictions, Oliva sees these them as mere fantasies, which don't conform with the present state of Spanish theater.[23] He bases this assertion on his belief that "the theater will always be the confrontation between an accepted belief and unaccepted belief made by artists representing it live before a public. The theater will never be virtual. It will be live, or it will not be."[24] It is not a far-reaching generalization to suggest that, on the whole, theater productions in Spain today confirm this stance. On any given night in the major independent or commercial theaters in Madrid, the representations of dramatic works remain generally unchanged: proscenium theater, public in seats, actors on stage. There are occasional efforts to modify this arrangement (such as the avant-garde possibilities built into the Teatro Valle-Inclán), but for the most part the actors remain on the stage and the public firmly in their seats.

Nonetheless, contemporary theater often has an interesting and important relationship with new media. For example, the performances of Animalario not only looked to unique urban spaces (banquet halls, squatted social centers, etc.) as a new way to engage with audiences and enrich the content of the work, but they also distributed recordings online through YouTube and other platforms. If dramatists like Bertold Brecht and Luigi Pirandello transformed modern theater through the breaking of the metaphoric fourth wall of the stage, then Animalario has shattered the four literal walls of the theater by creating highly mobile works disseminated in digital format.

Other contemporary playwrights have engaged with media in other ways that have made more fluid and elastic the spatial limitations of the theater space. José Antonio Pérez Bowie points to the use of movie screens as one of these tools, and suggests that they accomplish a number of objectives and functions on the stage. For example, they can add ambience and/or expand the physical limits of the stage, illustrate the dialogue of the actors, and offer opportunities to create flashbacks, amongst other functions. In works like *El arquitecto y el relojero*, López Mozo, for example, deploys a film screen as a central feature of the staging. Through the juxtaposition of archival images and archival newsreel shorts or "NODOs" (Noticiario y documentales) with the action on stage, López Mozo deftly weaves his concerns with historical memory into his dramas through the use of these technologies. As architecture is a principal concern of his play about the rehabilitation of the iconic clock tower of the Real Casa de Correos, the screen also allows for the treatment of a subject that might present logistical and economic challenges for the tight budgets of theater companies and set designers. Changes in the physical landscape of the city needn't be constructed and represented in elaborate sets. In this sense, the use of a film screen offers flexibility for representing different settings for the action of the play. The fluidity of the theatrical space on stage is echoed by the mobility of the work: freed from an elaborate set that requires construction for performances, the work may move amongst theaters more easily.[25]

There are also other market explanations for this increasing incorporation of new forms of media into the scenographic vocabulary of Spanish theater. Candyce Leonard and John Gabriele position contemporary theater between two challenges: "the need to explore and experiment with new dramatic forms and the impulse to attract the public without distancing the traditional spectator. The result is a curious phenomenon of artistic renovation and survival."[26] This dance between attracting a new media-savvy public and staying committed to the aesthetics of the past to consolidate the traditional theater audience is an issue very much at work in the two plays included in this study.

THE "TELEPOLITICS" OF AZNARISMO

Considered in the context of Germán Labrador Méndez's recent efforts to periodize the last quarter of the twentieth century in Spanish letters, this media issue gains further resonance. Writing in

2010, Labrador Méndez's formulation of the post-Francoist period can be loosely divided into three cultural moments: 1) the 1980s, associated with emerging democratic structures and the cultural hegemony of the Socialist Party (PSOE); 2) the early 1990s, during which the corruption scandals that destroyed the credibility of the PSOE would lead to a crisis of language and identity for intellectuals and writers on the left; and 3) the rise to power of José María Aznar and the conservative Popular Party from 1996 until their defeat in the elections of 2003, just after the bombing of the Atocha train station.[27] As discussed in the previous chapter, this period of *aznarismo* was characterized by its neo-liberal economic policies, a revanchist dedication to Spanish Catholicism, and an unwavering commitment to an Atlantic power axis from within which to project international influence.[28]

Though Labrador Méndez focuses mainly on how the neo-nationalist politics of the Popular Party "animates the construction of alterities" (i.e., sense of otherness), like a reinvigorated regional nationalism in Catalonia and the Basque country, it is important to consider the spectacular nature of their method – what he refers to as telepolitics.[29] This postmodern political spectacle, in Debordian terms, "is both the result and the project of the dominant mode of production. It is not mere decoration added to the real world. It is the very heart of this real society's unreality."[30] In other words, the use of the image is an effort to supplant reality and create what French philosopher Jean Baudrillard would call the "simulacrum." As has been discussed in earlier portions of this book, an important part of this strategy of "telepolitics" has included the transformation of urban space. Indeed, the city itself is a part of the media *massage* used by the national government to create a simulacrum of success and progress: the burgeoning financial capital of Europe, Latin America, and the Mediterranean should have an appropriately appointed capital city. The role of the national Ministry of Culture in these transformations in the urban core of Madrid underscores that these changes in the city were not driven solely by the municipal government.

The two plays from this period of *aznarismo* demonstrate how "telepolitics," as both a media and urban phenomenon, has become an increasingly important concern of contemporary Spanish theater. The coexistence of these discourses of urbanism and the media reflect the broader transformations occurring in the city during this period (as previously discussed in Chapter 3 and 4). This concern with urbanism is also important because urban space is an implicitly central concern for dramatists, particularly given that they craft dramatic texts with the intention – one would presume – of having them represented publicly. Therefore, the theater as an artistic medium is always pursuing public space in which to be actualized into living performance. How a given city develops is often intimately tied to the development of its cultural infrastructure. On this level, too, urban space is a concern of fundamental importance to dramatists.

In Oliva's characterization, the challenges to Spanish theater have been varied over the last thirty years, but its precarious situation hasn't changed. This problematic situation stems principally from the fact that "the life of the theater moves between public centers of production in which predominate the grand spectacle and its tendency towards the classical and private businesses that gamble only on safe works."[31] For a wide range of theatrical movements, both during and after Francoism, including Underground Theater and Social Realism, as well as more philosophically-driven drama, the same struggle persists: access to the stage. In other words, they all struggle with the need to have their works performed and attract a public willing to pay admission for these works.[32] This need to find performance space (implicitly found in urban space) and the competition from new media forced Oliva to ask in 2004 if Spanish theater was writing its "last scene" – the phrase that would form the title of his book on theater of the period. Thus, there is the ironic twist that the works that form the focus of this chapter – works that I argue are compelling and important – have minimal performance history. The López Llera drama, for example, has never been performed. While the content of the works reflects the changing urban landscape of contemporary Madrid, their performance histories also point to the difficult situation for Spanish theater in general. Just as *aznarismo* catalyzed the construction of alterities, I assert that this period in Spain's history pushed its dramatists to look for new themes and new avenues of expression. In the *lived* space that emerged, the relationship between culture, scale, and urban space persists as an important discourse in representations of the contemporary urban spectacles of Lavapiés and Madrid.

THE SPECTACLE OF NEW SPAIN: *BAZAR*

In David Planell's (b.1967) play *Bazar*, the characters navigate a world in which appearance, reality, and identity are always contingent. The characters – first-generation Moroccan immigrants – grapple with issues of assimilation and cultural isolation in Spain on the cusp of the twenty-first century. The central plot of this two-act play revolves around the relationship between Hassan, a Moroccan immigrant, and his nephew Rashid and their efforts to win a funniest-home-video television show called "You've Been Framed." Some weeks earlier, before the action of the play begins, Hassan, while trying out a new video camera for the shop, unintentionally filmed Rashid's friend Anton crashing his bike into a blonde woman passing by. After discovering in the first act that the submission has been accepted, but deemed "too real" by the studio, the characters are thrust into an elaborate plan to reconstruct and film the accident in order to win the contest. This effort to simulate reality for the actual event is echoed by Rashid's friend Anton's plan to have Hassan produce a fake receipt, so that he can make a fraudulent insurance claim. These tensions between reality and simulation also resonate with the issues of identity that thread throughout the play, as both Hassan and Rashid must confront and resolve their differing perceptions of authenticity and cultural autonomy as immigrants. In this thematic context, the urban space of Lavapiés serves as the setting for two concurrent spectacles: the media spectacle of the home-video performance and its potential to offer access to financial security as well as the spectacle of being "other" on Madrid's city streets.

The very fact that Planell uses Lavapiés as the setting is fraught with meaning. The author might have developed the action in other neighborhoods with large immigrant populations, such as Carabanchel or Tetuán. By taking place in Madrid's iconic *barrio bajo*, the play reproduces the popular myth of Lavapiés as a symbol of immigration in Madrid. Moreover, that Planell writes not from personal experience, but rather (problematically) with the intention of creating some kind of allegory for contemporary immigration, also emphasizes the symbolic weight that Lavapiés carries as a synecdoche for Spain and the emerging challenges of integrating new waves of international immigrants. As Jeffery Coleman succinctly summarizes in his treatment of this issue of immigration in contemporary Spanish theater, the 1990s were a particularly acute moment in Spain's fraught relationship with international immigrants.[33] As a result of Spain's economic success in the mid-1990s and its growing international profile after events like the 1992 Olympic games, there was an influx of construction and agricultural workers from various places in the global south, such as north Africa, sub-Saharan Africa, and Latin America. It is precisely in these years when media images of *pateras* (small boats crossing the Straits of Gibraltar) and *cayucos* (large boats heading to the Canary Islands from West Africa) began to circulate regularly in Spanish media. As has already been detailed earlier, many of these immigrants settled in Lavapiés because of its degraded housing stock (and resulting low rents). The symbolism of the setting is suggested implicitly, not only because of the contemporary cultural cachet of Lavapiés as an immigrant neighborhood, but also because of the neighborhood's historical association with the quasi-nationalist notion of *lo castizo*. The urban space of Lavapiés is embedded in metropolitan and national discourses. In the work, it is a synecdoche of the nation as a whole. That this synecdoche occurs in a world in which reality is often constructed via the media points to the ways that urban space in contemporary Spain is the stage on which the spectacle of both individual and national identity are enacted.

Mainly a scriptwriter for television and the movies, Planell's credits include many of the most successful series of the Spanish television lineup, like *Hospital Central, Lobos, El comisario, MIR*, etc., and multiple nominations for Goya Awards for his screenwriting. Nonetheless, as recently as 2009, Planell still conceived of himself as a dramatist, because "a dramatist is a person that tells stories: he makes them up, gives them order, puts some interest into them, and sends them into the world as a possible mirror of life. That idea can be applied to all formats ... Internet and television are perfect places for the dramatist. There is a lot of future in new media."[34] *Bazar* was his first foray into theater and was met with critical acclaim. It won the Comedias de Hogar de Theatre prize after its debut in Cádiz, Spain, in August 1997, and then went on to tour around Spain before being performed in English at the Royal Court Theatre Upstairs in November 1997.[35] Because of the author's background and interest in television, it is not surprising that television is central to both the plot and the themes of the play.

The malleability of reality as a thematic thread begins to develop in the very first scene of the play, as Rashid works in the back of the store pricing inventory, while his friend Anton proposes his insurance-scam plan. Rashid is cautious about accepting this plan and states plainly "Okay, but it isn't true." When Anton responds, "Of course it isn't. I mean that's the whole point," he seems to shrug off the need for an accurate representation of reality.[36] For Anton, who appears to be Spanish, this seems to be a minor detail. As a Moroccan immigrant in Spain, Rashid's relationship with reality is already tenuous, since "Police don't believe [him]. If [he] went into a police station and told them [he'd been] robbed, [he knows] what'd happen. They'd put [him] in jail."[37] The sheer presence of being Other keeps Rashid trapped in perceived stereotypes and undermines his ability to be accepted as an individual by the culture around him. For Coleman, this status as perpetual Other through forms of "social death" like forced assimilation, surveillance, or captivity contribute to their necropolitical captivity as kind of social Zombies: immigrants who have lost their homes, lost the rights over their body, and lost their political status (particularly if they are undocumented).[38] Much of the play – as Coleman has emphasized in his reading of *Bazar* – seeks to offer a compassionate and humanizing view of the immigrant experience, but ultimately works to ossify this necropolitical racial thinking about immigrants that makes non-whiteness antithetical to Spanish identity. It is notable that it is Lavapiés where a new vision of what it means to be Spanish is negotiated and delineated.

As the play unfolds and the characters are forced to manufacture a more "real-looking" bicycle accident to enter the competition, this theme takes on a farcical quality. The actual footage of Anton is deemed by the studio to be "set up," in part because "it's all too clear. 'The camera's got to move. It needs to be dirty. To look worse. More ... fuzzy.' That's what they say."[39] To be taken seriously, the event needs to be recreated so that it appears "like it was more of an accident."[40] The actual authenticity of the event has no bearing on its believability. Rather, the grittiness and presentation of the event becomes the testament to its authenticity. In other words, the spectacle itself supersedes the event being represented. "They have to *look* real. They don't have to *be* real" according to Hassan.[41]

As the need to reproduce/fabricate reality becomes one of the central elements of the plot, the characters are aware of the fact that now Hassan is going "to direct a film."[42] In this way, *Bazar* participates in the broader trend in Spanish theater to engage with the dominance of visual media culture. Yet the critique of Spain's participation in global media culture is not the only significance of the work's focus on spectacle. There is a deeper resonance here because of the characters' status as immigrants. Their commitment to this get-rich-quick scheme suggests that participating in the spectacle of media culture is seen as perhaps their only real means of gaining financial and social mobility.

Yet the notion of spectacle also has resonances with the life on the street. With the prize money, Hassan plans to expand his shop and, in particular, "put in a shop window. [Because] we need a proper shop window" in order to be "overrun with customers."[43] Hassan's ability to conform to the requirements of the media spectacle will provide him with the financial capital to alter the facade of the store. The spectacle of the new shop window will allow the space of consumption within his shop to penetrate the street.[44] Their incorporation into the mediatized spectacle on television will enable them to more fully reproduce the spectacle of consumer culture in the urban space of Lavapiés. The bazaar referenced in the title becomes, here, more resonate, as it refers to the literal shop, Bazaar Hassan, and its array of commercial products, those that ultimately drive the production of television shows through ad revenues. In this sense, the bazaar of the commercial television interacts with and projects into and onto urban space.

But the role of spectacle in the play is also central in other ways, as the work attempts to contemplate the immigrant experience in Spain. For example, in one of several confrontations between Hassan and Rashid about how to succeed and what it means to be an immigrant, Hassan criticizes Rashid for finding a simulated Moroccan experience in Madrid. "It's the same every day: you get together, you roll a joint, you spend all day sitting on your magic carpet drinking mint tea ... Morocco in Madrid. Welcome to the ghetto. All you need is a photo of King Hassan on the dining-room wall."[45] For Hassan, the tea-house of Madrid is the charade of life in Morocco and therefore a false space that prevents assimilation into mainstream Spanish society. For Rashid, the social experience of the tea-house is a part of his identity as a Moroccan, and therefore he declares that "[he doesn't] know any other way of living. [He] just [knows his] own."[46] For Hassan it is these connections to the country of origin that must be suppressed, a resistance exemplified by his unwillingness to listen to Rashid "talking Berber language back at [him]" and his insistence on the need to "forget that way of life."[47] The authentic reality

Figure 5.1 | Image from *Bazar* by David Planell.

of one's culture must be superseded by the demands of integrating into the host country by appearing less Moroccan, less immigrant, less Other. This rejection of his past has kept Hassan from visiting Morocco for many years, and he scoffs at those who return. In his mind, typical Moroccan immigrants are "living here like animals, sleeping five in a bed, and going about there like big pricks in their Mercedes, which they drive around the village so everyone can see them."[48] Hassan seemingly rejects the notion that he must create a mythical image of himself back home, and therefore chooses to reject his Moroccan identity by remaining in Spain. (See Figure 5.1.)

This issue of appearance and authenticity is also represented aptly in two other instances in the play. The first occurs when Anton and Rashid describe the reenactment of the accident. The attempts to recruit a new "blonde" are thwarted when she insists that "I'm not going nowhere to do nothing with no Moor."[49] The result of her racist refusal is that the filmmakers use a blond wig to allow the grocer from around the corner to fill the role. Thus, they dress a man as a woman to recreate and make more "real" the original event. In actuality, the result is a representation of reality in which "the greengrocer had it on crooked ... and ... you could see his bald patch from a mile off."[50] The fabricated reality is quite literally askew, with the ugliness showing through. This ugly reality is symbolic of the racism that is an undercurrent throughout the play and is often manifested in Hassan's own self-loathing.

These issues come to a head in the climax of the play, when Hassan, Rashid, and Anton realize that the one good take from the afternoon has been ruined because of a technical malfunction of the camera. Hassan begins to work frantically to save the project and makes desperate declarations that he will pay all the extras for their continued participation. During the frenzy of these last scenes, Hassan becomes so obsessed with the notion that this video will provide him with economic and social access to Spanish society that he even goes so far as to dress himself in a traditional *djellaba* and decides that he will ride the bike himself (after five takes, Anton now has two broken arms). From this point in the second act until the end of the play, Hassan remains dressed in his *djellaba*, and seems to have accepted his inability to be anything but a caricature of his own ethnic identity. He is willing to demean himself and his culture because "they're going to love this disguise."[51] Even when Hassan finds out that the studio is out of money to pay him, he remains committed to his plan to make a video in which the "Arab's going to give himself a smash on his bicycle."[52] His only justification at this point is that the studio is "going to transmit it, and that's all [he wants]."[53] Like a modern-day *penitente* seeking salvation in urban space through self-mortification, Hassan wants to defile both his body and his identity for the triumphant media-age objective of merely appearing on the television.

This cynicism within the play becomes more redemptive in the last scene of the play when Anton confronts Rashid and Hassan about the receipt that is central to the insurance scam. Hassan had provided it to Anton without knowledge of its purpose, and Rashid had subsequently stolen it from Anton to protect Hassan from any legal troubles. When Anton returns in search of the receipt, he launches racial epithets at Hassan, calling him "Mahomet" and beating him with his crutch. Notably, in the face of this racial attack Hassan shouts to Rashid and Anton in Arabic and proclaims "*Ismi Hasan, machi Muhammad*" ("My name's Hassan, not Muhammad") and insists that "*Magadish nat'leb esmah*" ("I'm not going to say I'm sorry").[54] This self-actualization becomes the climax of the play when Hassan grabs the receipt from Anton's hand, stuffs it in his mouth, and eats it. The moment recasts a story Hassan told earlier in the play about his apparent boldness on a train, when, in the face of racial slurs directed at him by a group of older women, he snatches one woman's ticket away and eats it just before the conductor arrives (thus leaving her with no ticket for the conductor). Earlier, Rashid had exposed this story to be an urban legend and a lie. But dressed in his *djellaba*, Hassan inverts the truth-fabrication theme of the play by making actual what was exposed to be a lie on his part.

The final image of the play creates a similar inversion of the spectacle. Infuriated, Anton uses the price gun to "price" Hassan, and storms out. Hassan realizes with pride that he has stood up to him and stood up for who he is, repeating twice "He wanted the receipt. I ate it."[55] This symbolic act of "standing up" is echoed by the injured Hassan literally getting to his feet to look for the slippers that will complete his *djellaba* outfit. Understanding that Hassan has re-engaged with his identity, Rashid helps him to the mirror, assists him as he puts on the "African slippers," insisting on their comfort.[56] Thus, the audience is left with the image of Hassan in front of the mirror, dressed from head to toe in the traditional dress symbolizing his ethnic identity. He has re-actualized his identity as a Moroccan, but it is unclear whether this will lead to a greater or lesser ability to assimilate.

This ambiguous ending is indicative of some of the broader cultural issues at work surrounding this play. To my knowledge, it is one of the few published plays to be found that engages directly with the immigrant experience in Lavapiés, even though portrayals of contemporary immigration began in 1991, with the production of *La mirada del hombre oscuro* (*The View of the Dark Man*) by Ignacio del Moral, and has continued to the present day.[57] While the work's focus on immigration is notable for the time period, it is not unique – as Coleman has demonstrated. What is significant is its use of Lavapiés as the setting to explore these issues, a choice that alludes to what Lefebvre would describe as the "representational space" of the city, that which "overlays physical space, making symbolic use of its objects."[58]

Some of this symbolic meaning derives from the play's very complicated and problematic issues of representation: it is the immigrant experience as told by a Spaniard from Madrid.[59] The dramatist's decision to choose Moroccan immigrants as his subject falls into certain crude stereotypes from that period – a point made so compellingly by Coleman in his treatment of the play and portrayals of immigration more generally on the Spanish stage.[60] There is no mention in the play of the broad diversity of immigration found in a neighborhood where residents hail from China, Senegal, Ecuador, Bangladesh, and other places. The cultural situation of the play is compounded by the fact that, after its initial debut in the Festival de Teatro de Comedias in Puerto de Santa María in 1997, it was subsequently produced in translation by the Royal Theatre Company in the United Kingdom and then later published (again in translation) in 1999 by the British publisher Nick Hern Books in the collection *New Spanish Plays*. As a result, the immigrant experience in Lavapiés has been exported for consumption abroad, but remains somewhat outside the view of contemporary Spanish readers.

STAGING IMMIGRATION IN THE STREET

One can contrast this treatment of the immigrant "subject" with a performance produced jointly by the Association of the Undocumented and The Support Network for the Underground Railroad that occurred in front of the Centro Dramático Valle-Inclán in May 2009 to support the rights of undocumented immigrants in Spain. In this performance, entitled "Because Life Is Not a Prison, Let's End Controls," volunteers read testimonials of anonymous immigrants that described their mistreatment and abuse at the hands of the Spanish police (see Figure 5.2). These included the experiences of María Luisa, from Ecuador, Lydia, from Africa, and Salma, from Morocco, interspersed with testimonials from Jewish refugees of Nazi Germany and victims of the apartheid in South Africa.[61] It is a somewhat unrefined performance that also used the stage of Lavapiés (and, notably, the plaza in front of the Teatro Valle-Inclán) to engage with Spain's immigration policy. Comparing Planell's use of Lavapiés with this street performance demonstrates a problematic perpetuation of stereotypes about the inhabitants of Lavapiés and the neighborhood's status as one of foreign "immigrants" – particularly those from North Africa. On one hand, this association with international immigrants has contributed to the neighborhood's image as a bastion of tolerance and progressive politics. On the other, this discourse of tolerance belies how immigrant bodies have

Figure 5.2 | Performance of "La vida no es una cárcel/Life Is Not a Prison" in front of the Teatro Valle-Inclán, 11 May 2009.

become sites of contestation, where state violence and the national imaginary converge. Planell's play foregrounds the symbolic value of Lavapiés over a genuine engagement with the neighborhood – indeed, the actual urban space of the neighborhood has nary a mention. Lavapiés is converted into mere symbolic placeholder for the idea of an immigrant neighborhood, and, arguably, the stage for contemplating immigration in Spain.

Finally, it is important to mention that *Bazaar* not only helps reinforce the notion of Lavapiés as a point of articulation amongst various geographies at different scales and scopes, but the play also illustrates my assertion earlier in this chapter that film and television media are increasingly (and, it seems, naturally) becoming an important part of Spanish theater. In many ways, this work is Planell's only foray into the world of theater. He has a well-developed Internet Movie Database (IMDB) page with a long list of credits writing for various television series and movies. Planell is basically a television scriptwriter who decided to write a play. The play's loose commitment to Aristotle's dramatic unities derives more from a television sit-com aesthetic, in which one setting is preferable to having several sets, than from some dedication to theatrical traditions of Greek tragedy.[62] One can conjecture that this "play" might have been dually conceived as a script to be peddled to the television network as much as it was written for the stage.

Nonetheless, Planell's problematic representation of Lavapiés still stands in stark contrast to actual television representations that appeared at this time. In 2002, TeleMadrid produced a short-lived television sit-com, entitled *Living Lavapiés*, that offered viewers a sanitized vision of the neighborhood. It focused on the lives of several twenty-somethings living and working in the neighborhood.[63] The representation elided the economic struggles of its inhabitants, as well as the neighborhood's diversity and political combativity. It was a whitewashed vision of Lavapiés that suggested that the neighborhood had begun to be imagined in new and problematic ways – ways that ignored the complications and contradictions of everyday life in the neighborhood. As in Planell's work, *Living Lavapiés* relied on Lavapiés as a symbol of youthful urban life in the city. The character of this program and Planell's drama both highlight how aesthetic, economic, and political trends in both Spanish theater and urban development were in the process of creating a representational space for Lavapiés that had less to do with the city space and more to do with its possibilities as a globalized media product.

THE CONCAVE MIRROR OF MADRID IN *UN CHIVO EN LA CORTE DEL BOTELLÓN O VALLE-INCLÁN EN LAVAPIÉS*

While David Planell's characters in *Bazar* grapple with personal ethnic identity and issues of representation in a mediatized and consumerist world, César López Llera (b. 1963), in his 2005 play *Un Chivo en la corte del botellón o Valle-Inclán en Lavapiés* (*A Bearded One in the Court of the Street Party or Valle-Inclán in Lavapiés*), navigates more explicitly the precarity of urban living in a globalizing city.[64] Notably, it is the setting of Madrid and Lavapiés upon which López Llera relies for this recontextualizing and recapitulating of Ramón María del Valle-Inclán's canonical play *Luces de bohemia* (*Bohemian Lights*) from 1924. The representations of the city in the play and its clear allusions to a number of canonical works from the visual and dramatic arts allow López Llera to rearticulate Lavapiés in allegorical terms that reflect the struggles of a city in profound transformation.

Earlier chapters of this book have demonstrated how the conflicting spectacles in Lavapiés of a national theater building (the Teatro Valle-Inclán) and the cultural activities of a squatted social center (el Labo 03) reflected broader conflicts over efforts to reimagine Madrid and Spain in the twenty-first century. I have posited these two examples within the framework of Lefebvre's triad of spatial production: the former associated with Lefebvre's idea of abstract space and the latter with spatial practice (perceived space). López Llera's play offers the most compelling vision of Lavapiés's representational space (lived space) and the difficult dynamics that occur between art and the city in the Madrid of the early 2000s. Like *Bazar, Un Chivo en la corte de Botellón o Valle-Inclán in Lavapiés* illustrates yet another example of the way in which a contemporary dramatist deployed the setting of Lavapiés for its symbolic associations as a synecdoche of Madrid, and arguably Spain. It is not only in spatial practice or the vision of technocrats where the production of space articulates various geographies, but also in the dramatic worlds of contemporary playwrights.

César López Llera received the Teatro Serantes Award in 2004 for the play that will be discussed, and has had additional success in recent years, including great acclaim for his 2006 play *Últimos días de una puta libertaria o La vieja y la mar*, for which he won the Tirso de Molina Award. More recently, in 2010, he was awarded the prestigious Lope de Vega Prize for *Bagdad, ciudad de miedo*, a dramatic treatment of the war in Iraq. The work that I will refer to as the *Chivo en la Corte* offers a recapitulation of Valle-Inclán's famous drama, which tells the story of the last night of the life of blind, alcoholic writer Max Estrella as he traverses the streets of Madrid in search of financial remuneration for a book that his compatriot Don Latino has sold. Over the course of the night, this Dante-esque journey carries Max Estrella and Don Latino through the urban landscape of early-twentieth-century Madrid – to taverns full of modernist writers, into street confrontations between anarchists and the police, and into the jail cells in the basement of the Real Casa de Correos in the Puerta del Sol.[65] The work relies on both colloquial language and more elevated literary prose, while lengthy stage directions offer descriptions of characters and settings that create a distorted and expressionistic world. This range of techniques and characteristics would become codified by Valle-Inclán into something altogether new, which he called the genre of the *esperpento*, or the grotesque.

In the twelfth scene of the drama – one of the most cited scenes in the play – the work self-consciously defines this notion of the *esperpento* and argues for its necessity to reflect Spain's reality. It occurs late in the drama, when Max and Don Latino encounter the carnival mirrors on the side street of the callejón del Gato near the calle de la Cruz. Estrella proposes that "classical heroes reflected in concave mirrors create the *esperpento*," and suggests that "the tragic quality of Spanish life can only be captured through an aesthetic of systematic deformation," an approach necessary because Spain itself is a "grotesque deformation of European civilization."[66] The darkness and playfulness that characterizes this distinctly Spanish aesthetic, for Max Estrella, is a world "invented by Goya."[67] Max's epiphany in this famous scene would become one of the defining images of the Spanish experience, a way to capture a society always seemingly on the margins of European modernity.[68] At the end of the play, when Max Estrella is not only left to die on the street but also relieved of his wallet by his "loyal" squire, Don Latino, Valle-Inclán transforms the loyalty and affection of Cervantes's classic duo into the pessimistic image of an artist left dead and penniless after attempting to navigate the cityscape of modern Madrid.

For Dru Dougherty, the work's use of Madrid's urban landscape is central to its deforming aesthetic. The verisimilitude of early-twentieth-century Madrid found in the play creates a "flat mirror," which grounds Valle-Inclán's critique in a recognizable setting.[69] Yet, the work also emphasizes the spectacle of the changing city; the allure of the modern elides a complementary, but potentially contrary, discourse. According to Dougherty, "it is an incessant spectacle of novelties whose arbitrary quality gives the impression of chaos; and the contrary sensation that behind so much variety exists an inflexible order and determinism that transforms life into, as Clarín observed, a 'piece of machinery.'"[70] Thus the city simultaneously functions as a concave mirror that reflects an ambivalence toward modernity and a flat one that reflects the political and economic turmoil it has produced.[71]

That López Llera looks to Valle-Inclán for the secondary title of his work implicitly puts López Llera's "burla trágica," or tragic mockery – as the author subtitles the work – within the tradition of the *esperpento*. Given the Madrid setting and the plot, it is hard not to see the work as a recasting of *Luces de bohemia*. Just as in the original, the work follows a pair of characters as they traverse urban space over the course of a night. Also, like the 1924 text, urban landscape not only grounds the work in a concrete reality, but also allows its deforming aesthetic to function more emphatically. The juxtaposition of the central characters contributes to this sense of deformation. The role of the errant knight falls to Pablo, a junky who is resuscitated from a heroin overdose in the first scene, and that of his loyal squire is none other than a clone of Valle-Inclán. The mere act of pairing a street junky and a titan of Spanish literature for a nocturnal foray is one that puts tradition and a decadent crumbling contemporary reality into direct dialogue.

This tension is compounded by other structural elements of the work. In this more contemporary version, the work is divided into three "*trancas*," instead of the fifteen scenes of the original. By utilizing this odd term, which colloquially means *borrachera*, or "drunken binge," López Llera disrupts traditional dramatic terminology. At the same time, the work is divided into three sections and consequently echoes the highly traditional division of drama into three acts. Over the course of these three *trancas*, the pair move through the urban space of Madrid. Interestingly though, in López Llera's twenty-first-century version of this nocturnal jaunt, the action is focused exclusively in Lavapiés and moves from the Plaza Lavapiés in the first *tranca* to a decrepit shanty in the neighborhood for the entirety of the second *tranca*. The third *tranca* reverses this trajectory, moving from the house to the plaza. Though the play relies on a more limited number of urban settings, the circular structure creates a sense of movement and flow that echoes the nocturnal journey found in *Luces de Bohemia*. For Franciso Gutiérrez Carbajo, the circularity in *Un chivo en la Corte* presents an inverse journey to that found in Valle-Inclán's play. Instead of traveling from home-street-home, as in the original, the modern characters begin on the street, travel home, and then finish in the street. As Carbajo points out, this choice is not by accident, and it speaks to the way in which the street has become the stage for the precarious life of many urban dwellers.[72]

It is significant that the locale chosen for the nocturnal journey is Lavapiés. Instead of romanticized images of jaunty *chulapos* and sharp-tongued women hanging laundry from the balconies of *corralas*, we find a plaza full of – almost literally – viscera: "sabores y olores mezclados: alcohol, tabaco, miasmas residuals de orgía: sudor, semen, flujos vaginales, orines, vomitadas y hasta chispazos de sangre mondonguera" (mixture of tastes and smells: alcohol, tobacco, the residual miasma of orgies: sweat, semen, vaginal fluid, urine, vomit, and even flecks of intestinal blood).[73] Cups, bottles, and cans also fill the plaza, the material effluvium of the previous night's *botellón*: "improvisado vertedero de papeles y bolsas multicolores, cascos, latas, vasos" (makeshift trashcan of paper and multicolor bags, empty bottles, cans, glasses).[74] The repetitive rhythm of these descriptions, the consonance of the /s/ sounds in both descriptions and the assonance of the vowel sounds lend an almost poetic quality to this incredibly base subject matter. Amidst this mix of human waste and trash are "semi-naked twenty-somethings"[75]: a young eighteen-year-old drinking the liquid from a can of olives and Pablo preparing his dose with a spoon. Like his predecessor Valle-Inclán and other dramatists (Antonio Buero Vallejo comes to mind), López Llera relies on long stage directions (almost a full page) to create this scene – a technique that suggests the dramatist is searching on some level for some hybrid form of representation that is both simultaneously drama and narrative.

Through the use of what we might call "narration," López Llera asserts authorial control over the setting of the play's scenography. It leaves little room for interpretation – not only for solitary readers of the drama as written text, but also for directors or actors hoping to perform the work. They must contend with the tensions between the harshness of street life and the mundane backdrop of the urban setting. Against the "flat mirror" of the work's social realism, "the embers of a night of drunkenness" create an image evocative of a Hieronymous Bosch triptych.[76] This reading becomes more prescient when, amidst the visual cacophony created by the detritus on stage, strolls not only the aforementioned "Valle-Inclán clone," but also a Great Beast (what the text refers to as "un Gran Cabrón") leading a Band of Sinners (Pecadora Compaña) of dragons, turtles, monkeys, mandarins, medieval princesses, and naked young men and women with their bodies painted half white and half black.[77] According to the stage directions, with the song "Demons," by the Spanish pop group Estopa, as the soundtrack to this "Spring-time dawn, the procession is to emerge from the back of the theater and ascend the stage.[78] The mise-en-scène shifts from a scene of mere youthful

Figure 5.3 | Francisco de Goya y Lucientes. *El aquelarre o Gran Cabrón/The Witches Sabbath or Great He-Goat*, 1820–1823. Oil on mural transferred to canvas. Museo del Prado.

decadence, into a "night" of earthly delight, in which a pagan rite has occurred with Satan as overseer. The play interweaves the world of myth with the very specific cultural and geographic context of Lavapiés at the turn of the millennia. The deformations of Spanish culture that emerge from the layering of myth, pop culture, urban space, canonical literary figures, and a ruptured fourth wall creates the concave mirror of López Llera's *esperpento*.

It is also worth lingering on this scene for a moment to recall how the mise-en-scène here also recalls the painting of Francisco de Goya (the "inventor" of the *esperpento*, according to Max Estrella). Entitled "El aquelarre," or "The Witches' Sabbath," the Gran Cabrón, or large male goat, is being venerated as the focus of a Black Mass (see Figure 5.3). The visual allusion made in López Llera's play is twofold. On the one hand, it reinforces the work's connection with the tradition of the *esperpento* genre and therefore with the canonical artistic tradition in Spain. On the other hand, it emphasizes how deviant behavior – both hedonistic and heretical – characterizes the setting in which the action takes place: the *barrio bajo* of Lavapiés. In line with the interplay of dark and light, humor and gravity, and flatness and concavity found in the play, the Gran Cabrón's intermittent appearances throughout suggest that the characters' confrontations with the social realities of living in an under-resourced neighborhood has some deviant element to it.

Given that these behaviors are often just strategies of survival, the Gran Cabrón serves as an ironic symbol; the individuals are not deviant, merely trying to get by.

Valle-Inclán's presence in the urban environment of the Plaza Lavapiés also adds an element of the absurd. The juxtaposition of the first two scenes makes this clear. The play opens with Pablo falling into the spasms of an overdose after injecting himself with heroin. Subsequently Valle-Inclán saunters onto the stage drinking the remains of the bottles scattered about, while reciting the tenth verse of his poem "La tienda del herbolario" – a handful of stanzas that ironically describe an opiate-induced vision of "Green dragons, Chinese shadows, wise Princesses on litters."[79] The images of Valle-Inclán's escapist *modernismo* seem hollow and far removed from the contemporary world of drug abuse and social neglect surrounding him.[80] The character of Valle-Inclán (called El Chivo in the play) and his poems add comic effect to the play, as the police and others harass this canonical figure of Spanish letters for identification and he continually seems to be smoking hashish, all the while sprinkling verses about fairies and princesses from far-off lands throughout several scenes.

This comic effect is particularly acute when the paramedics and the police arrive in response to Pablo's overdose. Their request for the poet's identification prompts him to offer a long monologue, in which he boasts that his photo graces "all of the Histories of Literature" and that statues of his likeness are found on both the Paseo Recoletos and the Paseo de la Herradura de Santiago.[81] Unconvinced, the police respond only with a request for his home address. In the marginal space of Lavapiés, even one of the most important writers of the twentieth century is reduced to mere citizen and subject to a citation for carrying an open container. It is a bizarre scene, made all the more so by the pulsing and flashing lights indicated in the stage directions. Within the action of the play, the light emanates from the emergency vehicles. For the spectators, though, it has the dual purpose of representing the lights of the city at night, while also creating a dreamscape that undermines the realism of the action taking place. This strange quality is heightened when the Band of Sinners returns to the stage for a dance number to the 1982 hit "Bailando" by the Spanish pop group Alaska y los Pegamoides, a musical interlude that coincides with Pablo's resuscitation.

The play's cruel social reality balances these comic moments in the *esperpento*. The resolution of the first *tranca* revolves around a confrontation between the players on the stage and a domestic abuser who charges onto the stage in mid-dispute and shoots his pregnant lover (a direct allusion to a similar scene in *Luces de Bohemia*). In the context of drug addiction, overdose, and murder, the term *tranca* loses its amusing connotations of a night of bacchanalia. The paramedics return to save the baby and, in the background of the scene, the Gran Cabrón appears, seated in a large chair. With Satan overseeing the violent birth of the baby, the scene becomes a cynical modern-day *auto sacramental*, in which Pablo's resurrection simultaneously evokes the story of Cavalry and the disciple's conversion on the road to Damascus. The crying baby – symbolically orphaned at this moment – also alludes to the Bible and the birth of the baby Jesus. El Chivo confirms this reading by describing Pablo as "Saul, who regained his vision in order to convert himself into a witness for the prosecution of lies."[82] The urban setting of the play keeps these biblical allusions firmly rooted in the social reality of contemporary life. As in the case of *Bazar*, there is a certain typecasting taking place with the setting. If, for *Bazar*, the neighborhood metonymically represented Madrid's "immigrant neighborhoods," here Lavapiés is put forth as a stereotypical neighborhood suffering from the challenges of economic precarity and social marginalization. In both cases, Lavapiés becomes a metonym for broader conflicts over urban space affecting the city as a whole. The social exclusion in Lavapiés and its cynical representation here belies the gleaming city of steel and glass that is rising and the boosterism of city leaders at the time.

At the opening of the second *tranca*, the city seems literally to be crumbling around the characters. The stage directions describe how the curtain opens and the "sound of broken glass, shouts and a dry thud are heard … Deathly silence." On stage, "in the center of a humble dormered room of a house in ruins in the neighborhood of Lavapiés lies a body with a pool of blood below his head."[83] As the characters move from the public street to a private domestic space, spilled blood links the two spaces. In the last scenes of the first *tranca*, it is the abuser and his victim that provide the blood for the demonic *auto sacramental*. In this subsequent scene, the blood comes from the crumpled body that has fallen through the skylight. As the scene unfolds, the injured "body's" companion, El Colgado (the Stoner), comes to retrieve him. The somber mood is undercut by their drug-induced banter. Together the Injured and the Colgado have no serious contribution to make to the proceedings, other than to perpetuate this tension between violence and humor and link the aesthetic of the first *tranca* with the second.

Also important in the opening description of the space in this second act is the fact that the walls are marked by "Graffitis, *okupa* symbols, posters against the war and the Wizard of Oz."[84] The house to which El Chivo, Pablo, and Pablo's friend Micaela return is a *casa okupada*. As the play reveals later, the house is Micaela's, but given that the posters on the wall include anti-war slogans and its location in Lavapiés, there is a reasonable conjecture to be made that this *casa okupada* could be an iteration of the Laboratorio – the most high-profile occupied social center in the neighborhood in the period during which the play was written and published. Later in the play there appear many of the classic slogans of the *okupa* movement and the Laboratorio, a fact that bolsters this reading. For example, when threatened with eviction in the third *tranca*, Pablo shouts "when living is a luxury, squatting is a right"[85] and "one eviction, another squatted house."[86] Additionally, the presence of the young Somalian and Ecuadorian girls in this *casa okupada* converts the space from a mere representation of the Laboratorio into a microcosm of the neighborhood itself. Through his spatial choices and representations of characters in those spaces, López Llera allows the discrete domestic space of the *casa okupada* to become a place where symbolically all these geographical spaces can articulate with one another.

For geographers, such as Helga Leitner, Eric Sheppard, and Kristin M. Sziarto, these issues of scale are particularly important. They reject thinking of geographic scale as a means of understanding the scope of one's political action or circumstance.[87] Rather, they see attention to scale, and particularly the articulations between geographic scales, as a way of uncovering the "social relations of empowerment and disempowerment," as Erik Swyngedouw so aptly puts it.[88] As Brenner suggests, "scalar structuration" is a series of produced spaces that articulate with one another to construct and deconstruct power relations. Ironically, it is in the domestic space of the apartment where the global economic forces affecting Lavapiés are thrown into relief.

The play reveals these articulations through its representations of what Sharon Zukin calls the Artistic Mode of Production, a process by which art and cultural production play a key role in the management and production of space in the city, and thereby create tensions between the practice of daily life and the urbanization of capital. The work's contemplation of this theme begins broadly, as Pablo,

El Chivo, and Pablo's friend Chusito discuss the merits of Art, while Pablo, the contrarian, complains of how boring it is. In response, El Chivo and Chusito hope that "another Art is possible" in the pursuit of avant-garde expression, a suggestion that prompts El Chivo to argue cynically that "For that Art another world would be needed ... Now, even though we experiment, artists are obliged to reflect the perversity of reality and to profess its wretchedness."[89] The conversation reveals one of the reasons that the play has followed Valle-Inclán's lead and relied on the *esperpento* as an aesthetic frame. The artist's need to engage with social reality potentially limits the space for experimentation. López Llera, like many artists before him, seems to use his work as a way to navigate this tension between social reality and artistic experimentation and exploration.

In the middle of the second *tranca*, the scenography of the work expresses spatially this discomfort with aesthetically driven art. Pablo has offered El Chivo the opportunity to stay in the *casa okupada* in the room of Pablo's recently deceased artist girlfriend – another victim of heroin – who worked making copies of paintings as well as her own art. To accommodate him, El Chivo, Pablo, Chusito, and the Pecadora Compaña swirl in and out of Elisa's room to the sounds of Rossini's "Tarantella." The classical music, like the pop music of earlier scenes, adds a comic air to the process of rearranging the apartment. As the whole troupe of characters reorganizes the set in a humorous interlude, the moment becomes a choreographed dance sequence evocative of one found in a *zarzuela*.

As the stage directions indicate, their work results in a set divided into two parts separated by folding screens.[90] On the right side of the stage, there is a green curtain covering the wall, while "in the background on the right an enormous reproduction of the work 'Cante Hondo' by Romero de Torres stands out."[91] This large painting is complemented by other reproductions by Julio Antontio, Rusiñol, Victorio Macho, Gutiérrez Solana, and caricatures of Valle-Inclán.[92] The left side of the stage has been converted into a small coffee house with its own array of art reproductions and Charlie Chaplin posters.[93] The set has been transformed into a space devoted to art, and upon completing this process of rearranging the space on the stage El Chivo, Pablo, and Chusito occupy different parts of the stage: El Chivo in the space devoted exclusively to art, while the two twenty-somethings remain in the less-clearly-delineated artistic space in which living and art converge.

The *casa okupada* as a place for the (re)production of art develops another significance when, later in the scene, the owner of an art gallery arrives. He has come to see the paintings of Elisa Valle, Pablo's deceased ex. After examining the art on display, he notes the mix of "Abstract and realist painting together, architecture, sculpture, the lamp, I love it! It only lacks poetry and dance."[94] The broad mix of mediums and genres found in the space prompts the gallery owner to suggest that, "instead of exposition halls or galleries of art, it is creation in process, in the studio of the artist ... We could charge admission for it."[95] The intervention of capital and the market not only commodifies the objects, but urban space itself. Once it becomes commodity, as Lefebvre observes, we see space being consumed in both the economic and the literal senses of the word, "not as consumption of the cultural past, but indeed as immediate practical 'reality.'"[96] As Zukin, Harvey, and even Florida have made clear, the production of culture is intimately linked to the material production of space. The play highlights this dilemma and the challenges of de-linking artistic production from "abstract space." In exploring these issues, López Llera attempts to create a representational space in which art might signify space free from capital.

López Llera's use of the domestic space of Lavapiés to explore the neighborhood's symbolic meaning – its representational space – echoes similar moves by the architectural studio of Andrés Jaque nearly a decade later. As a part of the Ministry of Culture's fourth annual Art is Action event exploring the intersection of art and architecture, in November 2011, the architectural collective created a performance piece called *Ikea Disobedients*. The installation recreated the fifteen-square-meter apartment on the calle Mesón de Paredes of longtime Lavapiés resident Candela Logrosán Pérez and asked community members to "perform their everyday talents, behaviors, and discussions" to demonstrate the political possibilities found in domestic spaces.[97] First exhibited in the self-managed social center La Tabacalera, the performance was acquired by New York's Museum of Modern Art in 2012 as a part of its "9 + 1 Ways of Being Political: 50 Years of Political Stances in Architecture and Urban Design." For Jacque and his colleagues, it was not the space itself that was of interest, but the spatial practice of Candela and her neighbors, who would convene at her kitchen table to pool knowledge and resources to navigate the economic precarity of contemporary Madrid. The installation was a perverse inversion of the very process proposed by the gallery owner. In this case, though, it was not the artist's home that became the spectacle for consumption, but rather the micro-democracy found in the spatial practices of everyday living. While the exhibit at MoMA had a clear progressive agenda, there is always an irony in exhibiting engaged art within the confines of a museum that charges admission in one of the most expensive cities on earth.

Alongside the play's representations of capital's role in the commodification of the artistic process, there are allusions in the play to the fact that capital's interest in Lavapiés is also more traditional. Micaela, an older friend of Pablo's who has brought him and El Chivo to the apartment, is constantly a source of pathos in the play. Not only is her imminent demise from diabetic complications a source of dramatic tension in the second *tranca*, but her complaints about her economic situation belie the broader problems of the neighborhood. She complains about the lack of medical facilities in the neighborhood and that she has had to go to a private doctor instead of "that crappy clinic on Tribulete."[98] Similarly, the plumber who appears intermittently throughout the work to repair the bathroom in the apartment observes "that in this neighborhood there are many homes without a bathroom or with only a communal one."[99]

Just as these references reflect the debilitated state of much of the neighborhood in the early 2000s, Micaela's imminent eviction also reflects tensions over real-estate speculation and gentrification occurring in this period. She describes how "they'll give me a little apartment in Rivas, the Councilor of Urban Affairs told me ... New, spacious, well-lit, with views of a park."[100] She is obstinate about not accepting the city's offer, because "I moved in here in '63 and I haven't moved since then."[101] Micaela is, to use Gómez's term, *un vecino de toda la vida* – an elderly lifelong resident of Lavapiés who has remained in the decrepit housing in a neighborhood devoid of services because it is their home.

Micaela's imminent eviction and her failing health begin to converge into a religiously tinged sacrificial discourse. Having seen the Gran Cabrón in the first *tranca*, she is convinced that death is coming for her, and she prepares her "last supper." This Christological allusion echoes Chusito's joke earlier in the *tranca* about Micaela's taking in of Ecuadorian and Somali prostitutes. He proclaims that "you honor your namesake because Saint Micaela consecrated her life to prostitutes."[102] Chusito refers to Santa Micaela, a Spanish nun who lived in the nineteenth century and established the organization Adoring Slaves of Charity and the Holy Sacrament.[103] Like Micaela's efforts in the play to save the two young immigrant girls from the streets, this organization was committed to rescuing women from the perils of prostitution and a life on the streets. According to Chusito, however, Micaela has founded what he calls the Sisterhood for Sheltering *Okupas*. In addition, El Chivo suggests that, because of her efforts – "she [rescues] drug addicts, beggars, immigrants, and prostitutes" – she should be considered "Santa Micaela de Lavapiés."[104]

These proclamations come in the wake of her death at the end of the second *tranca* and her beatification derives not only from her works, but also from her martyrdom. In particular, "she accomplished the miracles of not committing suicide, of growing old, of conserving her dignity, and of resisting the abandonment of her house."[105] In the context of a decaying city, "the virtues of domesticity and of daily life" are the inspirations for myth, tragedy, and art.[106] Through the religious discourse that underpins much of the dramatic action, the work becomes a manifestation of the ideal of theatrical expression described in the play itself. The idea was Elisa's, and therefore it is left to Pablo and El Chivo to summarize how she "conceived of the theater as total art … as a combination of concepts and explosive plasticity, in the manner of the Baroque *auto sacramental*."[107]

The pursuit of new avenues of theatrical innovation desired by Elisa and echoed by El Chivo and Pablo, of course, butts up against the ubiquitous limitations of the market, in which "the ticket box drives all, not artistic quality."[108] Through the voice of Elisa, López Lllera proposes that, to surmount these challenges, the theater must "adapt itself to modern visual language … to exploit the possibilities of new technologies [and] create in virtual spaces, change the way the actors act, gamble on more literary dialogues, revindicate a sensual theater for the enjoyment of the five senses."[109] The play is self-consciously aware of itself as artifact, and through these reflections of its own aesthetic agenda, becomes an effort to contemplate not just the dilemma of urban living, but also that of the dramatist in the urban marketplace.

It is the market that limits and instructs both urban space and contemporary dramaturgy. Micaela's reappearance and resistance to the Gran Cabrón early in the third and final *tranca* serves an allegorical purpose. El Chivo rests in bed smoking his pipe when "Micaela appears triumphantly dragging the Gran Cabrón kicking and screaming by his hair."[110] Having seen this display of resistance in which "weakness and suffering" have "humbled the Gran Cabrón,"[111] El Chivo feels that he now has "the necessary strength and valor to defeat the enemies of Justice."[112]

As the third *tranca* unfolds and the police enter to evict the inhabitants of the apartment, it becomes clear just who those enemies of Justice are: the state's security apparatus advancing the interests of capital. The conflation here of the Gran Cabrón and capital might make readers attuned to the pop-culture vocabulary of the text (Estopa and Alaska y los Pegamoides, for example) recall Alex de la Iglesia's parallel use of el Gran Cabrón in his 1995 film The *Day of the Beast*. Within Iglesia's film, Satan comically symbolized the corruption and cronyism that accompanied capital's speculative activity in Madrid during the Torres Kio scandal in the late 1980s.[113]

As in the film, the play uses the Gran Cabrón as a device to invert the dominant social order. Here, the deviance associated with the Witches' Sabbath and Lavapiés is inverted and shown as heroic, while the state does the work of the devil (i.e., speculative capital). During the confrontation with the police, El Chivo makes this connection between the Gran Cabrón, the police with their eviction order, and the work of capital more explicit. He decries the fact that "property is a robbery, the true evil. The land lacks an owner, and no man possesses more right to enjoy it than another."[114]

Fundamental to this "robo," El Chivo points out, is that "in spite of the principle of equality, force perpetuates difference as an ally of states, of armies, of the police, of false religions."[115] With the body of Santa Micaela de Lavapiés lying in state in the midst of this confrontation, the false religion should be understood to be the worship of the Gran Cabrón and the alignment of the state with the interests of the marketplace. As Lefebvre points out, "nationhood implies *violence* ... a political power controlling and exploiting the resources of the market ... in order to maintain and further its rule."[116] Contrasting the violence of the state, Santa Micaela represents the sacraments of charity, of dignity, and of resistance, to which urban space and artistic production should be devoted.

As if to illustrate this idea, the troupe of inhabitants holds a devotional to Santa Micaela. After barricading the door, the inhabitants of the apartment pray that Jesus Christ might offer Micaela's soul eternal life. The ritual is followed by an act of civil disobedience, in which the characters chain themselves to Micaela's coffin. The plumber, who has facilitated their plan, knows that "surely they will appear in the newspaper and the television."[117] Their devotional to Santa Micaela has been transformed into the potential for multimedia spectacle, one intended to bring attention to the violence necessary to maintain the inequalities of private property. Despite the characters' act of resistance, the police enter violently with tear gas and force the inhabitants to leave. Because they are chained to the coffin, their exit turns into "a funeral procession headed by the female police officer."[118] One can imagine that outside the building the journalists are waiting to capture this spectacle of state power, although this scene does not appear in the play. In addition to possibly capturing the media's attention, the group's actions distracted the police for long enough to allow the young Somali and Ecuadorian girls to escape. Their spectacular protest has kept the spirit of Santa Micaela alive by protecting her wards.

The final scene closes the circular structure of the play and returns the action to the Plaza Lavapiés. With the stage populated by partially nude twenty-somethings making love on the bench, an observer watching them and pleasuring himself, and Pablo, El Colgado, the Injured one, and El Chivo smoking hashish, it reprises the scene of bacchanalia from the opening. The scene ends with Pablo, who has revealed himself to be HIV positive, sharing a needle with the other addicts. In contrast to the opening scene, this time his overdose kills him. As the curtain drops, the song "Dark Shadow" by Luz Casal and Carlos Nuñez is heard, and the audience is left with the image of both El Chivo and Pablo sprawled in the plaza, their bodies being poked with a nightstick by the police.

López Llera's play about this tragic night in Lavapiés alludes to the many hidden stories to be found in the city of Madrid. The dual use of the *auto sacramental* and *Bohemian Lights* to frame the work position it firmly in the theatrical traditions of Madrid, and Spain more generally. This intertextual quality helps the play function as an allegory for the victims of an emerging global city as the urbanization of capital forces more and more Spaniards into precarity. For Lefebvre, "there is doubtless no such thing as a myth or symbol unassociated with a mythical or symbolic space which is also determined by practice."[119] If the Urban Plan of 1997 attempted to tie the myth of Madrid to Lavapiés, César López Llera's work also looks to this iconic neighborhood for its symbolic resonance. In the *esperpento* of Lavapiés – the spectacle of Madrid's most iconic neighborhood – he reveals the *burla trágica* of Madrid and of Spain.

AFTERMATH

Restaging Spanish Politics in the Theater and the Streets

On 14 January 2014, fiery sociology professor and political activist Pablo Iglesias took to the stage of the theater cooperative the Teatro del Barrio in Madrid's Lavapiés neighborhood to announce the creation of a new political party.[1] Evoking the rhetorical flourish of Barack Obama ("Yes, we can!") and the populist sentiment of labor-rights activist Dolores Huerta ("Sí, se puede"), they called themselves Podemos ("We can") and declared their intention to "transform citizen indignation into political change."[2] Podemos sought to mobilize the energy generated by the encampments and assemblies of the 15-M movement into actual electoral and political action. In the five years that followed this auspicious press conference, Podemos and affiliated coalitions like Ahora Madrid and Barcelona En Comú would achieve electoral success at the municipal, national, and supranational levels. They won seats in the European Parliament in 2014 and then triumphed in the mayoral races in 2015 in Madrid and Barcelona with candidates Manuela Carmena and Ada Colau (respectively). More recently, in 2019, Podemos garnered enough seats in the parliament to enable them to leverage a role in a governing coalition with the party of the establishment left, the Spanish Socialist Workers' Party (PSOE). These were tectonic shifts in Spain's political landscape, one that had been dominated by the two-party rule of the conservative Popular Party and the center-left PSOE since the country's transition to democracy in 1978.[3] From that auspicious day in Lavapiés through the municipal elections in 2015, there existed a hopefulness that the spirit of indignation created by the 15-M movement had brought about actual political change after many years of economic and political crisis.

The site of the press conference – the Teatro del Barrio – was no accident. The theater cooperative operates in a space formerly occupied by the independent theater la Sala Triángulo, in the heart of Lavapiés. In part, the space was a natural location for the event, given that the offices of Podemos were and are located in the commercial space directly in front of the theater along the steep, narrow calle Zurita. Yet the theater's physical proximity to the offices of Podemos also reflected an ideological proximity: the Teatro del Barrio is yet another iteration in a struggle over politics, culture, and the city that has been taking place since at least the 1970s in the neighborhood. As I have demonstrated at several points throughout this book, it is a struggle in which the democratization of cultural production and urban space have been paramount. I focus on Podemos here because it aligns with the overall objective of this book. Podemos should not be understood merely as a political movement, but rather as the culmination of a broader *cultural* movement, and, perhaps better put, of an *urban* cultural movement that has sought to consolidate cultural space in the city as a means for enacting social change. Both today and historically, Lavapiés has figured centrally in this process at the local, municipal, and often national scales.

This story begins in Madrid's recent history, not with Podemos or 15-M, but with perhaps one of the most classic episodes of political activism associated with Lavapiés, namely the Citizens' Movement in Madrid. Sociologist Manuel Castells's influential treatment of this movement focused on neighborhood mobilizations across Spain and demonstrated how the combination of grassroots organizing and the deployment of strategic cultural projects allowed citizens to reclaim both physical and political space during the last throes of the Franco regime. With no democratic institutions within which to work, these movements of urban social protest began to address a variety of concerns associated with the conditions of urban life. Castells's work paid particular attention to the use of these strategies by the (now) iconic neighborhood association from Lavapiés called La Corrala. Castells called particular attention to the association's tactics for reclaiming the streets through the reinvigoration of the city's *verbena* tradition: street fairs that used popular music, dress, and food to celebrate neighborhood patron saints like San Cayetano, San Lorenzo, La Virgen de la Paloma, and San Isidro. The revival of these cultural events, according to Castells – with a nod to Henri Lefebvre – "[awakened] residents' individual consciousness as to their right to the city."[4]

If the Citizens' Movement of the 1970s established Lavapiés in the popular imaginary as a space where cultural projects were intimately tied to grassroots mobilization, then it was in the mid-1980s through the early 2000s that this tradition began to consolidate into its current form. No longer was the unit of protest and political organization a network of neighborhood associations, rather it became manifest in the neighborhood's squatted social centers. From the worker-occupation of la Minuesa in the mid-1980s and the four iterations of the Laboratorio in the late-1990s to the officially sanctioned social center in the Tabacalera, Lavapiés would become one of the epicenters of the *okupa* movement in Madrid – both in practice and symbolically. The spirit of horizontality and self-management, or *autogestion*, led to the occupation of empty buildings, vacant lots, and other spaces left derelict by speculative capital. The *okupas* of this period made manifest Susan Larson's observation that "the manipulation of space is a form of social power for all classes."[5] As a result, the Laboratorio 03 became the stage not only for protesting local issues like the gentrification of the neighborhood, but also issues of national and international importance, such as the Prestige Oil tanker spill in 2002 and the invasion of Iraq in 2003. As was discussed, a central aspect of these various projects was the promotion of free culture, in the form of art exhibitions and theatrical performances, including Animalario's performance of Juan Mayorga and Juan Cavestany's *Alejandro y Ana*. It is not a coincidence then that many of those involved in that production played a key role in the founding of the Teatro del Barrio. It was also in the Laboratorio where some of Madrid's first Hack-labs were established, where the convergence of a "right to the city" ethos of the *okupa* movement would converge with free-culture movements like copyleft and the Creative Commons and help incubate the notion of *lo procomún*, or the commons, that would become a central tenet of the 15-M movement.

Following their eviction and dislocation, the *okupas* of the Laboratorio – Pablo Iglesias among them – would continue to use appropriations of urban space as a means to cultivate cooperative models of understanding the city and producing culture. These activists would, according to Alberto Corsín Jiménez, "[find] crevices in the contemporary metropolis that [allowed] for building-up collaboration."[6] These collaborations would sprout up in a variety of places: from the brief repurposing of a vacant lot on the calle Olivar called

El Solar as a space for the Laboratorio in exile, to other "occupations" that would become sanctioned by the city, such as the feminist social center Eskalera Karakola, the Self-Managed Social Center La Tabacalera, and, up the hill in La Latina, El Campo de la Cebada. These projects, as well as more typical squatted social centers like Casablanca, sought to repurpose the city as "open-source architectural interventions," as Corsín Jiménez has called them, that allowed for citizen contributions and management.[7] It is from this network of self-managed spaces that the DIY know-how of the 15-M movement emerged. Notably, it is to the CSOA Casablanca where many of the artifacts of the Acampada Sol would end up in the form of the BiblioSol and the ArchivoSol – the library and archives respectively – of the encampment in Sol. Henri Lefebvre has suggested that "every society – and hence every mode of production ... produces a space, its own space."[8] In Lavapiés, this intertwining of space, cultural production, and politics sought to find new ways of producing space – a mode of production that looked beyond the city as merely a site for capitalist accumulation.

THEATER IN CRISIS

Since 2008, the production of theater has been an important vehicle for the production of this new kind of space – a situation made all the more complicated by the challenges of the economic crisis. Perhaps most significant has been the surge in politically-oriented theater.[9] This development has been all the more notable given that it has occurred in the wake of a dramatic (some would say punitive) Valued Added Tax put in place by the conservative Popular Party in September 2012. In the months after the VAT went from 8 per cent to 21 per cent, the Spanish theater industry lost nearly 1.8 million spectators and six hundred theater jobs, according to *El País*.[10] As Scott Boehm details, the response of the Spanish theater industry was, well, dramatic. In order to call attention to the situation, theaters tried a number of tactics that included everything from selling carrots to retro pornographic magazines instead of tickets.[11] Yet, importantly, this theater of the crisis responded not only with a shift in subject matter, but also through new and creative uses of space. Cristina Oñoro Otero highlights several of these theatrical projects predicated on new uses of urban spaces, including the Teatro del Barrio, Microteatro por Dinero, la Kubik Fabrik o la MiniTea3, La

Casa de la Portera, and Àtic 22.[12] While most of these experiments have taken place in "traditional" areas of the city for alternative theater – namely Lavapiés and La Latina – Oñoro Otero points to the fact that many of them have sprung up in neighborhoods and districts that are seemingly on the periphery of the city's cultural center, albeit often modeled on projects in Lavapiés. Building on the work of Susan Bennet, Oñoro Otero suggests that these new theater spaces and formats have altered the experience of audiences as they navigate the city in new ways in pursuit of cultural offerings.[13] This "restaging of urban space," as I have referred to it in other contexts, has created a trend in socially engaged theater that comes as much from its subject matter as it does from its use of non-traditional spaces. The work of the theater group AlmaViva Teatro has been innovative in this regard, with its attempts to bring canonical theater to the public in a variety of unique spaces across the city. From 2011 to 2013, these performances included the free annual performances of *Don Juan Tenorio* in the self-managed space called el Campo de Cebada, as well as a performance of Lope de Vega's *Fuente Ovejuna* in a historic *corrala* on the outskirts of Madrid.[14]

Some of the more compelling responses to the situation include the conversion of a brothel in the Triball neighborhood near Gran Vía into Microtheater spaces, in which actors perform short ten-to-twelve-minute works in various rooms, each with only six to eight spectators. It is a theatrical business model reminiscent of the *género chico* in the late-nineteenth century, done under similar conditions of economic duress.[15] Other important developments include the collaboration of various theaters in Lavapiés to form a theater consortium that formalizes Lavapiés as the center for independent theater in Madrid. Created in 2014, this organization, Lavapiés Barrio de los Teatros (Lavapiés Neighborhood of the Theaters), offers the public nearly one thousand seats at nearly four hundred performances a month.[16] Via their website, the consortium offers memberships by which participants can receive discounts and stay more easily informed about theatrical events in the neighborhood.[17] The project, as described in the organization's dossier, seeks to "bring the theater to the neighborhood, to the street, to public space. Democratize the theater of reality."[18] As a way of achieving these objectives, there is an emphasis on horizontality and a rejection of hierarchy – an intentionality closely tied to the spirit of self-management that has been so essential to the *okupa* movement and to 15-M.

Figuring centrally in these pursuits of that new mode of production – one dedicated to cooperation and participation instead of profits – has been the Teatro del Barrio. Established in 2013 by the actor Alberto San Juan and others from the theater group Animalario, the project has "a will that is openly political: to participate in the citizens' movement that is already underway to construct another form of coexisting."[19] In this sense, the Teatro del Barrio, is not merely a theater space, but a meeting space that "intends to be a permanent assembly, whereby observing together the world stops and we can imagine another, where a good life is possible." Echoing the work of the Citizens' Movement and later the *okupas*, their tools in this effort "are culture and festivities."[20]

In this commitment to culture as a political tool, the Teatro del Barrio has often used dramatic works to respond to current events, often working within the Documentary Theater tradition that relies on actual documentary material as the basis of the dramatic text. For example, in *Ruz-Barcenas*, written by Jordi Casanovas and directed by Alberto San Juan, which debuted in 2014, the work is constructed from the redacted transcripts of the deposition in 2013 of Luis Bárcenas, the ex-treasurer of the Popular Party, regarding documents that revealed secret payments to the leadership of the party. This attempt to address current events beyond the discourse of traditional media conglomerates offered the audience a collective catharsis in their response to the down-is-up machinations of politicians and the media in our post-fact world. This catharsis was particularly true in moments when the Magistrate's facial expressions directed at the audience brought attention to the absurdity of the testimony, like Bárcenas's dissembling about the "mysterious" identity of one "M. Rajoy" amongst the list of payees.[21]

In another work, *El Rey* from 2015, the play appropriates historical content to create a counter-narrative to official history, a process that Nortan Palacio Ortiz has suggested makes the theater performance itself the historical document.[22] Recreating fictional conversations and monologues held by the now-abdicated King Juan Carlos I and narrated from an indeterminate future, the structure of the play flows back and forth across an historical arc that includes the young Juan Carlos in his first appearance before Francisco Franco in 1948, and even includes the king officiating at his own burial in the Pantheon of Kings in El Escorial. There are also encounters between the king (at various ages) and various important figures of the Transition like Adolfo Suárez (sometimes as the lucid ex-president and at other times ill with Alzheimer's), Carrero Blanco, Antonio Tejero, and Juan Luis Cebrián, the director of the PRISA media group. Through these dialogues, the play does not interact with historical documents, but rather poses questions about history as it is structured, about its gaps, blind spots, and permutations. It brings attention to history as constructed text. In remaking its hidden moments, it breaks down the monolithic historical narrative of the Transition and opens up new space to imagine a political narrative of the future beyond what some scholars have called the "Regime of 1978."

The Teatro del Barrio is just one of many cooperative spaces and projects across the city that have emerged in recent years. Nonetheless, as I hope this book has made clear, it should also be understood as yet another iteration in which Lavapiés has been the stage for enacting political change at the local, municipal, and national scales. When describing the neighborhood movement some forty years ago, Manuel Castells argued that "under the impact of the neighborhood movement ... Spanish cities changed, political institutions were turned upside down, social relationships in the neighborhoods dramatically improved, and perhaps most significantly the urban culture, namely society's conception of what a city should be, was fundamentally altered."[23] Castells's words seem just as applicable today. From Barcelona mayor Ada Colau's invigorated investment in Superblocks to Manuela Carmena's efforts at participatory budgeting, Spanish cities have seen many changes and efforts to remake the city.

As the example of the Teatro Valle-Inclán and others throughout this book have demonstrated, the dynamics between theatrical production and material conditions in the city always reflect the broader dialectics of urban power and change. As in the case of Lavapiés and Madrid, the co-opting of available cultural resources has become a consistent feature of urbanized capital across the industrialized world. And, as in the case of Lavapiés, this production of space relies not only on global flows of capital, but on the cultural cachet of the local. The local (the *terroir*, as Zukin would call it) has become a key strategy for intertwining the urban scale with more globalized urban practices. To consume the local cultural offerings and seek out their authenticity has been lent an air of cosmopolitanism that makes it an expression of global identities. In an age when cultural practice and economic development (particularly urban development) are so closely linked, the spectacle of urban space is fraught with conflict.

This book has explored the role of spectacle in the physical development of urban space and in the national imaginary in Madrid. My approach highlights the ways that cultural products (various kinds of theatrical texts in this case) have very concrete material impacts on city space. The misconception that the study of Literature deals with dusty books in a cloistered library is one that is ripe for disruption (a deconstruction of the Real World vs. Academia binary, if you will). Representations of space in literature contribute to our understanding of our physical environment and often generate the very "placeness" to which we devote so much emotional energy. In Lavapiés, the interaction between culture and the built environment reflects a broader interaction between the interests of the nation-state and notions of the "local." That is, the process of urban change occurring at the local level in Lavapiés, and the presence of national cultural institutions and global capital in that process, result in a synecdoche that undermines the very notion of the local as it is subsumed by broader municipal, national, and even global interests. For literary scholars, my efforts to chart the spatial and material contexts of Spain's rich theater tradition continues the important work that scholars like Enrique García Santo-Tomás, Edward Baker, Michael Ugarte, and Susan Larson have dedicated to earlier periods in the city's development. As has been stated at various points throughout this book, the spatial component of theater begs for it to be considered in the broadest spatial context possible.

By considering the dialogic relationship between urban space and theater, scholars will have opportunities to re-examine works from earlier periods that were often approached as merely dramatic (i.e., written) texts. Though using this approach to study earlier periods may present challenges, the important role of theater in urban development in Madrid suggests that we consider not only how texts *represent* urban space, but also *where* and *when* they have been represented as a means of exploring urban discourses in the city. In other words, I hope that the approach that I have laid out in this book will provoke more investigation into the actual theater spaces where performances "took/take place" and allow researchers to quite literally map the consumption of literature on the terrain of the city. Just as literary critics have much to share by elucidating the role that cultural production has on creating the signifiers that underpin urban space, it is also important to see how the production and consumption of those cultural products reveal conflicts over urban space itself.

 This book is also a call to cultural critics to be supportive, but wary, of urban art initiatives. A healthy art scene is indeed a worthy thing to support. Too often, though, that pleasant gallery hop, public art initiative, or proposed performing-arts center is intimately tied to the "abstract space" found in the plans for condominium complexes just around the corner. In these times of global pandemic, the need, hope, and desire for art that connects us has become all the more pressing. Theater companies across the globe have begun to explore the interpretive possibilities for performances via Zoom or other online platforms, but one takeaway from the pandemic is that congregating as spectators and physically sharing space creates community and connection in ways that are simply impossible with remote delivery. My hope is that the story of Lavapiés shows the important role that spaces of culture play in shaping cities and building connections within them. Finally, the shifts that have taken place in the ten years after the encampments in Sol – both re-energized leftist populism (i.e., 15-M, Occupy, etc.) and darker populisms of the far right in Spain (Vox) and the United States (Trumpism) – have brought to the fore with all the more urgency the importance of Humanistic study. Indeed, the profound rejection of art and culture as a means of sharing human experience and generating cultural empathy should give us pause. If we are to build more just and humane cities, the stories and dramas of the human beings within them need to be shared and told.

 By contextualizing cultural production in this way and emphasizing its material qualities, this approach might also provide another means for exploring the thorny theoretical issue of scale. In particular, understanding how cultural products articulate global and local identities might benefit researchers in Geography. Likewise, seeing the material aspects of cultural production as they are literally written across the landscape of the city remains imperative for Humanities scholars. Because the notion of the urban spectacle is a process that converts the material quite explicitly into metaphor, it allows scholars to embrace the mutable, variable, and powerful ways that language functions as a kind of connective tissue between people and places. Here in the intersection of Literary Studies and Cultural Geography we might examine the narratives that are so central to the production of space and that organize our society physically, politically, sociologically, ideologically, and culturally. For it is in the conceived, perceived, and lived spaces of the city that the spectacle of urban space articulates municipal, national, and global identities.

Notes

INTRODUCTION

1 These ideas are most carefully articulated in what is perhaps his most influential book, *The Production of Space*. See in particular Chapter 1, "Plan of the Present Work," and Chapter 2, "Social Space."
2 Jacobs, *Death and Life*, 428.
3 In Latin America, the term has often been used to indicate racial purity. For more on caste and race in Latin America, see Vinson, *Mestizaje and the Frontiers of Race and Caste in Colonial Mexico*, 134.
4 See the introduction to the volume *Cartographies of Madrid: Contesting Urban Space at the Crossroads of the Global South and Global North*, ed. Silvia Bermúdez and Anthony L. Geist, ix–xxviii.
5 See in particular *Hispanic Review* 80, no. 4 from 2012 for essays by Moreno Caballud, Labrador Méndez, and Fernández-Savater for useful interpretations of 15-M and what Fernández-Savater calls "the new social power."
6 Note that all translations are by the author unless otherwise indicated. See https://musicaypitanzas.com/2014/08/13/tapapies-2014/ for an archived poster of the 2014 event. More current information can be found at https://tapapies.com/.
7 Many of the people that dress in these folkloric costumes are members of groups like the Agrupación de Madrileños y Amigos los Castizos, which are dedicated to preserving *castizo* culture in Madrid. See https://loscastizos.es/ for more information and details about the various groups.
8 González Esteban, *Madrid: sinopsis de su evolución urbana*, 16.
9 Bravo Morata, *Los nombres de las calles de Madrid*, 307.

10 Nash, *Madrid: A Cultural History*, 116. Nash suggests that the name derives from the Hebrew *aba-puest*, supposedly meaning "place of Jews." I have found no other sources that suggest this etymology, nor does it respond to any modern Hebrew translation.
11 Bravo Morata, *Los nombres de las calles de Madrid*, 307.
12 See Fita, "La judería de Madrid en 1391," 439–66.
13 Viñuales Ferreiro, "Los judíos de Madrid en el siglo XV," 296. Andréu Mediero and Paños Cubillo suggest that the *judería* was actually located between the Palacio Real, the Almudena Cathedral, and the Campo del Rey, in what was formerly the Puerta Valnadú, just to the east of the site of the original Alcázar.
14 Ringrose, "Madrid, Capital Imperial," 234. Ringrose suggests that, between 1550 and 1600, Madrid saw its population explode from about 20,000 inhabitants to nearly 100,000, and that by 1630 the population had reached almost 130,000.
15 The *cercas* include that of Philip II in 1571 and of Philip IV in 1625. The *cercas* had no military purpose, but allowed city officials to combat the increasing problems of sanitation due to overcrowding and provided more tax revenue through the regulation of people and goods into and out of the city.
16 Répide, *Las calles de Madrid*, 344. Like other popular chroniclers of the neighborhood's history, Répide suggests that the variation of the name Avapiés, which appears with great frequency from the eighteenth century on, derives from a mere "phonetic error, influencing the spelling, which altered the traditional name." Ibid., 342.
17 Répide, *Las calles de Madrid*, 343. The term *converso* refers most often to Jews that converted to Christianity from approximately the thirteenth century onwards, though Muslims were also converts. Because these *cristianos nuevos*, or New Christians, lacked the required Certificate of Clean Lineage (Estatutos de Limpieza de Sangre), they were barred from certain titles, professions, guilds, and religious orders. See Roth, *Conversos, Inquisition, and the Expulsion of the Jews from Spain*. In particular, see Chapters 1 and 2.
18 Répide, *Las calles de Madrid*, 343.
19 Pérez-Agote, Tejerina, and Barañano, *Barrios Multiculturales*, 140. More specifically, these waves of rural immigration occurred from 1561 to 1654, 1720 to 1800, 1836 and 1877, and into the late-twentieth century. Ringrose, "Madrid, Capital Imperial," 298.
20 Ringrose, "Madrid, Capital Imperial," 253.
21 Mesonero Romanos, *El Antiguo Madrid*, 189.

22 Cited in Pérez-Agote, et al., *Barrios Multiculturales*, 137. The Centro district of Madrid is made up of six different administrative wards: Cortes, Palacios, Sol, Justicia, Universidad, and Embajadores. Lavapiés forms the northernmost tip of Embajadores and is immediately adjacent to the tourist-laden ward of Sol. The Carabanchel district southwest of Centro contains the highest number of immigrants in the city.
23 Gea, *Centro*, 59.
24 Zárate Martín, "Imágenes mentales," 405. In Lavapiés in 2002, 5,216 residents of the 42,273 were from other countries. This figure of 12.3 per cent compares to the 5 per cent ratio in the entire capital city.
25 Díaz Orueta, "Los grandes proyectos," 181–2.
26 Gómez, "El barrio de Lavapiés," 3. In recent years this loose association of groups has lost its collaborative spirit.
27 Gómez, "El barrio de Lavapiés," 4.
28 Time Out PR. "Embajadores and Euljiro are on the list of Time Out's coolest neighbourhoods right now – Hackney and Williamsburg are not," 20 September 2018. https://www.timeout.com/about/latest-news/embajadores-and-euljiro-are-on-the-list-of-time-outs-coolest-neighbourhoods-right-now-hackney-and-williamsburg-are-not-092018.
29 For a useful overview of this subject and its impact on Barcelona, see Rebecca Mead's 2019 article in *The New Yorker* magazine "The AirBnB invasion of Barcelona." *The New Yorker*, April 2019. www.newyorker.com/magazine/2019/04/29/the-airbnb-invasion-of-barcelona.
30 Gil and Sequera, "Expansión de la ciudad," 26–7. See also Sequera's recent book, *Gentrificación: Capitalismo cool, turismo y control del espacio urbano*, for more on this process in Madrid and other European cities. More information on resistance to AirBnB in the neighborhood can be found at https://lavapiesdondevas.wordpress.com/
31 Zukin, *Naked City*, 4.
32 Harvey, *Rebel Cities*, 42–5. I cite these pages in *Rebel Cities* for their concise overview of this concept, but these arguments were originally developed more fully in Harvey, *The Limits to Capital*, and Harvey, *The Urbanisation of Capital*. Notably, in this urbanization process, surplus capital seeks refuge from declining profits through investment in this "second circuit" of capital (i.e., real estate).
33 See Compitello, "A Good Plan Gone Bad," for a more detailed discussion of the rehabilitation of the Atocha train station and the Reina Sofia and its impact on Lavapiés.
34 Área de Rehabilitación Preferente. In most cases, while I will the translate names of institutions and the like, I will use the Spanish initials.

35 Empresa Municipal, *Áreas de Rehabilitación Preferente*, 19–20.
36 Readers will note that, given the socio-economic status of residents, the need for parking garages was less pressing than the need for better schools and health facilities. This investment points to the desire to attract new types of residents and/or visitors from other parts of Madrid.
37 Following the financial crash of 2008, Caja Madrid merged with six other savings banks to form the conglomerate Bankia.
38 García de Sola, "Introducción," 7.
39 See Chapters 4 and 6 in Sassen, *The Global City*, on the command-and-control functions served by global cities in the post-Fordist economy.
40 Scholars in Geography and other critical social sciences have debated the potential fixity or fluidity of the boundaries between various geographical scales and the difficulties that "scales" (i.e., the local, the national, the global) present as analytic categories. In general terms, most critics emphasize the discursive power of scale because of its capacity to reify dominant modes of spatial production (namely, neo-liberal notions of globalization). Two concepts at work here are Marston, Jones, and Woodward's idea of "flat ontology" (see "Human Geography without Scale"). Leitner et al. echo this contention that geographic scales do not exist discursively as separate ontological categories, but in place of "flattening" scales, they emphasize the "articulations" amongst them; they "unfold into one another because each scale only exists in relation to other scales." It is this idea of articulation that is most relevant here. See "Spatialities of Contentious Politics," 159.
41 Merrifield, *Metromarxism*, 5.
42 Also known as the *procomún*, the idea of the "commons" is typically attributed to ecologist Garrett Hardin's famous 1968 essay, "The Tragedy of the Commons," that argued for sustainable management of common resources that serve the whole community. The work of Nobel Prize-winning economist Elinor Ostrom brought even more attention to the idea by demonstrating the proliferation of communities that collectively manage resources. The cooperation implicit in the *procomún* ethos disrupts widely held dogmas regarding the efficiencies of the market and the palliative effects of privatization.
43 Notably, these tactics would also greatly influence the Occupy Wall Street movement in the United States that emerged in the fall of 2011, shortly after the events in the Puerta del Sol. See Castañeda "The *Indignados* of Spain."
44 The *mareas* were different protest movements organized against different forms of austerity cuts. For example, there was a *marea verde* (green

wave) against cuts in public education and the *marea blanca* (white wave) against cuts in public health, etc. See the website https://15-Mpedia.org/wiki/Lista_de_mareas for a full list of the thirteen different *mareas*.

45 Harvey, "From Managerialism," 6–8. See also 13–14. He suggests that this shift toward "spectacle and play" and "an attractive urban imagery" has been central to changes in emphasis in cities, from managing the conditions of urban living to a more entrepreneurial approach for competing within a system of interurban competition.

46 See in particular, Smith, "New Globalism, New Urbanism," and Lees et. al, "Introduction," amongst many other critics of neo-liberal urban development. See also, Lee, Slater, and Wyly's *Gentrification* for a recent overview and relevant bibliography on Gentrification.

47 Lefebvre, *The Production of Space*, 31.

48 Mumford, *The City in History*, 115–16; and Sennett, "The Public Realm," 265.

49 Delgado, *El animal público*, 182.

50 Delgado, *La ciudad mentirosa: fraude y miseria del "modelo Barcelona,"* 11–17. Readers might consider Delgado's playful and compelling use of the word "model" to refer to Barcelona as both a type of urbanism as well as its use of urban space as merely a life-size diorama (i.e., model) to be commodified.

51 Both Harvey, *Paris*, 230, and de Certeau have argued cogently on the importance of understanding place as a palimpsest. See for example de Certeau, *The Practice of Everyday Life*, 201–2.

52 Lefebvre, *Production of Space*, 86, emphasis in the original.

53 See Zukin, *Loft Living*; Zukin, *The Cultures of Cities*; Zukin, *Naked City*; Kearns and Philo, *Selling Places*; Peck, "Struggling with the Creative Class"; Peck, "The Cult of Urban Creativity"; Lees et al., *Gentrification*; Harvey, "The Art of Rent."

54 Lefebvre, *Production of Space*, 38.

55 Ibid., 42.

CHAPTER ONE

1 Saint Isidore the Laborer was canonized in the seventeenth century.

2 Moral Ruiz, "La mitificación de Madrid," 70.

3 It is important to note that this is a loaded term, fraught with imperialist connotations. Its deployment by Francoist historiographers to construct their National Catholic historical narrative makes it all the more problematic.

Notes to pages 27–31

4 Allen, *Reconstruction of a Spanish Golden Age Playhouse*, 19.
5 McKendrick, *Theatre in Spain*, 6.
6 McKendrick suggests that records of the earliest processions date back to 1418. *Theatre in Spain*, 8.
7 Flynn, "The Spectacle of Suffering in Spanish Streets," 163 (emphasis mine).
8 Greer, "The Development of National Theatre," 240.
9 Ibid.
10 Bairoch, *Cities and Economic Development: From the Dawn of History to the Present*, 176. See also Mumford, *The City in History*, 355.
11 See Ringrose, "A Setting for Royal Authority," 234, and Reyes Leoz, "Evolución de la población, 1561–1587," 140–4.
12 Caridad, "El arte escénico en la edad media," 62.
13 Ibid., 64.
14 The street also plays an important role in a variety of non-religious forms of public performances during the fifteenth and sixteenth centuries, such as troubadours and jongleurs who performed in both private palaces and public streets. McKendrick *Theatre in Spain*, 6.
15 Casey, *Early Modern Spain: A Social History*, 113.
16 The Alcázar of Madrid was the site of the original Muslim fort of the ninth century from which the city of Madrid grew. The Alcázar experienced a number of modifications to accommodate the needs of different Spanish royal families after Madrid was named the site of the royal court. It burned down on Christmas Eve of 1734, and construction on the new Royal Palace under the supervision of architect Francesco Sabatini was completed in 1764. Today, it is used only for ceremonial purposes and touristic visits.
17 Pinto Crespo and Madrazo, *Madrid: atlas histórico de la ciudad*, 329.
18 McKendrick, *Theatre in Spain*, 45.
19 Lefebvre, *The Production of Space*, 38. Lefebvre defines this "abstract space" as the space of "scientists, planners, urbanists, technocratic sub-dividers and social engineers." Also called "spaces of representation" and "conceived space," it is space as organized, imagined, sub-divided, and built for the dominant power structures.
20 Coso Marín and Sanz Ballesteros, "El corral de comedias de Alcalá de Henares," 24.
21 Arellano, *Historia del teatro español del siglo XVII*, 69.
22 Greer, "The Development of National Theatre," 243.
23 Allen, *Reconstruction of a Spanish Golden Age Playhouse*, 4–5. The location of the important Corral del Príncipe, the site of the National

Theater during the Second Republic, is today the site of the Teatro Español and operated by the municipal government.

24 Allen, *Reconstruction of a Spanish Golden Age Playhouse*, 56.
25 The word *comedia* refers to a "secular play in three acts, with certain patterns of versification, around 3,000 lines long." The terms *comedia* and dramatic text were often used interchangeably, regardless of the content of the work. Campbell, *Monarchy, Political Culture, and Drama*, 33.
26 McKendrick, *Theatre in Spain*, 72.
27 Ibid.
28 For more on the interrelated crises of the seventeenth century, see Maravall, *La cultura del barroco*, 104–25; Kamen, *Spain: 1469-1714*, 208–32; and Elliot, *Imperial Spain, 1469–1716*, 285–308.
29 McKendrick, *Theatre in Spain*, 74.
30 Allen, *Reconstruction of a Spanish Golden Age Playhouse*, 6.
31 Anderson, *Imagined Communities*, 46.
32 I emphasize that my use of Anderson is somewhat liberal here. There may not be a Habermassian public sphere of readers emerging, but I believe it is feasible to suggest that Spanish drama of the period contributes to the construction of a shared understanding of various cultural institutions, such as the Crown.
33 Casey, *Early Modern Spain: A Social History*, 164.
34 Maravall, *Teatro y literatura*, 105–35, and Díez Borque, *Sociología de la comedia española del siglo XVII*, 163–80, are good examples. McKendrick, *Playing the King*, Carreño-Rodríguez, *Alegorías del poder*, and Garcia Santo-Tomas, *Espacio urbano* offer compelling alternatives to this reading.
35 D'Antuono, "La comedia española en la Italia del siglo XVII," 179.
36 Ruiz Ramón, *Historia del Teatro Español*, 137–41.
37 Campbell, *Monarchy, Political Culture, and Drama*, 1. Campbell describes tragedy as characterized by the "rise and fall of a powerful figure, whether god, prince, or noble, while a comedy placed an ordinary man in an unpleasant or absurd situation."
38 Ibid., 7.
39 Surtz, *The Birth of a Theatre*, 192.
40 Lines 1881 and 1889 respectively.
41 McKendrick, *Playing the King*, 213.
42 Carreño, *Alegorías del poder*, 56.
43 Hansen and Stepputat, "Introduction," 2.
44 Ibid.

45 See Lorenz, *The Tears of Sovereignty*, 6–14, 146, for a discussion of the ways in which the term sovereignty came into regular usage, not only in the political arena, but also within many works of early-modern drama, including *Fuente Ovejuna*.
46 Castells, *The City and the Grassroots*, 4–15. The *comunero* revolt studied by Castells was an uprising by Castilian cities against the centralized power (and policies of taxation) of the Spanish monarch, Charles V. In addition to fiscal reforms, they sought to establish municipal elections, the winners of which would answer to popular committees at the ward level.
47 Ibid., 4.
48 Ibid., 14.
49 Ibid.
50 García Santo-Tomas argues that it is precisely this tenuous power structure that characterizes Madrid in this period. Far from being a monolithic space for monarchic power, it was a city in flux, straddling a feudal past and an emerging urban modernity.
51 Aguilera Sastre, *El debate sobre el Teatro Nacional*, 22.
52 Maravall, *La cultura del barroco*, 104–25.
53 García Santo-Tomás, *Espacio urbano y creación literaria*, 20.
54 See, for example, George Simmel's classic essay from 1903, "The Metropolis and the Mental Life."
55 After Philip II named Madrid as the site of the royal court, the city's population surged, in part from the arrival of functionaries associated with the court. The lack of housing led to the *regalía de aposento* (royal housing decree) that required any domicile of two stories to house government officials. See González Esteban, *Madrid: sinopsis de su evolución urbana*, 30, and Lozano Bartolozzi, *Historia del urbanismo en España II*, 378.
56 The Plaza Mayor that both locals and tourists know today has undergone various changes since its first inception, due to fires in 1631, 1672, and 1790.
57 Escobar, *The Plaza Mayor*, 142. Escobar connects the symbolism of the panadería to the work of political theorist Giovanni Botero, who in 1589 suggested that "nothing keeps the people as happy as a good bread mart," ibid., 116.
58 Ibid., 188. On Corpus Christi, see María José del Río Barredo, "Cultura popular y fiesta," 324–39, and Javier Portús Pérez, *La Antigua procesión del Corpus Christi en Madrid*.
59 Ibid., 142.
60 García Santo-Tomás, *Espacio urbano*, 28.
61 Escobar, *The Plaza Mayor*, 8.
62 Ibid., 220.

Notes to pages 43–7

63 Ringrose, "Madrid, Capital Imperial," 193.
64 Escobar, *The Plaza Mayor*, 205–9.
65 Ringrose, "A Setting for Royal Authority," 237–8.
66 García Santo Tomas, *Espacio urbano*, 31.
67 Ringrose, "Madrid, Capital Imperial," 299.
68 Ibid., 300.
69 Pinto Crespo and Madrazo, *Madrid: atlas histórico de la ciudad*, 330.
70 Lobato, "Nobles como actores," 96–7.
71 Williams, "'Un estilo nuevo de grandeza,'" 200.
72 González Esteban, *Madrid: sinopsis de su evolución urbana*, 35.
73 Aguilera Sastre, *El debate sobre el Teatro Nacional*, 208.
74 Ibid.
75 Ruiz Ramón, *Historia del Teatro Español*, 127.
76 On the website of the Compañía Nacional del Teatro Clásico, the organization describes itself as "the leading institution dedicated to the recuperation, preservation, production, and diffusion of the theatrical patrimony from before the twentieth century, with particular attention on the *Siglo de oro* and the prosody of classical poetry." Compañía Nacional del Teatro Clásico, "¿Qué es la CNTC?" Ministerio de Cultura y Deporte. http://teatroclasico.mcu.es/la-comp/que-es-la-cntc/.
77 My intent is not to disregard the problematic assumptions upon which canonicity is based. I speak here in general terms regarding popular understandings and not essentialist ones. I refer to these particular authors because of their continued prevalence in anthologies and traditional reading lists for graduate programs, undergraduate-survey courses, etc.
78 See Kasten *The Cultural Politics of Twentieth-Century Theatre*, xi–xiv, for a detailed treatment of this event.
79 Ibid., 45–52.
80 Ibid., 50.
81 Luna-García, "Cities of Spain," 377.
82 Santiáñez, *Topographies of Fascism: Habitus, Space, and Writing in Twentieth-Century Spain*, 17.
83 Pope, "Historia y novela en la posguerra española," 17. It should be noted that linguistically what is often considered "Spanish" is actually the language of Castile (i.e., Castilian or Castellano). In this sense, Castilian is one of several competing languages within the territorial boundaries of Spain, on a par with Catalan, Galician, and Basque. For historical and political reasons, the domination of Castilian culture and language over Spanish territory has often led to the conflation of "Spanish" and Castilian, both within Spain and outside of it.

84 Herzberger, *Narrating the Past: Fiction and Historiography in Postwar Spain*, 24.
85 For more on Fascist urban planning, see Sambricio, *El Plan Bigador, 1941–1946*.
86 Santiáñez, *Topographies of Fascism*, 237.
87 Ibid., 239.
88 Santiáñez cites the voice-over from the newsreel *El Gran Desfile* from the Departamento Nacional de Cinematografía that declared that the parade was "the war's last military event."
89 Ibid., 227–8.
90 Ibid., 228.
91 See Wheeler, *Golden Age Drama in Contemporary Spain*, 17–74, for more on the production history of *comedias* after 1940 during the Francoist period.
92 Aguilera Sastre, *El debate sobre el Teatro Nacional en España*, 29. Fires in 1802, in 1887, and later in 1980 resulted in extensive rehabilitations to the original structure at various times during its history.
93 Although the other statue in the plaza does not refer to the *Siglo de Oro*, the fact that it is still a dramatist, Federico García Lorca (1898–1936), emphasizes the important role that theater and theater culture play in the way that Madrid's cultural legacy is constructed.
94 Lefebvre, *The Production of Space*, 87.
95 Brenner, "The Limits to Scale," 593.
96 Sambricio, "La Real Casa De Correos," 30.
97 Sambricio, "En la segunda mitad," 17.
98 Ringrose, "A Setting for Royal Authority," 237.
99 Lefebvre, *The Production of Space*, 38.
100 Sambricio, "En la segunda mitad," 17.
101 Ringrose, "A Setting for Royal Authority," 245.
102 Lefebvre, *The Production of Space*, 117.
103 Not soon after, in the late-nineteenth century, the custom emerges across Spain in which people eat twelve grapes to ring in the New Year as marked by the clock tower in the Puerta del Sol. The clock and the plaza not only projected the rhythms of the city and capitalist time across the national terrain, but they also had a cultural instrumentality that nationalized space.
104 Castro-Rial Garrone, "Prólogo," 22.
105 This expansion of the city's infrastructure and resource footprint would mark the beginning of a long process of spatial reorganization around water resources and state intervention that later would become one of the

hallmarks of the Franco regime. See Swyengedouw, "Producing Nature, Scaling Environment."
106 See Parsons, *A Cultural History of Madrid*, 77–86, for particularly good treatment of the spectacle of technology in Madrid at the turn of the twentieth century. Other "firsts" include the first use of gas lights in 1860; the first public bathrooms in 1863; the first electric streetlights in 1881; the first horse-drawn trolley in 1871; and, somewhat later, the first metro train in 1919.
107 Sambricio, "La Casa de Correos," 44–5.
108 Gómez de la Serna, *La historia de la Puerta del Sol*, 7 and 10. See also Larson's treatment of the Carmen de Burgos story "Los negociantes de la Puerta del Sol" for passages by de Burgos that reflect the same sentiment, 92–100.
109 Cited in Castro Rial-Garrone, "Prólogo," 22. One thinks of the similar process carried out by Baron George-Eugène Haussmann during the rule of Napoleon III (1852–1870).
110 Hansen and Stepputat, "Introduction," 2.
111 See Feinberg, "Urban Space, Spectacle, and Articulations."
112 Larson, *Constructing Modernity*, 36. She provides analysis of both Federico Chueca's famous *zarzuela* entitled *Gran Vía* and the construction of the actual avenue in Chapter 2 of *Constructing Modernity*. She argues that Chueca's allegorical treatment of the city signaled "popular anticipation and fear of urban renewal," and reflected how the pursuit of solutions to urban problems in Madrid at this time, both practical ones and highly imaginative utopic ones, "created an ongoing tension that thematically and structurally shaped urban cultural production in significant ways."
113 Fernández Isla, "La Real Casa de Correos: rehabilitación," 55.
114 Bonet Correa, "La Puerta del Sol, corazón y 'cogollo' de Madrid," 19.
115 Ibid.
116 Agnew, "Dramaturgy of Horizons," 100.
117 Howitt, "Scale as Relation," 49.
118 Gómez de la Serna, *La historia de la Puerta del Sol*, 43.
119 Antebi and Sánchez, "Plazas Fuertes," 67.
120 Lefebvre, *The Production of Space*, 386.
121 Saint Isidore the Laborer is known for famously using prayer to produce a spring to irrigate his master's lands during a severe drought, as well as using prayer to raise the waters of the well into which his infant had fallen, thus saving him. Finally, he is most famous for the assistance of two angels to plow a miraculous amount of terrain in a short period of time.

122 See Castells, *Networks of Outrage*; Snyder, *Poetics of Opposition*; Taibo, *El 15-M en sesenta preguntas*; and Moreno-Caballud, *Cultures of Anyone* for additional summaries of the roots of 15-M and analysis.
123 Taibo, *El 15-M en sesenta preguntas*, 15.
124 Castells, *Network of Outrage*, 113.
125 See Martínez and García Martínez, "Ocupar las plazas, liberar edificios," regarding the tactical and ideological relationship between the *okupa* movement and 15-M. For more on the influence of social movements and 15-M, see Taibo, 30–1 and 50–1.
126 The tactics would inspire a similar assembly-led encampment strategy in the movement known as Occupy Wall Street. See Castañeda, "The *Indignados* of Spain: A Precedent to Occupy Wall Street." For discussion of Occupy Wall Street, see *Beyond Zuccotti Park*, particularly, Franck and Huang, "Occupying Public Space, 2011," and Shepard, "Occupy Wall Street, Social Movements, and Contested Public Space."
127 Agnew, "Space and Place," 316–30, offers a thorough treatment of these concepts, along with an extensive bibliography on the subject.
128 Tuan, *Space and Place*, 6.
129 Ibid.
130 For more treatment of the dynamics of space, open-source software, and social movements, see Vilaseca, "The TriBall Case."
131 *Cómo cocinar una revolución pacífica (v2.0)*, 6. takethesquare.net, 5 November 2011. http://takethesquare.net/wpcontent/uploads/2011/11/RollUp_eng_v2_reviewed.pdf.
132 Martinez and García, "Ocupar las plazas, liberar edificios," 2.
133 See for example Castells, *Networks of Outrage and Hope*, and Férnandez, Sevilla, and Urbán, eds., *¡Ocupemos el Mundo: Occupy the World!*
134 Castells, *Rise of the Networked Society*, 145.
135 Before serving as mayor of Barcelona, Ada Colau was launched into the national spotlight as the spokesperson for the Barcelona branch of this platform, a role that arguably led to her electoral success. For more on the various "platforms" and organizations that aligned in the wake of 15-M, see Castells, Caraça, and Cardoso, *Aftermath: The Cultures of the Economic Crisis*, and the extremely useful online archive Constellation of the Commons, developed by Palomar Álvarez-Blanco and others at https://constelaciondeloscomunes.org/en/home/.
136 Baker, "Historical Perspectives from Madrid," 178.
137 Larson, *Constructing and Resisting Modernity*, 27.

138 See *Hispanic Review*, 80, no. 4, for a number of important interpretations of 15-M. *The Journal of Spanish Cultural Studies* 15, no. 1–2, also provides a variety of perspectives on the impacts and meaning of 15-M.
139 See the work of Corsín Jiménez, for example, "The Right to Infrastructure: A Prototype for Open Source Urbanism." See also Feinberg and Larson on the "cultural ecology" of 15-M and post-crisis Madrid, and Feinberg, "Don Juan Tenorio in the Campo de Cebada: Restaging Urban Space after 15-M."
140 Taibo, *El 15-M en sesenta preguntas*, 30, 50.
141 Ibid., 30.
142 There will be more detailed treatment of this topic in Chapter 4. For information on the activities of the Tabacalera, see Durán and Moore, "La Tabacalera of Lavapiés: A Social Experiment or a Work of Art?"
143 Durán, personal interview with the author.
144 María Isabel Serrano, "El PP lamenta el 'oxígeno' que se da al 15-M en La Tabacalera." *www.abc.es*. 2 August 2011. https://www.abc.es/espana/madrid/abcp-lamenta-oxigeno-tabacalera-201108020000_noticia.html.
145 Joseba Elola, "Cómo el 15-M se exportó al mundo." *El País*, 15 October 2011. http://politica.elpais.com/politica/2011/10/16/actualidad/1318724728_043129.html.

CHAPTER TWO

1 Readers might recall the statement often attributed to French writer Alexandre Dumas (despite the dubiousness of the attribution) that "Africa begins at the Pyrenees."
2 Salaün, "El 'género chico' o los mecanismos de un pacto cultural"; and Moral Ruiz, "El género chico y la invención de Madrid: *La Gran Vía* (1886)" and "La mitificación de Madrid en el género chico."
3 Candela Soto, *Cigarreras madrileñas: trabajo y vida, 1888–1927*, 171–4.
4 Nash, *Madrid: A Cultural History*, 121.
5 According to a study in 1977, there were 440 corralas distributed amongst the neighborhoods of Lavapiés, Embajadores, and el Rastro. Berlinches Acín, *Arquitectura de Madrid*, 154.
6 See Feinberg, "The Violence of Everyday Life: Lope de Vega's *Fuente Ovejuna* as Urban Allegory," for a discussion of the way the setting of the *corrala* has been used more recently by the theater group AlmaViva Teatro for staging an adaptation of Lope de Vega's drama.

7   I once again direct readers to Castell's detailed study of this period, *The City and the Grassroots*, 217–76.
8   Chapter 4 focuses on the Laboratorio 03. First established in April of 1997, the Labo occupied three additional locations in the neighborhood until 2004, when it began targeting La Tabacalera as the permanent location for the activities (and spirit) of the Laboratorio.
9   See Feinberg, "From Cigarreras to Indignados: Spectacles of Scale in the CSA La Tabacalera of Lavapiés, Madrid," for more on this performance.
10 Images from this performance can be found at https://www.flickr.com/photos/tabacaleralavapies/sets/72157626096797052/.
11 La flor de Lavapiés, "Archive for diciembre 2010"; "La flor de Lavapiés: Otro sitio más de los blogs de la Tabacalera." 2010. http://blogs.latabacalera.net/laflor/2010/12/.
12 The word "costumbrist" refers to realist representations of daily life in the visual or literary arts, primarily in Spain and Latin America in the nineteenth century. For more on costumbrism, see Fernández de Montesinos, *Costumbrismo y novela*, and Fontanella, *La imprenta y las letras en la España romántica*. In the visual arts, the series of murals commissioned for the library of Archer M. Huntington's museum and painted by Joaquín Sorolla in 1911 might be a particularly representative example.
13 Parsons, *A Cultural History of Madrid*, 10.
14 "castizo." *Diccionario de la lengua española. Vigésima segunda edición.* Real Academia Española, 2021, https://dle.rae.es/castiz.o.
15 For more detailed consideration of the beginnings of Basque and Catalan nationalism, see Fox, *La invención de España*, 65–110, and Conversi, *The Basques, the Catalans, and Spain*, 11–35 and 44–73.
16 Unamuno, *En torno al casticismo*, 200.
17 Fox, *La invención de España*, 118.
18 Torrecilla, *España exótica*, 6.
19 See Lozano Barolozzi, *Historia del urbanismo en España II*, 384–8, for a more detailed treatment of the urban reforms of Ferdinand VI and Charles III. The extensive work of Carlos Sambricio also provides more in-depth context. See, for example, *Territorio y ciudad en la España de la Ilustración* or *La arquitectura española de la ilustración*.
20 Foucault develops his idea of Governmentality in *Security, Territory, Population*. While its definition is slippery, it refers to the range of tools and discourses used to discipline the population. In this case, the increased visibility of citizens and public space allowed for more careful surveillance of the city.

21 In *El soñador para un pueblo* (1959), Antonio Buero Vallejo (1916–2000) uses Esquilache's efforts to illuminate Madrid as a metaphor for the moral and intellectual improvement of the inhabitants. For Rivero, it is a thinly veiled critique of the anti-intellectual tradition in Spain that has its roots in the Inquisition and extends through the Francoist period of the twentieth century, "*Un soñador para un pueblo*, de Antonio Buero Vallejo, y la utopía el espíritu geométrico," 94–6.
22 Herr, "Flow and Ebb," 179. As discussed in the previous chapter, Castells offers compelling analysis of the *comuneros* revolt, *The City and the Grassroots*, 4–15.
23 Juan Ignacio González del Castillo of Cádiz is also given credit for establishing the *sainete* tradition. Romero Ferrer, "Introducción," 2005.
24 Noyes, "La maja vestida," 199.
25 Ibid.
26 Other examples from Goya include *La maja vestida* (*The Clothed Maja*) (1798–1800) and *Majas al balcón* (*Majas on a Balcony*) (1777).
27 Torrecilla's basic argument suggests that the "primitive" essence of Spanish identity was not imposed externally by foreign writers (namely the Romantics), but rather was very much produced domestically as a reaction to French influence. His later work on this subject can be found in his book *Guerras literarias del XVIII Español*.
28 Torrecilla, *España exótica*, 6.
29 Iarocci, "Romantic Prose, Journalism, and *costumbrismo*," 386. Iarocci suggests that this *proto-costumbrista* tendency can be found in Clavijo y Fajardo's journal, *El pensador*; the plays of Moratín; Goya's *caprichos*; the *sainetes* of Ramón de la Cruz; and the emphasis on folkloric music by collectors like Juan Antonio de Iza Zamácola. See also, Rinaldo Froldi's "Anticipaciones dieciochescas del costumbrismo romántico."
30 Haidt, "Los Majos, el 'españolísimo gremio' del teatro," 158.
31 Ibid., 163.
32 Webber, *The Zarzuela Companion*, 2.
33 Readers will recall from the Introduction that one of the nicknames historically for Lavapiés has often been *La manolería*.
34 de la Cruz, *Manolo*, 104.
35 Ibid., 105.
36 Gies, *The Cambridge History of Spanish Literature*, 339.
37 Tomás López de Vargas Machuca, "Plano geométrico de Madrid: dedicado y presentado al rey nuestro señor Don Carlos III por mano del Excelentísimo señor conde de Floridablanca," ca. 1:5.500. Catálogo

Cartoteca. Instituto Geográfico Nacional. 1785. 2015. http://www2.ign.es/MapasAbsysJPG/12-L-63_01_a.JPG/.
38 Cruz, "Bandos," line 219.
39 Ibid., lines 219–20.
40 Ibid., line 220.
41 Ibid., lines 336–7.
42 Ibid., lines 444–5.
43 Ibid., line 447.
44 Ibid., lines 502–3.
45 Notably this author came upon a handbill pasted on a wall in Lavapiés in 2011 inviting residents to a neighborhood assembly. At the top, the handbill read "Los bandos de Lavapiés."
46 Hendecasyllable is a poetic meter in which each line contains eleven syllables.
47 Noyes, "La maja vestida," 198.
48 Ibid., 214.
49 Iarocci, "Romantic Prose, Journalism, and *costumbrismo*," 387.
50 Also known as the Peninsular War, this conflict occurred from 1808 to 1814.
51 Haidt, "Visibly Modern Madrid," 25.
52 Ibid., 32–3.
53 Ibid., 39.
54 Fraser, *Henri Lefebvre and the Spanish Urban Experience*, 56–69.
55 Haidt, "Visibly Modern Madrid," 40.
56 Frost, *Cultivating Madrid*, 12.
57 Ibid., 383.
58 Mesonero Romanos, *Escenas Matritenses*, 5 (emphasis mine).
59 Harney, "Costumbrismo and the Ideology of Género Chico," 35.
60 del Moral, *Costumbrismo*, 44–6.
61 Alier, *La zarzuela*, 11.
62 Pinto Crespo and Madrazo, *Madrid: atlas histórico*, 364.
63 Alier, *La zarzuela*, 42.
64 Readers will note that the main residence and working offices of the Spanish monarchs today is the Zarzuela Palace. Thus, within certain contexts in the press, the term has become a metonym for the monarchy.
65 Alier, *La zarzuela*, 48.
66 Doménech, "El arte escénico en el siglo XVIII," 575. Regarding *majismo* and dancing, see also Haidt, "Los majos, 'el españolismo gremio' del teatro," 171–2.
67 Webber, *The Zarzuela Companion*, 3.

68 Alier, *La zarzuela*, 49.
69 Alier suggests that the *zarzuela* tradition might be understood more broadly as a variety of theatrical forms focused on mythologizing the popular life of the city (vs. its lyrical and musical character), a definition that includes the works of Ramón de la Cruz. Ibid., 50.
70 Ibid., 51.
71 Alier comments that Barcelona sought to be excluded from this prohibition because of the prolific nature of the Italian opera in the city, and therefore the Italian opera continued to be performed (with Italian singers) in the port city. Ibid.
72 Ibid., 53.
73 The *jota* is a folkloric dance from Aragon performed in various parts of Spain where more localized versions have developed (like the Basque *jota*). Similarly, the *sardana* is a traditional folkloric dance of Catalonia.
74 Alier, *La zarzuela*, 63.
75 The *ensanche de Madrid* (or *Plan de Castro*) refers to the plan developed for the government in 1857 by Carlos María de Castro to expand the city to the southeast and the northeast beyond the parameters of the old *cerca* and the established footprint of the capital. For more on the *Ensanche*, see Terán, *Historia del urbanismo en España III*, 62–3, and Juliá, "Madrid: Capital del Estado (1833–1993)," 370–84.
76 Salaün, "El 'género chico' o los mecanismos de un pacto cultural," 251.
77 Dougherty, "Theatre and Culture, 1868–1936," 214.
78 Espín Templado, "El Casticismo del género chico," 28, and Moral Ruiz, "La mitificación de Madrid en el género chico," 74.
79 Harney, "Controlling Resistance, Resisting Control," 158.
80 For more on the influence of the *género chico* on the dialect of Madrid, see Seco, *Arniches y el habla de Madrid*.
81 Vela, "El género chico," 364.
82 Harney describes how many of the *librettists* of the *género chico* were also journalists or low-level functionaries, who, despite being considered hacks, were able to feed the public frenzy for the genre due to their positions within the sensationalist press. "Controlling Resistance, Resisting Control," 153.
83 Gea, *Centro*, 54.
84 Terán, *Historia del urbanismo en España III*, 25. See also Ringrose, *Madrid and the Spanish Economy*, Chapter 3.
85 Ibid., 23.
86 Parsons, *A Cultural History of Madrid*, 10.
87 Ibid.

88 I am using the term *aleph* in reference to Jorge Luis Borges's famous short story "The Aleph" (1945). During the climax of the story, the narrator discovers the object of the story's title in his rival's basement. There, on the nineteenth step of the basement stairs, the narrator gazes upon the Aleph: "one of the points in space that contain all points." It was an object "probably two or three centimeters in diameter, but universal space was contained inside it, with no diminution in size." Borges, "The Aleph," 283.
89 Salaün, "El 'género chico' o los mecanismos de un pacto cultural," 18.
90 Parsons, "Fiesta Culture in Madrid Posters," 192.
91 Ibid., 196.
92 Gómez Labad, *El Madrid de la Zarzuela: visión regocijada de un pasado en cantables*, 12.
93 Moral Ruiz, "La mitificación de Madrid," 70.
94 Moral Ruiz, "El género chico y la invención de Madrid: *La Gran Vía* (1886)," 56.
95 Salaün, "El 'género chico' o los mecanismos de un pacto cultural," 251 and 365.
96 Herrera de la Mula, "*La verbena de la Paloma* y el mito popular madrileño," 1.
97 Stapell, *Remaking Madrid*, 16–18.

CHAPTER THREE

1 López Mozo, *El Arquitecto y el Relojero*, 57. López Mozo was born in 1942 and came of age as a dramatist during the last throes of the Francoist regime. His work is considered a part of the New Spanish Theater, a group of dramatists devoted to political critique and an avant-garde aesthetic that helped to bring Spain through the Transition to democracy.
2 Ibid., 12. López Mozo has discussed how the book *La Real Casa de Correos, 1756–1988*, published in honor of the building's rehabilitation, inspired the writing of the play. Jerónimo López Mozo, personal interview.
3 López Mozo, *El Arquitecto y el Relojero*, 58.
4 Ibid.
5 Ibid.
6 Ruggeri, "Review: *El Arquitecto*," 192.
7 López Mozo, *El Arquitecto y el Relojero*, 29.
8 Ibid.
9 López Mozo, personal interview.

Notes to pages 97–103

10 The Centro Dramático Nacional was managed by the Ministry of Culture until 2011, when the ministry was consolidated into the Ministry of Education, Sport, and Culture. There are currently two National Drama Center sites: the Teatro María Guerrero and the Teatro Valle-Inclán.
11 Lefebvre, *The Production of Space*, 38.
12 Aguilera Sastre, *El debate*, 18.
13 Fox, *La invención de España*, 118
14 Aguilera Sastre, *El debate*, 188.
15 Cited in ibid., 190. Sánchez Mazas would later become one of the intellectual architects of the fascist Falange movement, which would underpin the military coup led by General Francisco Franco.
16 Ibid., 322–3.
17 Dougherty, "Theatre and Culture," 220.
18 Ibid.
19 Aguilera Sastre, *El debate*, 333. It would maintain this designation until 1978, when it would be converted into the site of the Centro Dramático Nacional, a title which it continues to hold today.
20 Ibid., 337.
21 Kasten, *Cultural Politics*, xv.
22 Ibid., 48.
23 Oliva, *La última escena*, 45.
24 Ruiz Ramón, "Spanish Transition Theater," 91–3.
25 The building had two short-lived iterations as a theater space beginning in 1908, as Lo Rat Penat and later the Teatro Chueca. The building was rehabilitated in the proceeding years until eventually settling in as the movie house known as the Cine Olimpia in 1926.
26 Ruiz Ramón describes the environment of the Francoist period as a "stifling, completely neurotic atmosphere of prohibition and inquisition that had blocked all outlets for critical theater" ("Spanish Transition Theater," 91). During much of the Transition, Spanish theater was characterized by what Ruiz Ramón has called Operation Rescue and Operation Recovery. These two "cultural operations" sought to represent many authors and plays from the postwar period that had been victims of censorship.
27 Ibid., 99.
28 Juliá, "History, Politics, and Culture," 116.
29 Ibid., 117.
30 Oliva, *La última escena*, 66.
31 Stapell, *Remaking Madrid*, 17.
32 Oliva, *La última escena*, 71.

33 Centro Dramático Nacional. "¿Qué es el CDN?" Instituto Nacional de Artes Escénicas y de la Música. https://dramatico.mcu.es/.
34 Oliva, *La última escena*, 66.
35 Aurora Intxausti, "Entrevista: Gerardo Vera/Director del Centro Dramático Nacional." *El País*, 25 February 2006. https://elpais.com/diario/2006/02/26/cultura/1140908404_850215.html.
36 Ibid.
37 Ibid.
38 Ibid.
39 Echenagusia, *Madrid: cuatro años de gestión*, 140.
40 Liz Perales, "10 ideas para el CDN de Gerardo Vera," 30 September 2004. https://elcultural.com/Gerardo-Vera. According to their homepage, the Instituto Cervantes "is the public institution created by Spain in 1991 for the promotion and instruction of the Spanish language and for the diffusion of Spanish and Hispano-American culture." Instituto Cervantes, "Quiénes Somos." https://www.cervantes.es/sobre_instituto_cervantes/informacion.htm#:~:text=La%20instituci%C3%B3n,culturas%20hisp%C3%A1nicas%20en%20el%20exterior.
41 Liz Perales, "10 ideas para el CDN de Gerardo Vera," 30 September 2004. https://elcultural.com/Gerardo-Vera.
42 Ibid.
43 Often classified into three principal groups that include the generations of 1898, of 1914, and of 1927, this Silver Age includes such important artistic figures as Miguel de Unamuno, Antonio Machado, Salvador Dalí, Pablo Picasso, Federico García Lorca, and of course Ramón María del Valle-Inclán. It is arguably the most celebrated period of cultural production in Spain's history, next to the seventeenth century.
44 I rely here on Peter Bürger's notion of the avant-garde that sees the vanguard as a self-criticizing arm of bourgeois – although, it must be pointed out that Francisco Nieva does not pertain to the historical avant-garde of the teens and twenties in Spain. Nonetheless, his efforts to disrupt traditional modes of communication between reader-text/drama-spectator places him within a broader tradition of artistic experimentation associated with a more general definition of avant-garde art.
45 Instituto Nacional de Las Artes Escénicas y de la Música (INAEM). "Teatro Valle Inclán," Ministerio de Cultura, 2006. https://cdn.mcu.es/programacion/teatro-valle-inclan/.
46 García de Paredes, personal interview.
47 Pedrosa, "Teatro Olimpia," 161.
48 Ibid.

49 Ibid., 156.
50 Mugerauer, "Toward an Architectural Vocabulary," 104.
51 Pedrosa, "Teatro Olimpia," 158.
52 Tuan, *Space and Place*, 102.
53 Ibid., 107.
54 James Treceño, "Lavapiés vigilado por 48 cámaras." *elmundo.es*. 18 May 2009. https://www.elmundo.es/elmundo/2009/05/17/madrid/1242577241.html.
55 Octavio Fraile, "División entre los vecinos de Lavapiés por las cámaras de vigilancia." *20minuto.es*. 23 December 2009. https://www.20minutos.es/noticia/595015/0/division/lavapies/camaras/.
56 Tuan, *Space and Place*, 110.
57 Debord, I:12.
58 Juan Carlos Martínez, "Lavapiés en su estado original," *El País*, 27 February 2004. Propiedades: 10.
59 Gómez, "El barrio de Lavapiés," 4.
60 Juan Carlos Martínez, "Las dos caras de Embajadores," *El País*, 1 February 2002. Propiedades: 11.
61 Andrés Rubio Fernández and Rafael Fernández Bermejo, "Los nuevos iconos urbanos de Madrid," *El País*, 6 November 2004, El viajero: 3
62 Vera Gutiérrez, "El Ayuntamiento solo ha erradicado en seis años el 20% de las infraviviendas de Lavapiés," *El País*, 4 September 2003: 3.
63 Juan Carlos Martínez,. "Las dos caras de Embajadores," *El País*, 1 February 2002, Propiedades: 11.
64 Quoted in Pablo Guimón, "República de Lavapiés," *El País*, 27 June 2003, Tentaciones: 18
65 Quoted in Vega, Inmaculada de la Vega, "40 proyectos singulares en marcha," *El País*, 26 December 2003, Propiedades: 3
66 Carlos Vidania, personal interview.
67 Instituto Nacional de Las Artes Escénicas y de la Música (INAEM). "Teatro Valle-Inclán." Ministerio de Cultura, Madrid, 2006. Archives of the Teatro Valle-Inclán, 1.
68 Ibid.
69 Ibid.
70 Lefebvre, *Writings on Cities*, 65.
71 Ibid., 70.
72 Ibid., 72, emphasis in the original.
73 Ibid.
74 Readers might recall the sight of seemingly endless cranes that dotted Spain's Mediterranean coastline in the early 2000s, as foreign capital and

access to financing drove a construction boom. The "rural" communities of the Costa del Sol were urbanized within this mode of production as much as any gentrified neighborhood in the major cities.

75 Ibid., 73.
76 Ibid., 95.
77 Álvarez del Manzano, "Presentación," 5.
78 Ibid.
79 García de Sola, "Introducción," 7.
80 Álvarez del Manzano, "Presentación," 5.
81 The 2012 Summer Olympic Games were awarded to London, much to the chagrin of city leaders in Madrid.
82 Cited in Carmen Sánchez-Silva, "¿Unos Juegos rentables? Brasil afronta los Juegos Olímpicos de 2016 con 14.400 millones de dólares," *El País*, 11 October 2009. https://elpais.com/diario/2009/10/11/negocio/1255266868_850215.html.
83 Hill, *Olympic Politics*, 195–6. For more in-depth discussion of the 1992 games in Barcelona and of tourism in Catalonia in general, see also Pi-Sunyer "Tourism in Catalonia." Pi-Sunyer provides an interesting analysis of the ways the city government, the regional government of Catalonia, and the national government clashed over the symbolic use of the games for cultural and nationalistic ends.
84 See in particular Florida, *The Rise of the Creative Class*.
85 Álvarez del Manzano, "Presentación," 5.
86 Smith, "New Globalism, New Urbanism," 100.
87 Pasqual Maragall, "Madrid se ha ido," *El País*, 6 July 2003. https://elpais.com/diario/2003/07/07/opinion/1057528808_850215.html.
88 The political context of this article alludes to the fact that the Basque separatist group ETA (*Euskadi Ta Askatasuna*) [Basque Homeland and Freedom] had broken their treaty with the Spanish government in 2000. In addition, the nationalist policies of the ruling Popular Party had increasingly isolated politically the northern regions of Catalonia and the Basque country.
89 Echenagusia, *Madrid: cuatro años de gestion*, 16
90 Ibid.
91 Ibid., 56.
92 Ibid.
93 Ibid., 17.
94 Gómez, "El barrio de Lavapiés," 5.
95 These themes form the focus of the 2006 documentary *A ras de suelo*, directed by Alberto García Ortiz and Agatha Maciaszek. In particular, it

highlights that the Health Center in a neighborhood with a large elderly population was not located at the ground level and lacked an elevator.
96 Echenagusia, *Madrid: cuatro años de gestión*, 110.
97 Zárate Martín, "Imágenes mentales," 297.
98 Ibid., 295.
99 See Echenagusia, *Madrid: cuatro años de gestion*, 130–46.
100 Ibid., 111, emphasis mine.
101 Echenagusia, *Madrid: cuatro años de gestion*, 23.
102 Ibid.
103 Ibid., 50.
104 Ringrose, "Madrid, Capital Imperial," 193.
105 Echenagusia, *Madrid: cuatro años de gestion*, 124.
106 Ibid., 112.
107 Ibid.
108 Florida, *Flight of the Creative Class*, 145.
109 Echenagusia, *Madrid: cuatro años de gestion*, 111.
110 Ibid., 130, emphasis mine.
111 Ibid.
112 These subsidized areas are known as Áreas de Rehabilitación Preferentes as well.
113 Echenagusia, *Madrid: cuatro años de gestion*, 112.
114 Ibid.
115 Ibid.
116 Ibid., 132.
117 Ibid.
118 Ibid.
119 Ibid.
120 Ibid., 140.
121 Ibid., emphasis mine.
122 Ibid.
123 Ibid.
124 Ibid.
125 Echenagusia, *Madrid: cuatro años de gestion*, 130.
126 Ibid.
127 Gómez, "El barrio de Lavapiés," 1.
128 Ibid.
129 See the full listing of events at http://www.mrmonkey.es/tangopies/.
130 There is no longer an active link with information on the BollyMadrid festival, but an overview can be found at the following link, as well as in

myriad YouTube videos: https://www.casaasia.eu/actividad/7th-indian-culture-festival-in-madrid-bollymadrid/.
131 Echenagusia, *Madrid: cuatro años de gestion,* 130.
132 Lloyd and Clark, "The City as Entertainment Machine," 357–8.
133 Barrado Timón, "Gran ciudad y Turismo," paragraph 7.
134 AZCA stands for Asociación Mixta de Compensación de la Manzana A de la Zona Comercial de la Avenida del Generalísimo (Mixed Association for Compensation of the A Block of the Commercial Area of the Avenue of the Generalísimo). Readers will note that the avenue's name changed to the Castellana after the end of the Franco regime.
135 The four towers are the Torre Espacio, Torre de Cristal, Torre PwC, and Torre Cepsa.
136 Barrado Timón, "Gran ciudad y Turismo," paragraph 20.
137 Santiago Rodríguez, "Madrid, Global," 3.
138 Ibid.
139 Taylor et al., "Command and Control Centres," 20. The book *Global Urban Analysis* was produced by the collaboration between the Global Urban Competitiveness Project (GUCP) at the Chinese Academy of Social Sciences and the Globalization and World Cities (GaWC) Research Network housed at Loughborough University (UK). The index uses the top 2000 firms in the world, as designated in *Forbes* composite index, and scores cities based on the number of headquarters and the ranking of those firms (i.e., the city with a top 50 firm headquarters scores 12 points, firms ranked 51 to 100 score 11 points, etc.). The other index uses a similar methodology.
140 Taylor, "Advanced Producer Service Centres," 24–33.
141 Taylor et al., "European Cities in Globalization," 114–35.
142 Santiago Rodríguez, "Madrid, Global," 10.
143 Ibid., 6.
144 Ibid., 8.
145 Méndez Gutiérrez, Tébar Arjona, and Aragón, "Economía del conocimiento," paragraph 36.
146 Ibid.
147 Santiago Rodríguez, "Madrid, Global," 7. He presents data showing that, in the 1970s, only 28 per cent of banking entities were to be found in Madrid. This grew over the following decades to 49.6 per cent in 1985 and in 2004 to 63.4 per cent of the national banks having a presence in Madrid.
148 Ibid. In each of the years 2003, 2004, and 2005, the average level of foreign investment has been 58 per cent. It has also served as the exit point

for Spanish capital during these years, with over 55 per cent of the Spanish investment emanating from the city.
149 López and Rodríguez, "The Spanish Model," 10.
150 Méndez Gutiérrez, Tébar Arjona, and Aragón, "Economía del conocimiento," paragraph 36.
151 It is important to note that Madrid's economic dominance is not, by any means, complete. In 2000 Catalonia accounted for 28 per cent of the commercial transactions with the exterior, compared to Madrid's 19 per cent. Santiago Rodríguez, "Madrid, Global," 10.
152 Ibid., 8.
153 Pasqual Maragall, "Madrid se va," *El País*, 26 February 2001, https://elpais.com/diario/2001/02/27/opinion/983228408. The notion of a decentralized Spanish state to which Maragall alludes in 2001 has obviously been belied by the ongoing conflict between Catalonia and the central government, which entered a particularly acute phase in 2017 after the controversial referendum on independence called by the Catalonian government in October of that year and the subsequent invocation of Article 53 of the Spanish Constitution by the central government, which removed the autonomous political powers of Catalonia.
154 Santiago Rodríguez, "Madrid, Global," 52.
155 López and Rodríguez, "The Spanish Model," 5.
156 Ibid.
157 Harvey, *The Limits to Capital*, 235–8.
158 López and Rodríguez, "The Spanish Model," 14; Roch, "La deriva patológica del espacio social," paragraph 11; Roch, "El modelo inmobiliario español," 34; and García Pérez, "Gentrificación en Madrid," 77–8. Also see Observatorio Metropolitano publications like *Manifiesto por Madrid*, *Crítica y crisis del modelo metropolitano* and *Madrid, ¿La suma de todos? Globalización, territorio, desigualdad*.
159 "After the fiesta." Editorial. *The Economist*, 16.
160 Jonathan House, "Spain's Unemployment Rate Breaches 20%." *Wall Street Journal* (Online), 30 April 2010. https://www.wsj.com/articles/SB10001424052748703871904575215430811273278.
161 For more on the causes and consequences of the global financial crisis of 2007–08 for the United States, Spain, and the global economy, see Stiglitz, *Freefall, American*; and de la Dehesa, *La primera gran crisis financier*.
162 "Qué es." *Casa Encendida*. Caja Madrid. https://www.lacasaencendida.es/que-es-casa-encendida.
163 Ibid.

CHAPTER FOUR

1. Grupo Surrealista, "Aviso para la próxima demolición del Nuevo Teatro Olimpia," 91.
2. This description relies on both the video archives of the protest made by filmmaker Antonio Girón of Kinowo Media, acquired with the gracious help of local activist Jacobo Rivero, as well as scenes from the documentary *A ras de suelo* (2006), directed by Alberto García Ortiz and Agatha Maciaszek.
3. García Ortiz and Maciaszek, *A ras de suelo*, 1:26:12
4. Ibid., 1:29:18
5. Girón "Olimpia inauguración," 2:15
6. Rivero, personal interview. The term *okupa*, spelled with the non-standard "k" (as opposed to the standard spelling *ocupa* or *ocupar*) generally alludes to politically motivated acts of squatting, often with the intention of establishing a social center. Because of these very specific connotations, the term *okupa* will not be translated into English, since the English term "squatting" lacks the layer of meaning communicated by the subversive "k."
7. Girón "Olimpia inauguración," 3:15
8. For more on the Tabacalera, see Durán and Moore, "La Tabacalera of Lavapiés."
9. Merrifield, *Metromarxism*, 106.
10. Vilaseca, *Barcelona Okupas*, 5.
11. Cited in ibid.
12. Merrifield, *Metromarxism*, 96.
13. I rely here on Prujit's useful taxonomy of squatting. See "Okupar en Europa," 35–6, for more discussion. See also the abundance of materials published by the activist research collective Squatting Europe Collective (SQEK), such as *The Squatters' Movement in Europe: Commons and Autonomy as Alternatives to Capitalism* and *Squatting in Europe: Radical Spaces, Urban Struggles*.
14. For a more detailed explanation of these differences, see the helpful chart in Pruijt, 59–60. Pruijt cites the work of Lowe to develop this definition.
15. Martínez López, *Okupaciones de viviendas*, 26.
16. It is well beyond the scope of this study to discuss in detail the extensive bibliography in the field of sociology devoted to the term "social movement." Martínez López defines it as "a specific collective action that activates power relations within their contexts (not only political, but also spatial, social, or economic)," ibid.

17 Ibid., 99.
18 Ibid., 106.
19 For more on institutionalization in Amsterdam, see Owens, *Cracking under Pressure*. Martínez López, "How Do Squatters Deal with the State?" also provides a thorough overview of the relevant literature regarding institutionalized squatting.
20 Martínez López, *Okupaciones de viviendas*, 106–7.
21 In Germany, squatters are called *besetzers*. For additional commentary on *okupas*, see also Chapter 5 of Feixa, Costa, and Pallares, *Movimientos juveniles en la Península Ibérica: Graffitis, Grifotas, Okupas*.
22 Martínez López, *Okupaciones de viviendas*, 109.
23 Terán, *Historia del urbanismo en España III*, 262.
24 Adell Argilés, "Introducción," 22.
25 "'Aquellos maravillosos años': una historia de la okupación en Madrid." *Nodo50. contrainformación en red*. 19 October 2008, 2. https://info.nodo50.org/Aquellos-maravillosos-anos-una.html.
26 Martínez López, *Okupaciones de viviendas*, 142–3.
27 Martínez López includes the example of the *gaztetxe* squat in the city of Laudio, which was active for almost eleven years, and Gazteizkio Gaztetxea in Vitoria, which lasted thirteen years. *Okupaciones*, 143–4.
28 Martínez López, *Okupaciones de viviendas*, 144.
29 Rivero, personal interview, 8 June 2009.
30 Martínez López, *Okupacione de viviendas*, 146.
31 "'Aquellos maravillosos años': una historia de la okupación en Madrid." *Nodo50. contrainformación en red*, 19 October 2008, 3. https://info.nodo50.org/Aquellos-maravillosos-anos-una.html
32 Rivero, personal interview, 8 June 2009.
33 Ibid.
34 Martínez López, "Del urbanismo," 86.
35 Martínez López, *Okupaciones de viviendas*, 154; Almudena Flecha, "Son ya más de 200 las viviendas 'okupadas' en España, la mayor parte en Madrid y Barcelona." *ABC Madrid*, 8 December 2009, Sociedad: 34. https://www.abc.es/sociedad/abci-mas-viviendas-okupadas-espana-mayor-parte-madrid-y-barcelona-200108110300-39733_noticia.html.
36 Martínez López, *Okupacione de viviendas*, 155–7.
37 Rivero, personal interview, 8 June 2009.
38 Ibid.

39 Ibid.
40 For a more in-depth discussion of squatted social centers in Madrid, see *Okupa Madrid (1985–2011). Memoria, reflexión, debate y autogestión colectiva del conocimiento*, edited by Miguel Martínez and Angela García Bernardos.
41 Vilaseca, *Barcelona Okupas*, 4.
42 As noted in the Introduction, this idea of the *procomún* derives most explicitly from ecologist Garrett Hardin's famous 1968 essay "The Tragedy of the Commons" and the work of Nobel Prize–winning economist Elinor Ostrom. It also is central to the 15-M movement. See Moreno-Caballud, "Imaginación sostenible" and *Cultures of Anyone* for an overview of this subject.
43 Rivero, personal interview, 8 June 2009
44 Vidania and Padilla, "Okupar el vacío desde el vació," 53.
45 Rivero, personal interview, 8 June 2009.
46 Ibid.
47 Vidania and Marga Padilla, "Okupar el vacío desde el vacío," 53
48 Carlos Vidania, "El Labo como iniciativa social." *Viento sur*, no. 69 (2003). www.vientosur.info/spip.php?article1530.
49 Ibid.
50 Lefebvre, *Introduction to Modernity*, 116.
51 Rivero, personal interview, 8 June 2009. Readers will recall that change in the Penal Code made squatting a crime.
52 Ibid.
53 Ibid.
54 *Constitución española* Boletín Oficial de Estado, 29319.
55 Ibid., 29320.
56 "Informe de las actividades del centro social okupado El Laboratorio." Archives of Traficantes de Sueño, 15 May 2009. This document and others in this chapter come from the archives of the Laboratorios, a collection of papers, photographs, and newspapers clippings held in the offices of the now-defunct alternative newspaper *El Diagonal*, which was published in Lavapiés from 2005 to 2016, and the offices of the alternative bookstore Traficantes del sueño. Many thanks to Jacobo Rivero for providing me with access to these materials and the opportunity to photocopy relevant documents.
57 Ibid.
58 Smith, *Uneven Development*, 150.
59 "Manifiesto en defensa de la okupación y de los espacios autogestionados." Archives of Traficantes de Sueño. February 1999. Accessed 15 May 2009.

Notes to pages 142–8

60 Ibid.
61 Ibid.
62 Ibid.
63 Ibid.
64 Gelman, "Cuentos espaciales (apotegmas sobre la okupación)," 38.
65 Ibid. The ampersand is used in many *okupa* texts to make gendered nouns simultaneously masculine and feminine.
66 "Informe de las actividades del centro social okupado El Laboratorio." Archives of Traficantes de Sueño, 15 May 2009.
67 Ibid., 2.
68 Ibid.
69 Ibid.
70 Ibid.
71 Ibid.
72 Ibid. Readers might recall how this notion that you "cannot evict an idea" would enter into the discourse of 15-M and later the Occupy Wall Street movement.
73 The title in Spanish is "Un paseo (guiado) por Lavapiés: textos recopilados"
74 Rivero, personal interview, 8 June 2009.
75 Ibid.
76 Ibid.
77 This text is on a pamphlet inserted into the jacket cover of Julien Charlon's book of photographs. It is composed of several short texts, many of which are written anonymously or credited to an individual only by first name. Given that collectivity is such a key value for the *okupas* of the Laboratorio, I have used only one bibliographic citation and will cite Charlon, who edited the text, as the reference.
78 Charlon, *Labo 03 Lavapiés, Madrid*, 3.
79 Charlon, *Labo 03 Lavapiés, Madrid*, 2.
80 Ibid.
81 Ibid., 8.
82 Menéndez, *Laboratorio 03: Ocupando el vacío*, 11:11–11:20.
83 Ibid., 11:56–15:33.
84 Ibid., 9:34–9:40.
85 Laura Corcuera and Belén Rubira, personal interview with the author.
86 Belén Rubira and María Ruíz-Larrea, "Cedepalo Manifesto." Personal Archives of Laura Corcuera.
87 Laura Corcuera and Belén Rubira, personal interview.

88 Ibid.
89 Ibid.
90 Ibid.
91 Ibid.
92 Menéndez, *Laboratorio 03: Ocupando el vacío*, 25:50–26:40.
93 The full video of the event from 25 January 2003 can be found in the online archive compiled by Ana Sánchez found at: https://archive.org/details/revistacaminadalabo325enero.
94 "Revista Caminada y otras actividades en Labo03." Agencia de Noticias de Información Alternativa. 2 February 2003. Accessed 7 July 2010. http://ania.urcm.net/spip.php?article4475.
95 Ana Valera, "Encierro para salvar el Laboratorio." *El Mundo*, 26 June 2002, M2: 12
96 Menéndez, *Laboratorio 03: Ocupando el vacío*, 30:33–32:22.
97 Ibid., 30:55.
98 María José Olmo, "'El Laboratorio,' último cuartel de los 'okupas.'" *ABC Madrid*, 8 April 2001: 91.
99 Ana Valera, "Encierro para salvar el Laboratorio." *El Mundo*, 26 June 2002, M2: 12.
100 Menéndez, *Laboratorio 03: Ocupando el vacío*, 21:40–21:52.
101 Ibid., 32:05. The Spanish translation is "El Labo se queda in Lavapiés."
102 Ibid., 50:11.
103 In Spanish, the title is *Alejandro y Ana: lo que España no pudo ver de la boda de la hija del president*. After its debut, the work's title was shortened to *Alejandro y Ana* for simplicity's sake for its tour around Spain. I will rely on this shortened title to refer to the work during the course of this chapter.
104 Juan Mayorga, personal communication.
105 For more on the connection between the Teatro del Barrio and Animalario, see Vélez-Sainz, "En los alrededores del teatro document," and Boehm, "Popular Theatre as Space and Symbol of the Spanish Democratic Revolution."
106 He wrote *Gente de mala calidad (Low-Class People)* (2008), *Dispongo de barcos (Boats Available)*(2010), *El señor (Mr Man)* (2012), and won the Saint Jordi Prize for Best Film of 2013, *Gente en sitios (People in Places)* (2013). In more recent years, he has turned his attention to writing for streaming television, and in 2017 wrote the series *Vergüenza (Shame)*, which was awarded the Best Comedy Series in the Feroz Awards. The Saint Jordi Awards are awarded by the Catalonian region of Radio y Televisión Española (RTVE). The Feroz Awards are Spain's equivalent of

Notes to pages 156–60

the United States Golden Globes and are awarded by the Spanish Cinematographic Press Association.

107 He took possession of the seat "M" on 12 April 2018 after the previous occupant, scholar Carlos Bousoño Prieto, passed away.
108 His awards include the following: Europa Nuevas Realidades Teatrales (2016), the National Theater Award (2007), the National Dramatic Literature Award (2013), Teresa de Ávila National Award in Letters (2016), the Valle-Inclán Award (2009), the Ceres Award (2013), the Barraca Award for Performing Arts (2013), the National Radio Critical Eye Award (2000), and the Max Award for Best Author (2006, 2008, and 2009), and the Best Adaptation (2008 and 2013).
109 Vélez-Sainz, "En los alrededores del teatro documento," 366.
110 Weiss, "Fourteen Propositions for a Documentary Theatre," 375–7.
111 Martin, *Theatre of the Real*, 5.
112 Spain would ultimately support the United States through public statements and materially in the form of nine hundred troops and three ships designated for medical and anti-mine support. No Spanish troops participated in combat in Iraq.
113 *Nunca máis* is a phrase in Galician, the language spoken in the region where the Prestige oil spill occurred.
114 Labrador Méndez, "Afterword: Regarding the Spain of Others," 269. Bellicose Atlanticism refers to Aznar's allegiance to the aggressive, militaristic, and unapologetic foreign policy of the United States during the presidency of George W. Bush (2000–2008), including Spain's military involvement in the controversial invasion of Iraq in 2003.
115 Ibid., 270.
116 Animalario. "Alejandro y Ana." http://www.animalario.eu/shows/alejandroyana.html.
117 Campos, "Retrato del corrupto: 'Alejandro y Ana', la obra de teatro que destapó la trama Gürtel." *El confidencial*, 12 December 2014. https://www.elconfidencial.com/cultura/2014-12-12/retrato-del-corrupto-alejandro-y-ana-la-obra-de-teatro-que-destapo-la-trama-gurtel_588585/.
118 See, for example, Molanes Rial, "La ciudad y su doble en el teatro de Juan Mayorga" in *Espacios urbanos en el teatro español de los siglos XX y XXI*.
119 Mayorga, personal communication.
120 Mayorga, "Prólogo," 7.
121 Ibid.
122 Ibid.

123 Veléz-Saenz, "En los alrededores del teatro documento," 368.
124 Mayorga and Cavestany, *Alejandro y Ana*, 279.
125 Ibid.
126 Ibid., 284
127 Ibid.
128 Ibid., 285.
129 Ibid., 282.
130 Ibid., 288.
131 Ibid.
132 Belén Ginart, "El grupo Animalario parodia al PP en su montaje sobre la boda de la hija de Aznar." *El País*, 23 September 2003, Cultura y Espectáculos: 40.
133 Ibid.
134 A complete performance of the play is available at https://www.youtube.com/watch?v=1zTKhyZZkYo.
135 "Alejandro y Ana. Lo que España no pudo ver del banquete de la boda de la hija del presidente." 29 June 2016. https://www.youtube.com/watch?v=1zTKhyZZkYo, 0:33.
136 Vilaseca, *Barcelonan Okupas*, ix.
137 Snyder, "Practices," 65, and *Poetics of Opposition*, 5–6.
138 "PSOE e IU unen sus fuerzas para que los 'okupas' sigan en el Laboratorio III." ABC *Madrid*, 15 April 2003: 37. https://www.abc.es/espana/madrid/abci-psoe-unen-fuerzas-para-okupas-sigan-labotarorio-200304150300-174594_noticia.html.
139 Charlon, *Mundo Lavapiés*, 10.
140 Ibid., 13.
141 Sádaba Rodríguez and Roig Domínguez, "El movimiento okupación," 281.
142 For a detailed study of the current online activities of the *okupa* movement in Madrid in this period, see Vilaseca, "The TriBall Case," and Martínez López, "How Do Squatters Deal with the State?"
143 For more on this process, see Feinberg "From Cigarreras to Indignados: Spectacles of Scale in the CSA La Tabacalera of Lavapiés, Madrid."
144 "La Audiencia Provincial de Madrid ratifica la absolución de las 16 personas acusadas por la okupación de El Laboratorio 03. Archivada la causa de El Laboratorio 02." CSOA *Laboratorio: una experiencia multitudinaria, pública y autónoma*, https://sindominio.net/laboratorio/.
145 Charlon, *Laboratorio 03*, 1.

CHAPTER FIVE

1. Mesonero Romanos, *Escenas matritenses*, 93.
2. Baker, "Historical Perspectives," 174.
3. See Harvey, *The Urban Experience* and *The Condition of Postmodernity*, about this transformation.
4. For more on the PGOUM 1985 in general, see Compitello's "From Planning to Design: The Culture of Flexible Accumulation in Post-Cambio Madrid." For more about the changes in the late 1980s and early 1990s in Lavapiés, see Compitello, "A Good Plan Gone Bad."
5. Compitello, "A Good Plan, Gone Bad," 77.
6. Mesonero Romanos, 93.
7. Juanjo Martín Escriche, "El teatro de kif," line 3.
8. Ibid., line 5.
9. Ibid., lines 1 and 2.
10. Ibid., line 4.
11. Ibid. line 6.
12. Echenagusia, *Madrid: cuatro años de gestion*, 110.
13. Time Out PR, "Embajadores and Euljiro are on the list of Time Out's coolest neighbourhoods right now – Hackney and Williamsburg are not," 20September2018.https://www.timeout.com/about/latest-news/embajadores-and-euljiro-are-on-the-list-of-time-outs-coolest-neighbourhoods-right-now-hackney-and-williamsburg-are-not-092018.
14. Fraser, *Henri Lefebvre and the Spanish Urban Experience*, 17.
15. Ibid.
16. Delgado, *El Animal Público*, 183–4.
17. Ibid., 184
18. Delgado, *El Animal Público*, 46–58.
19. Oliva, *La última escena*, 185.
20. Martín-Estudillo and Spadaccini, "Introduction," ix.
21. Ibid., ix–x.
22. Both Valle-Inclán and Antonin Artaud take this position. See Dougherty's *Un Valle-Inclán olvidado*, 168, and Oliva, *La última escena*, 90.
23. Oliva, *La última escena*, 18 and 90.
24. Ibid. 90.
25. See Pérez Bowie, "Pantallas en el scenario," for a more thorough overview of the various functions of screens on the contemporary Spanish stage.
26. Leonard and Gabriele, "Fórmula para una dramaturgia," 7.
27. Labrador Méndez, "Afterword: Regarding the Spain of Others," 263.

28 Ibid., 269.
29 Ibid., 270. Labrador Méndez emphasizes how the "phallocentric rewriting of the nation" catalyzes a rise of regional nationalism, a re-energized feminist movement, amongst other consequences.
30 Debord, *Society of the Spectacle*, I:6.
31 Ibid., 263.
32 Oliva, Última Escena, 10.
33 Coleman, *The Necropolitical Theater*, 9.
34 David Planell, personal communication.
35 Dodgson and Peate, *Spanish Plays: New Spanish and Catalan Drama*, 105.
36 Planell, "Bazar," 10–12. The citations here refer to the translation by John Clifford.
37 Ibid., 11.
38 Coleman, *Necropolitical Theater*, 6.
39 Planell, "Bazar," 23.
40 Ibid.
41 Ibid.
42 Ibid., 30.
43 Ibid., 35.
44 Readers will likely recall German critic Walter Benjamin's meditations on the Paris Arcades.
45 Planell, "Bazar," 36.
46 Ibid.
47 Ibid.
48 Ibid., 37.
49 Ibid., 45.
50 Ibid., 49.
51 Ibid., 63.
52 Ibid.
53 Ibid., 73.
54 Ibid., 80.
55 Ibid., 83.
56 Ibid., 84.
57 Coleman, *The Necropolitical Theater*, 7. In addition to Jerónimo López Mozo's play *Ahlan*, which discusses the theme of immigration, there are also a number of recent narrative representations, including *Cosmofobia* (2007) by Lucía Etxeberría and *Esperando en un banco de Lavapiés* (2001) by Pako de Manuel. Also important is Básel Ramsis's 2002 documentary *El otro lado: un acercamiento a Lavapiés*. For a more complete list of films, literature, and criticism focused on the Moroccan immigrant

experience in Spain, see the appendix of the collection of *El retorno/el reencuentro: La inmigración en la literatura hispano-marroquí*. In recent years, these issues have gained visibility with the rise of the far-right political party Vox and events like the protests against police after the death of Senagalese street vendor Mame Mbaye in March 2018.

58 Lefebvre, *The Production of Space*, 39.
59 These issues are beyond the focus or scope of my discussion here, but Spivak's "Can the Subaltern Speak?" seems particularly relevant here.
60 Coleman, *Necropolitical Theater*, 62–8.
61 "Porque la vida no es una cárcel. Paremos los controles." La asociación de sin papeles de Madrid and La red de apoyo del ferrocaril clandestine, 28 May 2009. https://rebelion.org/la-vida-no-es-una-carcel-paremos-los-controles/.
62 Readers will recall that Aristotle proposed that tragedy should have a unity of action (one central plot), of place (one location), and of time (take place over twenty-four hours).
63 Readers can see a brief clip of the *Living Lavapiés* on YouTube at https://www.youtube.com/watch?v=JQ6iYwrG-SY.
64 "Botellón," according to the Real Academia Española, refers to the nocturnal practice of informal open-air gatherings of young people on street corners and in plazas to consume alcohol. See the online dictionary at https://dle.rae.es/botell%C3%B3n.
65 It is worth pointing out that this format of the nocturnal jaunt also evokes a similar set of scenes found in the costumbrist sketch "Madrid a la luna" (1842) by Ramón de Mesonero Romanos. See Paz Gago for a condensed overview of various locations in Madrid visited by Max Estrella during his *dérive* through Madrid.
66 Valle-Inclán, *Luces de Bohemia*, 162.
67 Ibid. The reference here is to Francisco José de Goya y Lucientes (1746–1828), the Spanish painter who is often considered the last of the old masters and one of the first modern painters because of his impressionistic style and his darkly cynical view of Spanish society.
68 For more on Spain and modernity, see the edited volume by Graham and Labanyi and Fusi and Palafox's *España, 1808–1996: el desafío de la modernidad*. For issues around modernity, urban development, and Madrid, see Larson, *Constructing and Resisting Modernity: Madrid 1900–1936*.
69 Dougherty, "La ciudad moderna," 134.
70 Ibid., 135–6. Dougherty refers here to Leopoldo Alas, also known as Clarín, a Spanish writer from the nineteenth century who often employed

his realist narrative to critique the decadence of Spain's emerging modernity.
71 Ibid., 133–4.
72 Carbajo, "La ciudad como utopia," 335.
73 López Llera, *Un Chivo en la Corte del botellón*, 9.
74 Ibid.
75 Ibid.
76 Ibid.
77 Ibid.
78 Estopa's self-titled first album, "Estopa," came out in 1999.
79 López Llera, *Un Chivo en la Corte del botellón*, 11.
80 "Modernismo" is a literary trend in Spanish letters closely associated with the Nicaraguan poet Rubén Darío (1867–1916), a writer who appears as a character in *Luces de Bohemia*. Despite the *modernismo* of these stanzas, the book of poems from which it derives, *La pipa de Kif* (1919), has been seen by some, such as Borelli, as a part of Valle-Inclán's aesthetic shift toward the *esperpento* preceding the publication of *Luces de Bohemia* and the novel *Tirano Banderas* (1926).
81 López Llera, *Un Chivo en la Corte del botellón*, 15.
82 Ibid., 20.
83 Ibid., 35.
84 Ibid., 34.
85 Ibid., 79.
86 Ibid.
87 Sheppard and Sziarto, "The Spatialities of Contentious Politics," 159.
88 Swyngedouw, "Excluding the Other: The Production of Scale and Scaled Politics," 169.
89 Ibid., *Un Chivo en la Corte del botellón*, 50
90 Ibid., 54.
91 Ibid.
92 Ibid.
93 Ibid.
94 Ibid., 58.
95 Ibid., 59.
96 Lefebvre, *Production of Space*, 123.
97 Andrés Jaque, "Ikea Disobedients," 2011, 9 + 1 *Ways of Being Political: 50 Years of Political Stances in Architecture and Urban Design*, Museum of Modern Art, 12 September 2012–25 March 2013. https://www.moma.org/collection/works/156886?sov_referrer=artist&artist_id=41431&page=1.

98 López Llera, *Un Chivo en la Corte del botellón*, 60.
99 Ibid., 62.
100 Ibid.
101 Ibid.
102 Ibid., 61.
103 In Spanish the name is Adoratrices Esclavas del Santísimo Sacramento y Caridad
104 López Llera, *Un Chivo en la Corte del botellón*, 82.
105 Ibid.
106 Ibid.
107 Ibid., 66.
108 Ibid.
109 Ibid.
110 Ibid., 71.
111 Ibid.
112 Ibid.
113 For more on this reading of de la Iglesia's film, see Compitello "From Planning to Design."
114 Ibid., 79–80.
115 Ibid., 80.
116 Lefebve, *The Production of Space*, 112.
117 López Llera, *Un Chivo en la Corte del botellón*, 86.
118 Ibid., 88.
119 Lefebvre, *Production of Space*, 118.

AFTERMATH

1 Readers will note that, in a historical twist, Pablo Iglesia Turrión shares his name with Pablo Iglesias Posse, the founder of the Spanish Socialist Workers' Party. Often considered the godfather of Spanish socialism, he established the PSOE in 1879 and the General Workers' Union (UGT) in 1888.
2 Rivero, *Podemos. Objetivo: asaltar los cielos*, 144.
3 These changes on the left have been accompanied by similar – albeit more unsettling – changes on the right driven by the rise of the far-right party Vox and its supposedly more center-right competition, Ciudadanos.
4 Castells, *The City and the Grassroots*, 254.
5 Larson, *Constructing and Resisting Modernity*, 27.
6 Corsín Jiménez, "Three Traps Many," 12.
7 Corsín Jiménez, "The Right to Architecture," 346.

8. Lefebvre, *The Production of Space*, 31.
9. Boehm, "Popular Theatre as Space and Symbol of the Spanish Democratic Revolution," 1086. See Muñoz Caliz for a brief overview of notable dramas of the twenty-first century. It is beyond the scope of this book to treat these works, as my concern is with urban space and Lavapiés. See also the issue of *Romance Quarterly* (2018) edited by Esther Fernández and David Rodríguez-Solás, focused on marginalized theater practices in Spain.
10. Rocío García, "El sector del teatro se desangra por el 'devastador' aumento del IVA.' *El País*, 21 March 2013. https://elpais.com/cultura/2013/03/21/actualidad/1363872815_952612.html.
11. Boehm, "Popular Theatre as Space and Symbol of the Spanish Democratic Revolution," 1087.
12. Oñoro Otero, "Otras maneras de habitar el espacio urbano," 377–93.
13. Ibid., 379–81.
14. See Feinberg, "*Don Juan Tenorio* in the Campo de Cebada" and "The Violence of Everyday Life."
15. See Vilaseca, "Triball Case: 'Okupación Creativa ¡Ya!' vs. Okupa Hacktivismo" for more information about issues of gentrification in the TriBall neighborhood.
16. The theaters included in the consortium include the Teatro del Barrio, La escalera de Jacob, el Umbral de primavera, Teatro Circo Price, Sala la Mirador, Centro Dramático Nacional Teatro Valle-Inclán, La Casa Encendida, Mínima Espacio Escénico, la Tortuga de Lavapiés, Sala-bar OFF Latina, El Paticano de Leo Bassi, Nuevo Teatro Fronterizo.
17. See the Dossier and Manifiesto of the organization at their home page http://www.lavapiesbarriodeteatros.es/.
18. Teatro del Barrio, "Dossier." http://www.lavapiesbarriodeteatros.es/.
19. Ibid., "Proyecto Barrio," 2019. https://teatrodelbarrio.com/proyecto-barrio/.
20. Ibid.
21. Mariano Rajoy was Spanish prime minister from 2011 to 2018 and the head of the Popular Party when this scandal unfolded.
22. Palacio Ortiz, "*El Rey*, de Alberto San Juan," 377.
23. Castells, *The City and the Grassroots*, 216.

Bibliography

ARCHIVAL MATERIAL

Girón, Antonio. "Olimpia inauguración." Archives of Antonio Girón. 21 February 2006. DVD.
"Informe de las actividades del centro social okupado El Laboratorio."Archives of Traficantes de Sueño, 15 May 2009.
Instituto Nacional de Las Artes Escénicas y de la Música (INAEM).
"Teatro Valle-Inclán." Ministerio de Cultura, Madrid, 2006. Archives of the Teatro Valle-Inclán.
"Manifiesto en defensa de la okupación y de los espacios autogestionados." Archives of Traficantes de Sueño. February 1999. Accessed 15 May 2009.
"Revista Caminada y otras actividades en Lab003." Agencia de Noticias de Información Alternativa. 2 February 2003. Accessed 7 July 2010. http://ania.urcm.net/spip.php?article4475.

FILMS AND DOCUMENTARIES

Animalario. "Alejandro y Ana. Lo que España no pudo ver del banquete de la boda de la hija del presidente." 99 min. 29 June 2016. https://www.youtube.com/watch?v=1zTKhyZZkYo.
García Ortiz, Alberto, and Agatha Maciaszek, *A ras de suelo*. Documentary, 93 min. 2006. https://www.youtube.com/watch?v=zJThpnqdP9U.
Menéndez, Fernando, co-dir. *Laboratorio 03: Ocupando el vacío*. Spain, Kinowo Media, 2007. DVD. 72 mins. https://vimeo.com/37888018.

Ramsis, Básel. *El otro lado: un acercamiento a Lavapiés*. Dayra Arts, 2002. 111 minutes. DVD.

INTERVIEWS AND PERSONAL COMMUNICATION

Corcuera, Laura, and Belén Rubira, 15 June 2009.
Durán, Gloria, 11 June 2012.
García de Paredes, Ángela. 10 June 2009.
López Mozo, Jerónimo, 20 May 2009.
Mayorga, Juan. Personal Communication, 19 November 2009.
Planell, David. Personal Communication, 9 March 2009.
Osana, Manuel, 5 June 2009.
Rivero, Jacobo. Personal Communication, 8 June 2009.
Vidania, Carlos, 9 June 2009.

NEWSPAPERS AND MAGAZINES

ABC Madrid
20 minutos
El Confidencial
The Economist
Fortune
El Mundo
The New Yorker
El País
The Wall Street Journal

PUBLISHED SECONDARY SOURCES

Adell Argilés, Ramón. "Introducción." In *¿Dónde están las llaves? El movimiento okupa: prácticas y contextos sociales*, edited by Ramón Adell Argilés and Miguel Martínez López, 21–2. Madrid: La Catarata, 2004.

Adell Argilés, Ramón, and Miguel Martínez López, eds. *¿Dónde están las llaves? El movimiento okupa: prácticas y contextos sociales*. Madrid: La Catarata, 2004.

Agnew, John. "The Dramaturgy of Horizons: Geographical Scale in the 'Reconstruction of Italy' by the New Italian Political Parties." *Political Geography* 16, no. 2 (1997): 99–121.

–. "Space and Place." *The Sage Handbook of Geographical Knowledge*, edited by John Agnew and David Livingstone, 316–30. London and Thousand Oaks, CA: Sage Publications, 2011.

Aguilera Sastre, Juan. *El debate sobre el Teatro Nacional en España (1900–1939): ideología y estética*. Madrid: Centro de Documentación Teatral, 2002.

Alier, Roger. *La zarzuela*. Barcelona: Robinbook, 2002.

Allen, John J. *Reconstruction of a Spanish Golden Age Playhouse: el corral del Príncipe, 1583–1744*. Gainesville, FL: University Press of Florida, 1983.

Álvarez del Manzano y López del Hierro, José María. "Presentación." In *Madrid: cuatro años de gestión del Plan General de Ordenación Urbana de Madrid 1997*, edited by Javier Echenagusia, 5. Madrid: Gerencia Municipal de Urbanismo del Ayuntamiento de Madrid, 2002.

Anderson, Benedict. *Imagined Communities: Reflections on the Origin and Spread of Nationalism*. 2nd ed. London and New York: Verso, 1991.

Andréu Mediero, Esther, and Verónica Paños Cubillo. "Nuevas propuestas de ubicación espacial de la judería medieval de Madrid." *Revista Historia Autónoma* 1 (2012): 53–72.

Antebi, Andrés, and José Sánchez. "Plazas Fuertes: de Midán Tahrir a la Plaça de Catalunya, Espacio público y revueltas populares contemporáneas." In *¡Ocupemos el mundo: Occupy the World!* edited by Joseba Fernández, Carlos Sevilla, and Miguel Urbán, 67–83. Barcelona: Icaria Editorial, 2012.

Arellano, Ignacio. *Historia del teatro español del siglo XVII*. Madrid: Cátedra, 1995.

Bairoch, Paul. *Cities and Economic Development: From the Dawn of History to the Present*. Translated by Christopher Braider. Chicago: University of Chicago Press, 1991.

Baker, Edward. "Historical Perspectives: From Madrid as *Villa y Corte* to *After Carmena, What?*" In *Cartographies of Madrid: Contesting Urban Space at the Crossroads of the Global South and Global North*. Hispanic Issues, no. 43, edited by Silvia Bermúdez and Anthony L. Geist, 173–85. Nashville, TN: Vanderbilt University Press, 2019.

–, and Malcolm Compitello, eds. *Madrid de Fortunata a la M-40: un siglo de cultura urbana*. Madrid: Alianza, 2003.

Barrado Timón, Diego. "Gran ciudad y turismo en la transición postindustrial: nuevos y viejos procesos, nuevas y viejas teorías. El ejemplo del área metropolitana de Madrid." *Scripta Nova: Revista electrónica de geografía y ciencias sociales* 14, no. 317 (2010). https://revistes.ub.edu/index.php/ScriptaNova/article/view/1623.

Baudrillard, Jean. *Simulacra and Simulation.* 1981. Translated by Sheila Faria Glaser. Ann Arbor: University of Michigan Press, 1994.

Bauer-Funke, Cerstin, ed. *Espacios urbanos en el teatro español de los siglos XX y XXI.* Hildesheim: Georg Olms Verlag, 2016.

Berlinches Acín, Amparo, ed. *Arquitectura de Madrid: casco histórico.* Madrid: Fundación COAM, 2003.

Berman, Marshall. *All That Is Solid Melts into Air: The Experience of Modernity.* London: Penguin, 1982.

Bermúdez, Silvia, and Anthony L. Geist. *Cartographies of Madrid: Contesting Urban Space at the Crossroads of the Global South and Global North.* Hispanic Issues, no. 43. Nashville, TN: Vanderbilt University Press, 2019.

Boehm, Scott. "Popular Theatre as Space and Symbol of the Spanish Democratic Revolution." *Bulletin of Hispanic Studies* 95, no. 10 (2018): 1085–106.

Bonet Correa, Antonio. "La Puerta del Sol, corazón y 'cogollo' de Madrid." In *La Real Casa de Correos, 1756/1998: Sede de la Presidencia de la Comunidad de Madrid,* edited by Antonio Bonet Correa, Carlos Sambricio, and José María Fernández-Isla, 17–27. Madrid: Dirección General de Arquitectura y Vivienda, 1998.

–. Carlos Sambricio, and José María Fernández-Isla, eds. *La Real Casa de Correos, 1756/1998: Sede de la Presidencia de la Comunidad de Madrid.* Madrid: Dirección General de Arquitectura y Vivienda, 1998.

Borges, Jorge Luis. "The Aleph." 1945. In *Collected Fictions/Jorge Luis Borges.* Translated by Andrew Hurley, 274–86. New York: Viking, 1998.

Borreli, Mary. "Valle-Inclán: Poet of Sarcasm." *Hispania* 44, no. 2 (1961), 266–8.

Bravo Morata, Federico. *Los nombres de las calles de Madrid.* 1970. 2nd ed. Madrid: Fenicia, 1984.

Brenner, Neil. "The Limits to Scale? Methodological Reflections on Scalar Structuration." *Progress in Human Geography* 25, no. 4 (2001): 591–614.

–, and Nik Theodore. *Spaces of Neoliberalism: Urban Restructuring in North America and Northern Europe.* Oxford: Blackwell Publishers, 2002.

Bürger, Peter. *Theory of the Avant-Garde.* 1974. Translated by Michael Shaw. Minneapolis, MN: University of Minnesota Press, 1984.

Campbell, Jodi. *Monarchy, Political Culture, and Drama in Seventeenth-Century Madrid: Theater of Negotiation*. Burlington, VT: Ashgate, 2006.

Candela Soto, Paloma. *Cigarreras madrileñas: trabajo y vida, 1888–1927*. Madrid: Tecnos, 1997.

Carbajo Isla, María F. *La población de la Villa de Madrid: desde finales del siglo XVI hasta mediados del siglo XIX*. Madrid: Siglo XXI, 1987.

Caridad, Eva Castro. "El arte escénico en la edad media." In *Historia del teatro español I: de la edad media a los siglos de oro*, edited by Javier Huerta Calvo, 55–83. Madrid: Gredos, 2003.

Carreño-Rodríguez, Antonio. *Alegorías del poder: crisis imperial y comedia nueva (1598–1659)*. Suffolk, UK: Tamesis, 2009.

Casey, James. *Early Modern Spain: A Social History*. New York: Routledge, 1999.

Castañeda, Ernesto. "The *Indignados* of Spain: A Precedent to Occupy Wall Street." *Social Movement Studies: Journal of Social, Cultural, and Political Protest* 12, no. 1 (2012): 309–19.

Castells, Manuel. *The City and the Grassroots: A Cross-Cultural Theory of Urban Social Movements*. Berkeley: University of California Press, 1983.

–. *Networks of Outrage and Hope: Social Movements in the Internet Age*. New York: Polity, 2012.

–. *The Rise of the Network Society*. Oxford: Blackwell Publishers, 1996.

–, João Caraça, and Gustavo Cardoso, eds. *Aftermath: The Cultures of the Economic Crisis*. Oxford: Oxford University Press, 2012.

Castro-Rial Garrone, Amalia. "Prólogo." In *La Real Casa de Correos, 1756/1998: Sede de la Presidencia de la Comunidad de Madrid*, edited by Antonio Bonet Correa, Carlos Sambricio, and José María Fernández-Isla, 13–24. Madrid: Dirección General de Arquitectura y Vivienda, 1998.

Certeau, Michel de. *The Practice of Everyday Life*. Translated by Steven Rendall. Berkeley: University of California Press, 1984.

Charlon, Julien, ed. *Labo 03 Lavapiés, Madrid*. Madrid: Traficantes de Sueños, 2004.

–. *Mundo Lavapiés. Libro-DVD Participativo*. Madrid: Atelier, 2006.

Coleman, Jeffrey K. *The Necropolitical Theater: Race and Immigration on the Contemporary Spanish Stage*. Evanston, IL: Northwestern University Press, 2020.

Compitello, Malcolm. "A Good Plan Gone Bad: From Operation Atocha to the Gentrification of Lavapiés." *International Journal of the Constructed Environment* 2, no. 2 (2012): 75–93.

—. "From Planning to Design: The Culture of Flexible Accumulation in Post-Cambio Madrid." *Arizona Journal of Hispanic Cultural Studies* 3 (1999): 199–219.

Constitución española. *Boletín Oficial de Estado*, no. 311, 29 diciembre de 1978, 29313–424 https://www.boe.es/eli/es/c/1978/12/27/(1).

Conversi, Daniele. *The Basques, the Catalans, and Spain: Alternative Routes to Nationalist Mobilization*. Reno and Las Vegas: University of Nevada Press, 1997.

Corsín Jiménez, Alberto. "Three Traps Many." *Culturas tecnocientíficas*. 16 May 2013. Accessed 10 December 2020. https://etnografiatecnociencias.wordpress.com/2013/04/24/three-traps-many-por-alberto-corsin-jimenez-16-de-mayo-miercoles/.

—. "The Right to Infrastructure: A Prototype for Open Source Urbanism." *Environment and Planning D: Society and Space* 32 (2014): 342–62.

—, and Adolfo Estalella. "The Atmospheric Person: Value, Experiment, and Making Neighbors." HAU: *Journal of Ethnographic Theory* 3, no. 2 (2013): 119–39

Coso Marín, Miguel Ángel, and Juan Sanz Ballesteros. "El corral de comedias de Alcalá de Henares y los corrales de Madrid." In *Cuatro siglos de teatro en Madrid: Museo Municipal, Teatro Albéniz, Teatro Español, Teatro María Guerrero, mayo-junio 1992*, edited by Andrés Peláez and Fernanda Andura, 21–32. Madrid: Consorcio para la Organización de Madrid, Capital Europea de la Cultura, 1992.

Cruz, Ramón de la. "Los bandos de Lavapiés." In *Doce Sainetes*, edited by José-Francisco Gatti, 243–64. Barcelona: Editorial Labor, 1972.

—. "Manolo, tragedia para reír o sainete para llorar." In *Doce Sainetes*, edited by José-Francisco Gatti, 103–21. Barcelona: Editorial Labor, 1972.

D'Antuono, Nancy L. "La comedia española en la Italia del siglo XVII: la commedia dell'arte." In *La comedia española y el teatro europeo del siglo XVII*, edited by Henry W. Sullivan, Raúl A. Galoppe, and Mahlon L. Stoutz, 1–36. Suffolk, UK: Tamesis, 1999.

Debord, Guy. *The Society of the Spectacle*. Translated by Ken Knabb. London: Rebel, 1992.

Dehesa, Guillermo de la. *La primera gran crisis financiera del siglo XXI: orígenes, detonante, efectos, respuestas y remedios*. Madrid: Alianza, 2009.

Delaney, David, and Helga Leitner. "The Political Construction of Scale." *Political Geography* 16, no. 2 (1997): 93–7.

Delgado, Manuel. *El animal público: hacia una antropología de los espacios urbanos*. Barcelona: Anagrama, 1993.

–. *La ciudad mentirosa: fraude y miseria del "Modelo Barcelona."* Madrid: Catarata, 2010.

Díaz Orueta, Fernando. "Los grandes proyectos de desarrollo urbano y la reconfiguración socio-espacial de las ciudades: el barrio de Lavapiés (Madrid)." *Cuaderno urbano* 6 (2007): 169–94.

Díez Borque, José María. *Sociología de la comedia española del siglo XVII.* Madrid: Cátedra, 1976.

Dodgson, Elyse, and Mary Peate, eds. *Spanish Plays: New Spanish and Catalan Drama.* London: Nick Hern Books, 1999.

Doménech, Fernando Rico. "El arte escénico en el siglo XVIII." In *Historia del teatro breve en España*, edited by Javier Huerta Calvo, 519–46. Madrid: Iberoamericana, 2008.

Dougherty, Dru. "La ciudad moderna y los esperpentos de Valle-Inclán." *Anales de la literatura española contemporánea*, 22, no. 1 (1997): 131–47.

–. "Theatre and Culture, 1868–1936." In *The Cambridge Companion to Modern Spanish Culture*, edited by David T. Gies, 211–21. Cambridge: Cambridge University Press, 1999.

–. *Un Valle-Inclán olvidado.* Madrid: Fundamentos, 1983.

Durán, Gloria G., and Alan W. Moore. "La Tabacalera of Lavapiés: A Social Experiment or a Work of Art?" *Field: A Journal of Socially-Engaged Art Criticism*, no. 2 (2015): 49–75.

Echenagusia, Javier, ed. *Madrid: cuatro años de gestión del Plan General de Ordenación Urbana 1997.* Madrid: Gerencia Municipal de Urbanismo del Ayuntamiento de Madrid, 2002.

Empresa Municipal de la Vivienda. Áreas de Rehabilitación Preferente: intervenciones en el centro histórico y barrios periféricos de Madrid (España), *1994–1999*. Madrid: Ayuntamiento de Madrid, 1999.

Elliot, John H. *Imperial Spain, 1469–1716.* London: Penguin Books, 2002.

Escobar, Jesús. *The Plaza Mayor and the Shaping of Baroque Madrid.* Cambridge: Cambridge University Press, 2003.

Escriche, Juanjo Martín. "El teatro de kif." In *Mundo Lavapiés. Libro-DVD Participativo*, edited by Julien Charlon, 99. Madrid: Atelier, 2006.

Espín Templado, Pilar. "El casticismo del Género Chico." In *Casticismo y literatura en España*, edited by Ana-Sofía Pérez-Bustamente Mourier and Alberto Romero Ferrer, 25–58. Cádiz: Servicio de Publicaciones, Universidad de Cádiz, 1992.

Etxeberría, Lucía. *Cosmofobia.* Madrid: Destino, 2007.

Feixa, Carlos, Carmen Costa, and Joan Pallarés. *Movimientos juveniles en la Península Ibérica: graffitis, grifotas, okupas.* Barcelona: Ariel, 2002.

Feinberg, Matthew I. "*Don Juan Tenorio* in the Campo de Cebada: Restaging Urban Space after 15-M." *Journal of Spanish Cultural Studies* 15, no. 1–2 (2014): 143–59.

–. "From Cigarreras to Indignados: Spectacles of Scale in the CSA La Tabacalera of Lavapiés, Madrid." *International Journal of Iberian Studies* 26, no. 1–2 (2013): 21–39.

–. "Urban Space, Spectacle, and Articulations of the Local and the National in Jerónimo López Mozo's *El arquitecto y el relojero.*" *Romance Quarterly* 60, no. 3 (2013): 125–36.

–. "The Violence of Everyday Life: Lope de Vega's *Fuente Ovejuna* as Urban Allegory." *Revista de Estudios Hispánicos* 53, no. 2 (2019): 727–51.

–, and Susan Larson. "Cultivating the Square: Trash, Recycling, and the Cultural Ecology of Post-Crisis Madrid." *Ethics of Life: Contemporary Iberian Debates.* Hispanic Issues Series 42 (2016): 113–42

Fernández, Esther, and David Rodríguez-Solás. "Marginality in Spanish Theater, Part 1" *Romance Quarterly* 65, no. 1 (2018): 175–9.

Férnandez, Joseba, and Carlos Sevilla y Miguel Urbán, eds. *¡Ocupemos el mundo: Occupy the World!* Barcelona: Icaria, 2012.

Fernández de Montesinos, José. *Costumbrismo y novela: ensayo sobre el redescubrimiento de la realidad española.* Berkeley: University of California Press, 1960.

Fernández-Isla, José María. "La Real Casa de Correos: rehabilitación." In *La Real Casa de Correos 1756/1998: Sede de la Presidencia de la Comunidad de Madrid*, edited by Antonio Bonet Correa, Carlos Sambricio, and José María Fernández-Isla, 55–60. Madrid: Dirección General de Arquitectura y Vivienda, 1998.

Fernández-Savater, Amador. "El nacimiento de un nuevo poder social." *Hispanic Review* 80, no. 12 (2012): 667–81.

Fita, Padre Miguel. "La judería de Madrid en 1391." *Boletín de la Real Academia de la Historia* 8 (1886): 439–66.

Florida, Richard. *Flight of the Creative Class: The New Global Competition for Talent.* New York: Harper Collins, 2005.

–. *The Rise of the Creative Class.* New York: Basic Books, 2002.

Flynn, Maureen. "The Spectacle of Suffering in Spanish Streets." In *City and Spectacle in Medieval Europe*, edited by Barbara Hanawalt and Kathryn Reyerson, 153–68. Minneapolis: University of Minnesota Press, 1994.

Fontanella, Lee. *La imprenta y las letras en la España romántica.* Berne: Peter Lang, 1982.

Foucault, Michel. "*Security, Territory, Population: Lectures at the Collège de France, 1977–1978.*" Edited by Michael Senallart. Translated by Graham Burchell. New York: Palgrave Macmillan, 2009.
Fox, Inman. *La invención de España: nacionalismo liberal e identidad nacional*. Madrid: Cátedra, 1997.
Franck, Karen A., and Te-Sheng Huang. "Occupy Wall Street, Social Movements, and Contested Public Space." In *Beyond Zuccotti Park: Freedom of Assembly and the Occupation of Public Space*, edited by Ron Shiffman, Rick Bell, Lance Jay Brown, and Lynne Elizabeth, 3–20. New York: New Village Press, 2012.
Fraser, Benjamin. *Henri Lefebvre and the Spanish Urban Experience*. Lewisburg, PA: Bucknell University Press, 2011.
Froldi, Rinaldo. "Anticipaciones dieciochescas del costumbrismo romántico." *Romanticismo* 6 (1996): 163–70.
Frost, Daniel. *Cultivating Madrid: Public Space and Middle-Class Culture in the Spanish Capital, 1833–1890*. Lewisburg, PA: Bucknell University Press, 2008.
Fusi Aizpurúa, Juan Pablo, and Jordi Palafox Gámir. *España, 1808–1996: el desafío de la modernidad*. Madrid: Espasa-Calpe, 1997.
Ganelin, Charles, and Howard Mancing. eds. *The Golden Age Comedia: Text, Theory, and Performance*. West Lafayette, IN: Purdue University Press, 1994.
García, Bernardo J., and María Luisa Lobato, eds. *Dramaturgia festiva y cultura nobiliaria en el siglo de oro*. Madrid: Iberoamericana, 2007.
García de Sola, Ignacio del Río. "Introducción." In *Madrid: cuatro años de gestión del Plan General de Ordenación Urbana de Madrid 1997*, edited by Javier Echenagusia, 6–7. Madrid: Gerencia Municipal de Urbanismo del Ayuntamiento de Madrid, 2002.
García Pérez, Eva. "Gentrificación en Madrid: de la burbuja a la crisis." *Revista de Geografía Norte Grande* 58 (2014): 71–91.
García Sánchez, María Luísa. "Las cigarreras madrileñas." *Revista de Folklore* 13, no. 147 (1993): 91–7.
García Santo-Tomás, Enrique. *Espacio urbano y creación literaria en el Madrid de Felipe IV*. Madrid: Iberoamericana, 2004.
Gea, María Isabel. *Centro*. Madrid: La Librería, 2000.
Gelman, Juan. "Cuentos espaciales (apotegmas sobre la okupación)." *El viejo topo*, no. 122 (1998): 38–43.
Gies, David T., ed. *The Cambridge History of Spanish Literature*. Cambridge: Cambridge University Press, 2004.

—. *The Cambridge Companion to Modern Spanish Culture*. Cambridge: Cambridge University Press, 1999.
Gil, Javier, and Jorge Sequera. "Expansión de la ciudad turística y nuevas resistencias. El caso de Airbnb en Madrid." *Empiria: Revista de Metodología de Ciencias Sociales*, no. 41 (2018): 15–32. DOI/ empiria.41.2018.22602.
Gómez, Mayte. "El barrio de Lavapiés, laboratorio de interculturalidad." *Dissidences: Hispanic Journal of Theory and Criticism* 1, no. 2, (2006): 1–42. https://digitalcommons.bowdoin.edu/dissidences/vol1/iss2/12.
Gómez de la Serna, Ramón. *La historia de la Puerta del Sol*. 3rd ed. 1920. Madrid: Almarabu, 1998.
Gómez Labad, Jose María. *El Madrid de la Zarzuela: visión regocijada de un pasado en cantables*. Madrid: Editorial Tres, 1983.
González Esteban, Carlos. *Madrid: sinopsis de su evolución urbana*. Madrid: La librería, 2001.
Graham, Helen, and Jo Labanyi. "Culture and Modernity: The Case of Spain." In *Spanish Cultural Studies: An Introduction. The Struggle for Modernity*, edited by Helen Graham and Jo Labanyi, 1–18. Oxford: Oxford University Press, 1995.
Greer, Margaret. "The Development of a National Theater." In *The Cambridge History of Spanish Literature*, edited by David Gies, 238–50. Cambridge: Cambridge University Press, 2009.
Grupo Surrealista de Madrid. "Aviso para la próxima demolición del Nuevo Teatro Olimpia." In *Mundo Lavapiés. Libro-DVD Participativo*, edited by Julien Charlon, 90–2. Madrid: Atelier, 2006.
Gutiérrez Carabajo, Franciso. "La ciudad como utopía y antiutopía en el teatro español actual." In *Espacios urbanos en el teatro español de los siglos XX y XXI*, edited by Cerstin Bauer-Funke, 323–51. Hildesheim: Georg Olms Verlag, 2016.
Haidt, Rebecca. "Los Majos, el 'españolísimo gremio' del teatro popular dieciochesco: sobre casticismo, inestabilidad y abyección." *Cuadernos de Historia Moderna* 10 (2011): 155–73.
—. "Visibly Modern Madrid: Mesonero, Visual Culture, and the Apparatus of Urban Reform." In *Visualizing Spanish Modernity*, edited by Susan Larson and Eva Woods, 24–45. Oxford and New York: Berg, 2005.
Hanawalt, Barbara, and Kathryn Reyerson, eds. *City and Spectacle in Medieval Europe*. Minneapolis: University of Minnesota Press, 1994.
Hansen, Thomas Blom, and Finn Stepputat, eds. *Sovereign Bodies: Citizens, Migrants, and States in the Postcolonial World*. Princeton, NJ: Princeton University Press, 2005.

Hardin, Garrett. "The Tragedy of the Commons." *Science* 162 (1968): 1243–8.
Harney, Lucy D. "Costumbrismo and the Ideology of Género Chico." *Ojáncano* 22 (2002): 33–58.
–. "Controlling Resistance, Resisting Control: The *género chico* and the Dynamics of Mass Entertainment in Late Nineteenth-Century Spain." *Arizona Journal of Hispanic Cultural Studies* 10 (2006): 151–67.
Harvey, David. "The Art of Rent: Globalization and the Commodification of Culture." In *Spaces of Capital. Towards a Critical Geography*, 394–411. New York: Routledge, 2001.
–. *The Condition of Postmodernity*. Oxford: Blackwell Publishers, 1990.
–. "From Managerialism to Entrepreneurialism: The Transformation in Urban Governance in Late Capitalism." *Geografiska Annaler. Series B. Human Geography* 71, no.1 (1989): 3–17.
–. *The Limits to Capital*. 1982. London: Verso, 1999.
–. *Paris, Capital of Modernity*. New York: Routledge, 2003.
–. *Rebel Cities: From the Right to the City to the Urban Revolution*. London: Verso, 2012.
–. *The Urban Experience*. Baltimore, MD: Johns Hopkins University Press, 1989.
Herr, Richard. "Flow and Ebb." In *Spain: A History*, edited by Raymond Carr, 173–204. Oxford: Oxford University Press, 2000.
Herrera de la Muela, María Teresa. "*La verbena de la Paloma* y el mito popular madrileño." PhD diss., University of Kentucky, 2004.
Herzberger, David K. *Narrating the Past: Fiction and Historiography in Postwar Spain*. Durham, NC: Duke University Press, 1995.
Hill, Christopher. *Olympic Politics: Athens to Atlanta, 1896–1996*. 2nd ed. Manchester, UK: Manchester University Press, 1996.
Howitt, R. "Scale as Relation: Musical Metaphors of Geographical Scale." *Area* 30 (1998): 49–58.
Iarocci, Michael. "Romantic Prose, Journalism, and *costumbrismo*." In *The Cambridge History of Spanish Literature*, edited by David T. Gies, 381–91. Cambridge: Cambridge University Press, 2004.
Ibarra, Pedro, and Benjamin Tejerina, eds. *Los movimientos sociales: Transformaciones políticas y cambio cultural*. Madrid: Trotta, 1998.
Jacobs, Jane. *The Death and Life of Great American Cities*. New York: Vintage, 1992.
Juliá, Santos. "History, Politics, and Culture, 1975–1996." In *The Cambridge Companion to Modern Spanish Culture*, edited by David T. Gies, 104–20. Cambridge: Cambridge University Press, 1999.

–. "Madrid Capital del Estado (1833–1993)." In *Madrid: historia de una capital*, edited by Juliá Santos, David Ringrose, and Cristina Segura, 317–576. Madrid: Alianza, 2000.

–. David Ringrose, and Cristina Segura. *Madrid: historia de una capital*. Madrid: Alianza, 1994.

Kamen, Henry. *Spain: 1469–1714*. 3rd ed. London: Pearson Longman, 2005.

Kasten, Carey. *The Cultural Politics of Twentieth-Century Theater: Representing the Auto Sacramental*. Lewisburg, PA: Bucknell University Press, 2012.

Kearns, Gerry, and Chris Philo. *Selling Places: The City as Cultural Capital, Past and Present*. Oxford: Pergamon Press, 1993.

Labrador Méndez, Germán. "Afterword: Regarding the Spain of Others: Sociopolitical Framing of New Literatures/Cultures in Democratic Spain." In *New Spain, New Literatures*, edited by Luis Martín-Estudillo and Nicholas Spadaccini, 261–76. Nashville, TN: Vanderbilt University Press, 2010.

–. "Las vidas 'subprime': la circulación de 'historias de vida' como tecnología de imaginación política en la crisis española (2007–2012)." *Hispanic Review* 80, no. 4 (2012): 557–81.

Larson, Susan. *Constructing and Resisting Modernity: Madrid, 1900–1936*. Madrid: Iberoamericana, 2011.

Lees, Loretta. "Rethinking Gentrification: Beyond the Positions of Economics or Culture." *Progress in Human Geography* 18, no. 2 (1994): 137–50.

–. Tom Slater, and Elvin Wyly. *Gentrification*. New York: Routledge, 2008.

–, Hyun Bang Shin and Ernesto López Morales. "Introduction: 'Gentrification' – a Global Urban Process?" In *Global Gentrifications: Uneven Development and Displacement*, edited by Loretta Lees, Hyun Bang Shin, and Ernesto López Morales, 1–18. Bristol, UK: Policy Press, 2015.

Lefebvre, Henri. *Introduction to Modernity*. 1962. Translated by John Moore. London: Verso, 1995.

–. *The Production of Space*. 1974. Translated by Donald Nicholson-Smith. Oxford, UK: Blackwell Publishers, 1991.

–. *Writings on Cities*. Edited by Eleonore Kofman and Elizabeth Lebas. Oxford, UK: Blackwell Publishers, 1996.

Leitner, Helga, and Byron Miller. "Scale and the Limitations of Ontological Debate: A Commentary on Marston, Jones, and

Woodward." *Transactions of the Institute of British Geographers* 32, no. 1 (2007): 116–25.

–, Eric Sheppard, and Kristin M. Sziarto. "The Spatialities of Contentious Politics." *Transactions of the Institute of British Geographers* 33, no. 2 (2008): 157–72.

Leonard, Candyce, and John P. Gabriele, eds. *Panorámica del teatro español actual*. Madrid: Editorial Fundamentos, 1996.

–. "Fórmula para una dramaturgia española de finales de siglo." *Panorámica del teatro español actual*, edited by Candyce Leonard and John P. Gabriele, 7–21. Madrid: Editorial Fundamentos, 1996.

Ley de Memoria Histórica. Boletín Oficial del Estado (BOE). 27 December 2007. Accessed 10 April 2011. http://www.boe.es/boe/dias/2007/12/27/pdfs/A53410-53416.pdf.

Lloyd, Richard, and Terry Nichols Clark. "The City as Entertainment Machine." In *Critical Perspectives on Urban Redevelopment* (Research in Urban Sociology, Vol. 6), edited by Kevin Fox, 357–78. Bingley, UK: Emerald Group, 2001.

Lobato, María Luisa. "Nobles como actores: el papel activo de las gentes de palacio en las representaciones cortesanas de la época de los Austrias." In *Dramaturgia festiva y cultura nobiliaria en el siglo de oro*, edited by Bernardo J. García and María Luisa Lobato, 89–114. Madrid: Iberoamericana, 2007.

López, Isidro, and Emmanuel Rodríguez. "The Spanish Model." *New Left Review* 69 (2011): 5–29.

López Llera, César. *Un chivo en la Corte del botellón o Valle Inclán en Lavapiés*. Elorrio, Spain: Artezblai, 2005.

López Mozo, Jerónimo. *Ahlán*. Madrid: Ediciones Cultura Hispánica, Agencia Española de Cooperación Internacional, 1997.

–. *El arquitecto y el relojero*. Alicante, Spain: Edita Muestra de Teatro Español de Autores Contemporáneos de Alicante, 2001.

–. "El 'Nuevo Teatro Español' durante la transición: una llama viva." In *Entre Actos: Diálogos sobre teatro español entre siglos*, edited by Martha T. Halsey and Phyllis Zatlin, 17–22. University Park, PA: Estreno, 1999.

Lorenz, Philip. *The Tears of Sovereignty: Perspectives of Power in Renaissance Drama*. New York: Fordham University Press, 2013.

Lowe, Stuart. *Urban Social Movements: The City after Castells*. London: Macmillan, 1986.

Lozano Barolozzi, María del Mar. *Historia del urbanismo en España II: siglos XVI, XVII y XVIII*. Madrid: Cátedra, 2011.

Luna-García, Antonio. "Cities of Spain: Localities on the Edge of an Identity Breakdown." *Cities* 20, no. 6 (2003): 377–9.
Madroñal Durán, Abraham, and Héctor Urzáiz Tortajada. "Introduction." In *Historia del teatro español I: de la edad media a los siglos de oro*, edited by Javier Huerta Calvo, 35–54. Madrid: Gredos, 2003.
Maravall, José Antonio. *La cultura del barroco: análisis de una estructura histórica*. Barcelona: Ariel, 1975.
–. *Teatro y literatura en la sociedad barroca*. Madrid: Benzal, 1972.
Marston, Sallie A. "The Social Construction of Scale." *Progress in Human Geography* 24, no. 2 (2000): 219–42.
–, John Paul Jones II, and Keith Woodward. "Human Geography without Scale" *Transactions of the Institute of British Geographers* 30, no. 4 (2005): 416–32.
Martin, Carole. *Theatre of the Real*. New York: Palgrave Macmillan, 2013.
Martín-Estudillo, Luis, and Nicholas Spadaccini. "Introduction: Contemporary Spanish Literature: Enduring Plurality." In *New Spain, New Literatures*, edited by Luis Martín-Estudillo and Nicholas Spadacini, ix–xvii. Nashville, TN: Vanderbilt University Press, 2010.
–, eds. *New Spain, New Literatures*. Nashville, TN: Vanderbilt University Press, 2010.
Martínez López, Miguel. "Del urbanismo a la autogestión: una historia posible del movimiento de okupación en España." In *¿Dónde están las llaves? El movimiento okupa: prácticas y contextos sociales*, edited by Ramón Adell Argilés and Miguel Martínez López, 61–88. Madrid: La Catarata, 2004.
–. "How Do Squatters Deal with the State? Legalization and Autonomous Institutionalization in Madrid." *International Journal of Urban and Regional Research* 38, no. 2 (March 2014): 646–74.
–. *Okupaciones de viviendas y de centros sociales: Autogestión, contracultura y conflictos urbanos*. Barcelona: Virus, 2002.
–, and Ángela García Bernardos. "Ocupar las plazas, liberar edificios." *ACME: An International E-Journal for Critical Geographies* 14 (2015): 157–84.
–, eds. *Okupa Madrid (1985–2011). Memoria, reflexión, debate y autogestión colectiva del conocimiento*. Madrid: Edita, 2014.
Mayorga, Juan. "Prólogo." In *Animalario: Bonitas historias de entretenimiento sobre la humillación cotidiana de existir*, edited by Animalario (Grupo teatral), 7. Madrid: Plaza Janés, 2005.
–, and Juan Cavestany. "Alejandro y Ana. Lo que España no pudo ver del banquete de la boda de la hija del presidente." In *Animalario: bonitas*

historias de entretenimiento sobre la humillación cotidiana de existir, edited by Animalario (Grupo teatral), 277–301. Madrid: Plaza Janés, 2005.

McKendrick, Melveena. *Theatre in Spain, 1490–1700*. Cambridge: Cambridge University Press Archive, 1992.

–. *Playing the King: Lope de Vega and the Limits of Conformity*. Suffolk, UK: Tamesis, 2000.

Méndez Gutiérrez del Valle, Ricardo, Jesús Tébar Arjona, Luis Daniel Abad Aragón. "Economía del conocimiento y calidad del empleo en la región metropolitana de Madrid: una perspectiva crítica." *Scripta Nova: Revista electrónica de geografía y ciencias sociales* 15, no. 380 (2011): n.p.

Merrifield, Andy. *Metromarxism: A Marxist Tale of the City*. London: Routledge, 2002.

Mesonero Romanos, Ramón. *El Antiguo Madrid: paseos histórico-anecdóticos por las calles y casas de esta villa*. 1861. Madrid: Dossat, 1986.

–. *Escenas matritenses: panorama matritense, escenas matritenses, tipos y caracteres*. 1842. Edited by María del Pilar Palomo. Barcelona: Planeta, 1987.

Molanes Rial, Mónica. "La ciudad y su doble en el teatro de Juan Mayorga." In *Espacios urbanos en el teatro español de los siglos XX y XXI*, edited by Cerstin Bauer-Funke, 209–16. Hildesheim: Georg Olms Verlag, 2016.

Moral Ruiz, Carmen del. "El género chico y la invención de Madrid: *La Gran Vía* (1886)." In *Madrid de Fortunata a la M-40: un siglo de cultura urbana*, edited by Edward Baker and Malcolm Compitello, 27–57. Madrid: Alianza, 2003.

–. "La mitificación de Madrid en el género chico." *Revista de Occidente*, no. 128 (1992): 69–82.

Morales Lomas, Francisco. "La lírica de Valle-Inclán: sistema rítmico y aspectos temático-simbólicos." *Anales de la literatura española contemporánea* 32, no. 3 (2005): 855–8.

Moreno-Caballud, Luis. *Cultures of Anyone: Studies on Democratization of Culture in the Spanish Neo-liberal Crisis*. Liverpool, UK: University of Liverpool Press, 2015.

–. "La imaginación sostenible: culturas y crisis económica en la España actual." *Hispanic Review*. Special Issue: *La imaginación sostenible: culturas y crisis económica en la España actual* 80, no. 4 (2012): 535–55.

Mugerauer, Robert. "Toward an Architectural Vocabulary: The Porch as Between." In *Dwelling, Seeing, and Designing: Towards a*

Phenomenological Ecology, edited by David Seamon, 103–28. Albany, NY: SUNY University Press Albany, 1993.

Mumford, Lewis. *The City in History: Its Origins, Its Transformations, and Its Prospects*. New York: Harcourt, Brace & World, 1961.

Muñoz Cáliz, Berta. "Madrid en el teatro español del siglo XXI." In *Espacios urbanos en el teatro español de los siglos XX y XXI*, edited by Cerstin Bauer-Funke, 281–99. Hildesheim: Georg Olms Verlag, 2016.

Nash, Elizabeth. *Madrid: A Cultural History*. Northampton, MA: Interlink Books, 2012.

Navarrete Moreno, Lorenzo. *La autopercepción de los jóvenes okupas en España*. Madrid: Ministerio de Trabajo y Asuntos Sociales, Instituto de Juventud, 1999.

Noyes, Dorothy. "La maja vestida: Dress as Resistance to Enlightenment in Late-18th-Century Madrid." *Journal of American Folklore* 111, no. 440 (1998): 197–217.

Observatorio Metropolitano. *Fin de ciclo: financiarización, territorio y sociedad de propietarios en la onda larga del capitalismo hispano (1959–2010)*. Madrid: Traficantes de Sueños, 2010.

–. *Madrid: ¿La suma de todos?: globalización, territorio, desigualdad*. Madrid: Traficantes de Sueños, 2007.

–. *Manifiesto por Madrid: crítica y crisis del modelo metropolitano*. Madrid: Traficantes de Sueños, 2009.

Oliva, César. *La última escena: teatro español de 1975 a nuestros días*. Madrid: Cátedra, 2004.

Oñoro Otero, Cristina. "Otras maneras de habitar el espacio urbano: los Nuevos Espacios y Formatos teatrales de Madrid (2008–2014)." In *Espacios urbanos en el teatro español de los siglos XX y XXI*, edited by Cerstin Bauer-Funke, 377–93. Hildesheim: Georg Olms Verlag, 2016.

Ostrom, Elinor. *Governing the Commons: The Evolution of Institutions for Collective Action*. Cambridge, UK: Cambridge University Press, 1990.

Owens, Linus. *Cracking under Pressure: Narrating the Decline of the Amsterdam Squatter's Movement*. Amsterdam: Amsterdam University Press, 2009.

Palacio Ortiz, Nortan. "*El Rey*, de Alberto San Juan como documento histórico." In *El teatro como documento artístico, histórico y cultural en los inicios del siglo XXI*, edited by José Romera Castillo, 375–84. Madrid: Editorial Verbum, 2017.

Parsons, Deborah. *A Cultural History of Madrid*. New York: Berg, 2003.

Paz Gago, José María. "Fiesta Culture in Madrid Posters, 1934–1955." In *Constructing Identity in Contemporary Spain: Theoretical Debates and Cultural Practice*, edited by Jo Labanyi, 178–206. Oxford: Oxford University Press, 2002.

—. "Luces de la ciudad: el Madrid imaginado en *Luces de bohemia*, de Ramón del Valle-Inclán." In *Espacios urbanos en el teatro español de los siglos XX y XXI*, edited by Cerstin Bauer-Funke, 23–32. Hildesheim: Georg Olms Verlag, 2016.

Peck, Jamie. "The Cult of Urban Creativity." In *Leviathan Undone: Towards a Political Economy of Scale*, edited by Roger Keil and Rianne Mahon, 159–76. Vancouver: University of British Columbia Press, 2009.

—. "Struggling with the Creative Class." *International Journal of Urban and Regional Research* 29, no. 4 (2005): 740–70.

Pedrosa, Ignacio G., and Ángela García de Paredes. "Teatro Olimpia en Lavapiés (Madrid)." *On diseño* 276 (2006): 154–67.

Perales, Liz. "10 ideas para el CDN de Gerardo Vera." *El cultural.es*. 30 September 2004. Accessed 5 January 2010. https://elcultural.com/Gerardo-Vera.

Pérez-Agote, Alfonso, Benjamín Tejerina, and Margarita Barañano, eds. *Barrios multiculturales: relaciones interétnicas en los barrios de San Francisco (Bilbao) y Embajadores/Lavapiés*. Madrid: Trotta, 2010.

Pérez-Bustamente Mourier, Ana-Sofía. "Cultura popular, cultura intelectual y casticismo." In *Casticismo y literatura en España*, edited by Ana-Sofía Pérez-Bustamente Mourier and Alberto Romero Ferrer, 125–62. Cádiz: Servicio de Publicaciones, Universidad de Cádiz, 1992.

—, and Alberto Romero Ferrer, eds. *Casticismo y literatura en España*. Cádiz: Servicio de Publicaciones, Universidad de Cádiz, 1992.

Pinto Crespo, Virgilio, and Santos Madrazo. *Madrid: atlas histórico de la ciudad siglos IX–XIX*. Madrid: Lunwerg Editores, 1995.

Pi-Sunyer, O. "Tourism in Catalonia." In *Tourism in Spain: Critical Issues*, edited by Michael Barke, J. Towner, and Michael T. Newton, 231–64. Oxford: Oxford University Press, 1996.

Planell, David. "Bazar." Translated by John Clifford. In *Spanish Plays: New Spanish and Catalan Drama*, edited by Elyse Dodgson and Mary Peat, 105–68. London: Nick Hern Books, 1999.

Pope, Randolph. "Historia y novela en la posguerra española." *Siglo XX: 20th Century* 5 (1987–88): 16–27.

Portús Pérez, Javier. *La antigua procesión del Corpus Christi en Madrid*. Madrid: Comunidad de Madrid, Consejería de Cultura, Centro de Estudios y Actividades Culturales, 1993.

Pruijt, Hans. "Okupar en Europa." In ¿Dónde están las llaves? El movimiento okupa: prácticas y contextos sociales, edited by Ramón Adell Argilés and Miguel Martínez López, 35–60. Madrid: La Catarata, 2004.

–. "Squatting in Europe." In Squatting in Europe: Radical Spaces, Urban Struggles, edited by Squatting Europe Kollective, 17–60. New York: Minor Compositions, 2013.

Répide, Pedro de. Las calles de Madrid. Edited by Federico Romero. Madrid: Afrodisio Aguado, 1972.

Riechman, J., and F. Fernández Buey. Redes que dan libertad: Introducción a los nuevos movimientos sociales. Barcelona: Paidós, 1995.

Ringrose, David. "A Setting for Royal Authority: The Reshaping of Madrid, Sixteenth-Eighteenth Centuries." In Embodiments of Power: Building Baroque Cities in Europe, edited by Gary B. Cohen and Franz A.J. Szabo, 230–48. Oxford and New York: Bergham Books, 2008.

–. "Madrid, Capital Imperial (1561–1833)." In Madrid: historia de una capital, edited by Santos Juliá, David Ringrose, and Cristina Segura, 155–314. Madrid: Alianza, 2000.

–. Madrid and the Spanish Economy. Berkeley, CA: University of California Press, 1983.

Río Barredo, María José del. "Cultura popular y fiesta." In Madrid: atlas histórico de la ciudad siglos IX–XIX, edited by Virgilio Pinto Crespo and Santos Madrazo, 324–39. Madrid: Lunwerg Editores, 1995.

Río García de Sola, Ignacio del. "Introducción." In Madrid: cuatro años de gestión del Plan General de Ordenación Urbana 1997, edited by Javier Echenagusia, 6–7. Madrid: Gerencia Municipal de Urbanismo del Ayuntamiento de Madrid, 2002.

Rivero, Carmen. "*Un soñador para un pueblo,* de Antonio Buero Vallejo, y la utopía del espíritu geométrico." In Espacios urbanos en el teatro español de los siglos XX y XXI, edited by Cerstin Bauer-Funke, 93–106. Hildesheim: Georg Olms Verlag, 2016.

Rivero, Jacobo. Podemos. Objetivo: asaltar los cielos. Barcelona: Editorial Planeta, 2015.

Roch, Fernando. "El modelo inmobiliario español." In Desigualdad social y vivienda, edited by Fernando Díaz Orueta and Maria Luisa Lourés Seoane, 31–52. Alicante: Editorial Club Universitario, 2004.

– "La deriva patológica del espacio social en el modelo inmobiliario neoliberal madrileño." Scripta Nova: Revista electrónica de geografía y ciencias sociales 12, no. 270 (40) (2008): n.p.

Rodríguez, Emmanuel. "La ciudad global o la nueva centralidad de Madrid." In Madrid ¿La suma de todos? Globalización, territorio *desigualdad*, edited by Observatorio Metropolitano, 41–93. Madrid: Traficantes de Sueños, 2007.

Romero Ferrer, Alberto. "Introducción." In *Antología del género chico*, edited by Alberto Romero Ferrer, 11–63. Madrid: Cátedra, 2005.

Roth, Norman. *Conversos, Inquisition, and the Expulsion of the Jews from Spain*. Madison, WI: University of Wisconsin Press, 2002.

Ruano de la Haza, José María. "Siglo de Oro." *Historia de los espectáculos en España*, vol. 1, edited by Andrés Amorós and José M. Díez Borque, 37–66. Madrid: Castalia, 1999.

Rueda, Ana, ed. *El retorno/el reencuentro: la inmigración en la literatura hispano-marroquí*. Madrid: Iberoamericana Editorial Vervuert, 2010.

Ruggeri Marchetti, Magda. "Review: '*El arquitecto y el relojero* de Jerónimo López Mozo.'" *Acotaciones*, no. 8 (enero-junio 2002): 192–5. Madrid: Editorial Fundamentos, 2002.

Ruiz Ramón, Francisco. *Historia del Teatro Español (Desde sus orígenes hasta 1900)*. 10th ed. Madrid: Cátedra, 2000.

–. "Spanish Transition Theater and Theater Transition, 1975–1985." In *Literature, the Arts, and Democracy: Spain in the Eighties*, edited by Samuel Amell and translated by Alma Amell, 90–101. Madison, NJ: Fairleigh Dickinson University Press, 1990.

Sádaba Rodríguez, Igor, and Gustavo Roig Domínguez. "El movimiento okupación ante las nuevas tecnologías: okupas en las redes." In *¿Dónde están las llaves? El movimiento okupa: prácticas y contextos sociales*, edited by Ramón Adell Argilés and Miguel Martínez López, 267–91. Madrid: La Catarata, 2004.

Salaün, Serge. "El 'género chico' o los mecanismos de un pacto cultural." *El teatro menor en España a partir del siglo XVI. Actas del Coloquio celebrado en Madrid, 20–22 de Mayo 1982*, 251–62. Madrid: Consejo Superior de Investigaciones Científicas, 1983.

Sambricio, Carlos. "De nuevo sobre el Plan Bigador." In *Plan Bigador, 1941–1946. Plan General de Ordenación de Madrid*, edited by Carlos Sambricio, 12–18. Madrid: Nerea, 2003.

–. "En la segunda mitad del s. XVIII." In *La Real Casa de Correos: un edificio en la ciudad*, edited by Carlos Sambricio, 5–28. Madrid: Consejería de Política Territorial, 1988.

–. *La arquitectura española de la Ilustración*. Madrid: Consejo Superior de los Colegios de Arquitectos de España, 1986.

–. "La Real Casa de Correos y la Puerta del Sol." In *La Real Casa de Correos, 1756–1998: Sede de la Presidencia de la Comunidad de Madrid*, edited by Antonio Bonet Correa, Carlos Sambricio, and José

María Fernández-Isla, 29–53. Madrid: Dirección General de Arquitectura y Vivienda, 1998.

–. *Territorio y ciudad en la España de la Ilustración*. Madrid: Ministerio de Obras Públicas y Transportes, Instituto del Territorio y Urbanismo, 1991.

Santiago Rodríguez, Eduardo de. "Madrid, Global: la región urbana madrileña como nodo relacional en el contexto de la centralidad global." *Scripta Nova: Revista Electrónica de Geografía y Ciencias Sociales* 12, no. 270 (2008): n.p.

Santiáñez, Nil. *Topographies of Fascism: Habitus, Space, and Writing in Twentieth-Century Spain*. Toronto: University of Toronto Press, 2013.

Sassen, Saskia. *Cities in a World Economy*. 4th ed. Thousand Oaks, CA: Sage Publications, 2011.

–. *The Global City: New York, London, Tokyo*. Princeton, NJ: Princeton University Press, 1991.

Seco, Manuel. *Arniches y el habla de Madrid*. Barcelona: Alfaguara, 1970.

Sennett, Richard. "The Public Realm." In *The Blackwell City Reader*, 2nd edition, edited by Gary Bridge and Sophie Watson, 260–72. West Sussex, UK: Wiley-Blackwell 2010.

Sequera, Jorge. *Gentrificación: capitalismo cool, turismo y control del espacio urbano*. Madrid: La Catarata, 2020.

–, and Michael Janoschka. "Gentrification Dispositifs in the Historic Centre of Madrid: A Reconsideration of Urban Governmentality and State-Led Urban Reconfiguration." In *Global Gentrifications: Uneven Development and Displacement*, edited by Loretta Lees, Hyun Bang Shin, and Ernesto López Morales, 375–94. Bristol, UK: Policy Press, 2015.

Shepard, Ben. "Occupy Wall Street, Social Movements, and Contested Public Space." In *Beyond Zuccotti Park: Freedom of Assembly and the Occupation of Public Space*, edited by Ron Shiffman, Rick Bell, Lance Jay Brown, and Lynne Elizabeth, 21–33. New York: New Village Press, 2012.

Simmel, Georg. "The Metropolis and Mental Life." In *The Blackwell City Reader*, 2nd ed., edited by Gary Bridge and Sophie Watson, 103–10. Oxford: Blackwell Publishers, 2002.

Smith, Neil. "Gentrification and the Rent Gap." *Annals of the Association of American Geographers* 7, no. 3 (1987): 462–78.

–. "Gentrification, the Frontier, and the Restructuring of Urban Space." In *Gentrification of the City*, edited by Neal Smith and P. Williams, 15–34. Boston: Allen & Unwin, 1986.

–. "New Globalism, New Urbanism: Gentrification as Global Urban Strategy." In *Spaces of Neoliberalism: Urban Restructuring in North America and Northern Europe*, edited by Neil Brenner and Nik Theodore, 80–103. Oxford: Blackwell Publishers, 2002.

–. *The New Urban Frontier: Gentrification and the Revanchist City*. London and New York: Routledge, 1996.

–. "Toward a Theory of Gentrification: A Back to the City Movement by Capital, not People." *Journal of the American Planning Association* 45, no. 4 (1979): 538–48.

–. *Uneven Development: Nature, Capital, and the Production of Space*. Oxford: Blackwell Publishers, 1991.

Snow, David A., Sarah A. Soule, and Hans Peter Kriesi, eds. *Blackwell Companion to Social Movements*. Malden, MA: Blackwell Publishers, 2007.

Snyder, Jonathan. *Poetics of Opposition in Contemporary Spain: Politics and the Work of Urban Culture*. Hispanic Urban Studies. New York: Palgrave Macmillan, 2015.

–. "Practices of Oppositional Literacy in the 15-M Movement in Madrid." In *Cartographies of Madrid: Contesting Urban Space at the Crossroads of the Global South and Global North*, edited by Silvia Bermúdez and Anthony L. Geist, 49–71. Hispanic Issues, no. 43. Nashville, TN: Vanderbilt University Press, 2019.

Spivak, Gayatri Chakravorty. "Can the Subaltern Speak?" In *Marxism and the Interpretation of Culture*, edited by Cary Nelson and Lawrence Grossberg, 271–313. Urbana, IL: University of Illinois Press, 1988.

Squatting Europe Kollective. *The Squatters' Movement in Europe: Commons and Autonomy as Alternatives to Capitalism*. London and Chicago: Pluto Press, 2014.

–. *Squatting in Europe: Radical Spaces, Urban Struggles*. New York: Minor Compositions, 2012.

Stapell, Hamilton M. *Remaking Madrid: Culture, Politics, and Identity after Franco*. New York: Palgrave Macmillan, 2010.

Stiglitz, Joseph. *Freefall, American, Free Markets, and the Sinking of the World Economy*. New York: Norton, 2010.

Sullivan, Henry W., Raúl A. Galoppe, and Mahlon L. Stoutz, eds. *La comedia española y el teatro europeo del siglo XVII*. Suffolk, UK: Tamesis, 1999.

Surtz, Ronald. *The Birth of a Theater: Dramatic Convention in the Spanish Theater from Juan del Encina to Lope de Vega*. Madrid: Castalia, 1979.

Swyngedouw, Erik. "Excluding the Other: The Production of Scale and Scaled Politics." In *Geographies of Economies*, edited by R. Lee and J. Wills, 167–76. London: Arnold, 1997.

–. "Producing Nature, Scaling Environment: Water, Networks, and Territories in Fascist Spain." In *Leviathan Undone: Towards a Political Economy of Scale*, edited by Roger Keil and Rianne Mahon, 121–39. Vancouver: University of British Columbia Press, 2009.

Taibo, Carlos. *El 15-M en sesenta preguntas*. Madrid: La Catarata, 2011.

Taylor, Peter J. "Advanced Producer Service Centres in the World Economy." In *Global Urban Analysis: A Survey of Cities in Globalization*, edited by Peter J. Taylor, Pengfei Ni, Ben Derudder, Michael Hoyler, Jin Huang, and Frank Witlox, 22–39. London: Earthscan, 2011.

–, Pengfei Ni, Ben Derudder, Michael Hoyler, Jin Huang, Kathy Pain, Frank Witlox, Xiaolan Yang, David Bassens, and Wei Shen. "Command and Control Centres in the World Economy." In *Global Urban Analysis: A Survey of Cities in Globalization*, edited by Peter J. Taylor, Pengfei Ni, Ben Derudder, Michael Hoyler, Jin Huang, and Frank Witlox, 17–21. London: Earthscan, 2011.

–, Ben Derudder, Michael Hoyler, Kathy Pain, Frank Witlox. "European Cities in Globalization." In *Global Urban Analysis: A Survey of Cities in Globalization*, edited by Peter J. Taylor, Pengfei Ni, Ben Derudder, Michael Hoyler, Jin Huang, and Frank Witlox, 114–35. London: Earthscan, 2011.

Terán, Fernando de. *Historia del urbanismo en España III. Siglos XIX y XX*. Madrid: Cátedra, 1999.

Torrecilla, Jesús. *España exótica: la formación de la imagen española moderna*. Boulder, CO: Society of Spanish and Spanish-American Studies, 2004.

–. *Guerras literarias del XVIII Español: la modernidad como invención*. Salamanca: Ediciones Universidad de Salamanca, 2008.

Tuan, Yi-Fu. *Space and Place: The Perspective of Experience*. Minneapolis: University of Minnesota Press, 2001.

Ugarte, Michael. *Madrid 1900: The Capital as Cradle of Culture*. University Park, PA: Pennsylvania State University Press, 1996.

Unamuno, Miguel de. *En torno al casticismo*. 1895. Madrid: Biblioteca Nueva, 1996.

Valle-Inclán, Ramón María del. *Luces de bohemia*. 1924. Edited by Alonso Zamora Vicente. Madrid: Espasa-Calpe, 2004.

Vega y Carpio, Félix Lope de. *Fuente Ovejuna*. Madrid: Castalia, 1996.

Vela, Fernando. "El género chico." *Revista de Occidente* 10 (1965): 364–9.
Vélez-Sainz, Julio. "En los alrededores del teatro documento: Animalario y Teatro del barrio." *El teatro como documento artístico, histórico y cultural en los inicios del siglo XXI*, edited by José Romera Castillo, 365–74. Madrid: Editorial Verbum, 2017.
Vidaniana, Carlos. "El Labo como iniciativa social." *Viento sur*, no. 69 (2003). www.vientosur.info/spip.php?article1530.
–, and Marga Padilla. "Okupar el vacío desde el vacío." Interview by Áreaciega in *Autonomía y metrópolis: del movimiento Okupa a los centros sociales de segunda generación*, edited by Javier Toret, Nicolás Sguiglia, Santiago Fernández Patón, and Mónica Lama, 53–6. Málaga: Cedma, 2008.
Vilaseca, Stephen Luis. *Barcelonan Okupas: Squatter Power!* Madison, NJ: Fairleigh Dickinson, 2013.
–. "Patio Maravillas' Anti-gentrification Campaign against the TriBall Group." In *Making Room: Cultural Production in Occupied Spaces*, edited by Alan Moore and Alan Smart, 272–5. Barcelona: Journal of Aesthetics and Protest, 2015.
–. "The TriBall Case: 'Okupación Creativa ¡Ya!' vs. Okupa Hacktivismo." *Arizona Journal of Hispanic Cultural Studies* 14 (2010): 11–30.
Vinson, Ben, III. *Before Mestizaje: The Frontiers of Race and Caste in Colonial Mexico*. Cambridge: Cambridge University Press, 2018.
Viñuales Ferreiro, Gonzalo. "Los judíos de Madrid en el siglo XV: las minutas de los escribanos." *Espacio, Tiempo y Forma. Serie III, Historia Medieval* 15 (2002): 287–306.
Webber, Christopher. *The Zarzuela Companion*. Lanham, MD: Scarecrow Press, 2002.
Weiss, Peter. "Fourteen Propositions for a Documentary Theatre." *World Theatre* 17, no. 5–6 (1968): 375–89.
Wheeler, Duncan. *Golden Age Drama in Contemporary Spain: The Comedia on Page, Stage, and Screen*. Wales, UK: University of Wales Press, 2012.
Williams, Patrick. "'Un estilo nuevo de grandeza' El Duque de Lerma y la vida cortesana en el reinado de Felipe III (1598–1621)." In *Dramaturgia festiva y cultura nobiliaria en el siglo de oro*, edited by Bernardo J. García García and María Luisa Lobato, 169–202. Madrid: Iberoamericana, 2007.
Zarate Martín, M. Antonio. "Imágenes mentales del centro de Madrid: el barrio de Lavapiés." *Boletín de la Real Sociedad Geográfica* 137–138 (2001–2002): 404–21.

–. "Medio siglo de cambios en los centros urbanos españoles." *Estudios Geográficos* 67, no. 260 (2006): 283–315.

Zatlin, Phyllis. "Theater and Culture, 1936–1996." In *The Cambridge Companion to Modern Spanish Culture*, edited by David T. Gies, 222–36. Cambridge: Cambridge University Press, 1999.

Zukin, Sharon. *The Culture of Cities*. Oxford: Blackwell Publishers, 1995.

–. *Loft Living: Culture and Capital in Urban Change*. 1982. New Brunswick, NJ: Rutgers University Press, 1989.

–. *Naked City: Death and Life of Authentic Urban Places*. Oxford: Oxford University Press, 2011.

Index

Acampada Sol, 23, 56, 58–9, 62, 164–5, 180, 205
AirBnB, 29. *See also* short-term rental; Vrbo
Alejandro y Ana: as Documentary Theater, 157; origins, 155–6; as social critique, 162–4; use of urban space, 159–60. *See also* Animalario; Mayorga, Juan
Aleph, the, 92
Alier, Roger, 81, 84, 229n69, 229n71
AlmaViva Teatro, 206, 225n6
Álvarez del Manzano, José María, 114–15. *See also Madrid: Four Years of Management of the PGOUM 1997*.
Amparo, 103, 129, 139, 148, 152. *See also* Laboratorio 03
Animalario, 154, 204; on *Alejandro y Ana*, 159, 163; at the Goyas, 158; origins and members, 155–6; and Teatro del Barrio, 157, 207, 242n105; and urban space, 174. *See also Alejandro y Ana*
aplebeyamiento, 74, 77

Arab Spring, 56
Area of Integrated Rehabilitation, 119
Area de Rehabilitación Preferente (ARP), 16, 17, 215n34
Argumosa Street, 97, 109–10, 137, 147
El arquitecto y el relojero, 54, 96–7, 175, 230n. *See also* López Mozo, Jerónimo
Artistic Mode of Production, 195
Art of Rent, 169. *See also* Harvey, David
Assembly, General, 18, 57, 60, 134, 137, 139, 143, 207, 224n126, 228n45. *See also autogestión*; self-management
autogestión, 18, 58. 60, 129, 136, 143, 166, 204. *See also* Assembly, General; self-management
autonomy, 37, 54, 133–7, 139, 143–4, 178. *See also* horizontality
auto sacramental, 41, 46, 101, 173, 194, 199, 201
AZCA complex, 123, 236n134

Aznar, José María, 154, 158, 160–3, 176, 243n114. See also *aznarismo*
aznarismo, 159–63, 176–7

Baker, Edward, 59, 168, 182, 209
Barajas Airport, 124
El barberillo de Lavapiés, 85, 87
Barbieri, Francisco Asenjo, 84, 85, 91. See also *El barberillo de Lavapiés*
Barcelona, 57, 59, 96, 114, 126, 135, 138–9, 158, 161; Barcelona Model, 21, 217n50; municipal elections 2014, 202, 208, 224n135; Olympic Games 1992, 114–15, 126; *zarzuela*, 229n71
La Barraca, 100
Barrado Timón, Diego, 123
Barrio de los Teatros, 206
Bazar, 23, 173–87, 194
Berg, Peter, 132
Bizet, Georges, 63
Boehm, Scott, 156
Bohemian Lights. See *Luces de bohemia*
BollyMadrid, 6–7, 122, 235n130
Borges, Jorge Luis, 230n88
Brecht, Bertold, 161, 174
Brenner, Neil, 51, 195
Bretón, Tomás, 89, 91
Brunet, Ferrán, 114–15

Carmen, 63–4, 68, 89
Carreño-Rodríguez, Antonio, 36, 219n34
Casa Encendida, 15, 17, 128,
casa de malicia, 39
Castells, Manuel, 37, 59; and Citizens' Movement 203, 208;

and *comunero* revolt, 38, 220n46, 227n22
Castile, 35–7, 45, 47–8, 69–72, 79–80, 91–3, 221n83
castizo, 4, 7, 9, 23, 69–71, 74, 80, 82, 88–91, 123, 213n7; definition, 47, 63–4; and Francoism 92–4; and theater, 25, 95, 168
Castro Urban Plan, 85
Catholic Monarchs, 35
Cavestany, Juan, 155–6, 158–9, 204
Cedepalo, 148, 150
Centro Dramático Nacional, 17, 23, 95, 97–8, 103–5, 156, 170, 231n10, 250n16. See also Teatro Valle-Inclán
Centro social okupado autogestionado. See also self-managed social center; *okupas*
cerca; 214n15; of Philip II, 10; of Philip IV, 91
chabolismo vertical, 141
Chapí, Ruperto, 89–91
Charles III, 71–2, 75, 85, 226n19
Charlon, Julien, 145–6, 170, 241n77
chivo en la Corte del botellón o Valle Inclán en Lavapiés, Un, 170, 173, 187–201. See also López Llera, César
chulapos, 8, 70, 88, 90, 92, 190
cigarreras, 63–6, 68
Cigarreras: Tiempo y Método, 68. See also Tabacalera
Cine Princesa, 138
Citizens' Movement, 135, 203–4, 207. See also Castells, Manuel
Colau, Ada, 202, 208, 224n135
Coleman, Jeffery, 178, 180, 184–5. See also necropolitical theater

Commons, 18, 139, 204, 216n42, 224n135, 242n42. See also *procomún*
Compitello, Malcolm, 168–9, 215n33, 245n4, 249n113
comunero revolt, 37–8, 72
Constitution of 1978, 102, 115; Article 33, 141; Article 47, 141; Article 53, 237n153
Corcuera, Laura, 148–9. See also Cedepalo
corrala: housing, 65, 66, 191, 206, 225n5; in *género chico*, 88–91; Neighborhood Association 13, 103, 149, 203
corrales de comedia, 27, 29–31, 33–4, 38–9, 45–6, 49
Corsín Jiménez, Alberto, 204, 205, 225n139
costumbrismo, 6, 9, 79, 80, 87, 89, 226n12, 227n29, 247n65
Creative City, 115. See also Florida, Richard
Cruz, Ramón de la, 7, 21, 23, 70–2, 74–5, 80, 82–3, 85, 91; *Manolo*, 75; *Los Bandos de Lavapiés*, 75–7, 227n29
cultural bunker, 111

Debord, Guy, 21–2, 97, 109, 132, 176, 247
de Certeau, Michel, 217n51
Delgado, Manuel, 18, 20, 172, 217n50
Documentary Theater, 157, 207
Dougherty, Dru, 189
Durán, Gloria, 61

economic crisis 2008, 5, 24, 56–9, 125; impact, 128; lead up to, 127

entertainment machine, 123
entremés, 75
Escobar, Jesús, 40–1, 75, 220n57
Esperpento, 105, 171, 189–90, 192–3, 196, 201, 248n80

Ferdinand II. See Catholic Monarchs
Ferdinand VI, 71–2, 75, 82, 226n19
Ferdinand VII, 83,
Fernández Shaw, Carlos, 89
15-M movement, 26, 33 164, 210; and electoral politics, 5, 24, 155, 202, 224n135; and Lavapiés, 18, 60–2, 155, 166, 203–6; and Occupy Wall Street, 61; origins, 5, 57–9; and self-management, 18, 58, 60, 204; Sol encampment, 23, 59, 62; and Teatro del Barrio, 204–6
flat ontology, 216n40. See also geographic scale
Florida, Richard, 110, 115, 117, 119, 197
Foucault, Michel, 226n20
Four Towers Business Complex, 123
Francoist regime, 6, 46, 64–6, 96, 113, 161; and *castizo* culture, 47, 93; historiography, 49, 174, 217n3; and Puerta del Sol, 54, 56; and theater, 46, 103, 177, 207, 222n91, 227n21; and tourism, 64, and the Transition, 101–2, 176; and urban space, 48, 50, 203, 222n5
Fraser, Benjamin, 79, 172
Fuente Ovejuna, 34–8, 76, 206, 220n45. See also Lope de Vega y Carpio, Félix de

Gabriele, John, 175
García Paredes, Ángela, 106, 108
García Santo-Tomás, Enrique, 39–41, 209, 220n50
García de Sola, Ignacio del Río, 17, 114
gaztetxe, 135
Generation of 1898, 70, 92
genéro chico, 8, 25, 168, 206, 229n82; and *castizo* culture, 69, 80–1, 88–95
gentrification, 16, 18–19, 59, 65, 111, 115, 118, 129, 151, 198, 204
geographic scale, 4, 18, 20, 23–4, 195, 216n40
Global City, 6, 17, 126, 201, 216n39
Golden Age, 26, 30, 46, 101. See also *siglo de oro*
Gómez, Mayte, 13, 35, 36, 110, 116, 121–2, 171, 198
Goya y Lucientes, Francisco de, 73–4, 77–8, 158, 163, 189, 192, 227n29, 247n67
Gutiérrez Carbajo, Franciso, 190
Gran Vía: street 54, 206; *zarzuela*, 223n112

Hacktivism, 144, 154, 165
Haidt, Rebecca, 74, 78–9
Hansen, Thomas Blom, 36–7
Harney, Lucy D., 80, 89, 229n82
Harvey, David, 18, 22, 197; art of rent, 169; creative destruction, 58; from management to entrepreneurialism, 45, 123, 168–9; palimpsest, 217n52; urbanization of capital, 16, 127, 215n32; urbanization of consciousness, 53

Haussmanization, 54
Hola, 157, 160

Iglesias Posse, Pablo, 64, 249n1
Iglesias Turrón, Pablo, 202, 204
Ikea Disobedients, 197. See also Jacque, Andrés
infravivienda, 13, 110
Inquisition, 42, 227n21
Integral Rehabilitation Plan of Lavapiés, 110
Isabella of Castile, 35, 37, 47
Isabella II, 53–4, 85

Jacque, Andrés, 197
Juan Carlos I, 207
Juliá, Santos, 102, 207

Kasten, Carey, 46
Kearns, Gerry, 36
krakker, 134. See also *okupas*

Laboratorio: chronology, 136; cultural events, 144; and geographic scale, 142–3; Laboratorio 01, 145; Laboratorio 02, 142, 145; origin, 136–9; philosophy, 139–40; and spectacle, 141–2
Laboratorio 03, 23, 68, 129–31, 136; and *Alejandro y Ana*, 155–64; connections to Lavapiés, 146–7; eviction, 165; and 15-M, 166; history, 145–7; origins, 144–6; and theater, 148–54. See also *okupas*.
Laboratorio 03: ocupando el vacío, 145, 147, 152
Labrador Méndez, Germán, 5, 159, 175–6, 213n5, 243n114

Larson, Susan, 54, 60, 204, 209, 223n108, 223n112
Lavapiés: as *barrio* bajo, 9, 25, 166, 169, 178, 192; boundaries, 15; etymology and history, 9–11; and *castizo* culture, 9, 16, 23, 25, 62, 64, 69, 71; and the Citizens' Movement, 135, 203–4; demographics, 12–13; and 15-M, 204–6; and *género chico*, 88–94; and gentrification, 15–16, 109–11; and housing, 13, 110; immigration, 6, 11, 122, 178–9, 184; maps, 14, 15; and Ramón de la Cruz, 23, 70–8, 85; and theater, 15, 21, 90, 101–4, 123, 203, 206; and urban planning, 16–18, 97, 111–20
Lavapiés Network, 13, 149–50, 149
Lefebvre, Henri, 18, 167, 200, 201; abstract space, 29, 98, 112, 171, 188, 218n19; geographic scale, 22, 51; lived space, 24, 201; perceived space, 171; production of space, 3, 26, 19–20, 52, 56, 140, 142, 205; representational space, 24, 184; right to the city, 18, 113, 203; spatial practice, 24, 52, 60, 79, 93, 146, 166, 188, 197; spatial triad, 23, 172, 188; urban fabric, 113
Leitner, Helga, 195, 216n40
Leonard, Candyce, 175
Ley sinde, 165
Lima, Andrés, 155–6, 159–60, 162
Lloyd, Richard, 122
Lope de Vega y Carpio, Félix de, 32–6, 38, 45, 76, 206, 225n6. See also *Fuene Ovejuna*

López, Isidro, 126
López Llera, César, 24, 170, 173, 177, 187–92, 95–7, 20. See also *Un chivo en la Corte de botellón*
López Mozo, Jerónimo, 96, 175, 230n1, 230n2. See also *El arquitecto y el relojero*
Luces de bohemia, 24, 187, 190, 194. See also Valle-Inclán, Ramón María
Lucha autónoma, 137

Madrid, 3–6; architecture, 40–4, 124; and Baroque spectacle, 26–32, 40, 42–6; and *castizo* culture, 94–6; and early-modern theater, 29, 38–9; and *costumbrismo*, 78–80, 122–7, 167; demographics, 10, 11–12, 27–8, 91, 214n14; globalization and economic growth, 122–7, 236n139; housing, 30, 39, 65, 117, 127–8; and Kilometer Zero, 50; and the Spanish Civil War, 46–9; Royal Court, 168; and urban planning, 52–3, 65, 72, 79, 85, 111–22, 169, 176, 229n75; and *zarzuela*, 80–4, 88–93
Madrid: Four Years of Management of the General Plan for Urban Ordinance for Madrid 1997, 104, 111, 114–16; issues of geographic scale, 119–23. See also Urban Plan of 1997
majos/majas, 70–2, 74, 77–8, 80, 82, 85. See also Cruz, Ramón de la
majísmo, 71–2, 74, 77
Manolo, 80, 85, 92; origin of name, 11; theatrical work, 75, 77

mantón de manila, 8, 64, 68, 89
Maravall, José Antonio, 39
Marston, Sallie A., 26n40
Martín Escriche, Juanjo, 170
Martín Estudillo, Luis, 173
Martínez López, Miguel, 134, 238n16
Mayorga, Juan, 155–6, 158–60, 204. See also *Alejandro y Ana*
McKendrick, Melveena, 32, 36, 218n6, 218n14
Merrifield, Andy, 18
Mesonero Romanos, Ramón, 11, 78–80, 167, 170
Moral Ruiz, Carmen del, 25, 64, 88, 91, 94
Moratín, Fernández Leandro, 83
Moreno-Caballud, Luis, 5, 213n5
Museum of Modern Art (New York), 198

Nash, Elizabeth, 214n10
necropolitcal theater, 180. See also Coleman, Jefferey 9 + 1 Ways of Being Political, 197
nunca máis 158, 243n113. See also Prestige Environmental Disaster
No pasarán, 47

Observatorio Metropolitano, 127
Occupy Wall Street, 59, 61–2, 216n43, 224n126, 241n72
okupas, 4, 13, 19, 62; and *autogestión*, 143; in Lavapiés, 139–52; in Madrid, 136–9; overview, 132–5; and technology, 165. See also Laboratorio; squatters
Oliva, César, 103, 173–4, 177, 204
Oñoro Otero, Cristina, 205–6
Olympic Games, 17, 20, 114–15, 117, 179, 234n81, 234n83

Palacio Ortiz, Nortan, 207
Paredes Pedrosa Architects, 106
Parsons, Deborah, 91–3, 223n106
Partido Popular. See Popular Party
Partido Socialista Obrero Español (PSOE). See Spanish Socialist Workers' Party
Patio Maravillas, 61
Pedrosa, Ignacio G., 106, 108. See also Paredes Pedrosa Architects
Pérez Bowie, José Antonio, 175
petimetre, 74
PGOUM 1997. See Urban Plan of 1997
Philip II, 10, 26, 30, 40, 43, 88, 168, 214n15, 220n55
Philip III, 41
Philip IV, 39, 43, 65, 81, 214n15
Philip V, 71–2, 85–6
Pinto Crespo, Virgilio, 28, 44
Pirandello, Luigi, 174
Plan General de Ordenación Urbana de Madrid 1997 (PGOUM 1997). See Urban Plan of 1997
Plannel, David, 173, 178–9, 182, 185–7. See also *Bazar*
Plaza Mayor, 8, 93, 120, 151 220n56; in the seventeenth century, 23, 28, 40–3, 45, 52
Podemos, 19, 24, 202–3. See also Iglesias Turrón, Pablo
Popular Party, 115–16, 157–9, 163–4, 168, 176, 202, 207. See also Aznar, José María
Prestige Environmental Disaster, 158
procomún, 139, 204, 216n42, 240n42. See also commons
Puerta de Sol, 23, 96, 120, 188, 222n103; history, 51–6; and 15-M, 18–9, 57, 59, 62, 151

Real Casa de Correos: in *El arquitecto y el relojero*, 96–7, 175, 230n2; history, 52–6; as symbol, 50, 56, 59, 188
Red de Lavapiés. *See* Lavapiés Network.
Regime of 1978, 208
Revista Kaminada, 151, 155
La revoltosa, 89, 90. *See also género chico*
El rey, 207
Ringrose, David, 11, 43, 44, 214n14
Rivero, Carmen, 227n21
Rivero, Jacobo, 138–40, 145, 147
Roch Peña, Fernando, 127
Rodríguez, Emmanuel, 126–7
Rubira, Belén, 148–9, 165
Ruiz-Gallardón, Alberto, 130
Ruz/Barcenas, 207. *See also* Teatro del Barrio

sainete, 7, 23, 69–70, 75–7, 82–3, 85, 88, 90–3
Saint Micaela, 198–200
Sala triángulo, 203
Sambricio, Carlos, 52
Sánchez Mazas, Rafael, 100, 231n15
San Juan, Alberto, 155–8, 207. *See also* Animalario; Teatro del Barrio
San Isidro, 8, 25, 56, 64, 90, 93, 203
Santiago Rodríguez, Eduardo, 124, 125, 236n147, 237n151
Santiáñez, Nil, 47, 48, 222n88
Sassen, Saskia, 31, 216n39
scalar structuration, 51, 195
Second Republic, 100, 219n23

Sennet, Richard, 172
Sequera, Jorge, 16, 215n30
short-term rental. *See* AirBnB
Siglo de Oro, 26, 45, 49, 84, 101, 221n76, 222n93. *See also* Golden Age
Situationist, 21, 130, 132
Smith, Neil, 129, 142
Spadaccini, Nicholas, 173
Spanish Civil War, 46–8, 100
Spanish Model, 126
Spanish Miracle, 127
Spanish Socialist Workers' Party, 56, 64, 102–3, 164, 176, 202, 249n1.
Spanish War of Independence, 78, 83
spectacle, 4, 18, 20; counter-spectacles 215–16, 62, 69, 139; and Debord, Guy, 21–2, 132
spectator architecture, 34
self-managed social centers: history and philosophy, 134–6, 143; Casablanca, 61, 205; Cine Princessa, 138; Eskalera Karakola, 149, 205; La Guindalera, 138, 143; Haffenstrasse, 137; El Solar, 136, 166, 205. *See also* Laboratorio; *okupas*; Tabacalera
Snyder, Jonathan, 164
Squatter Assembly of Madrid, 137
squatting: definition and history, 133–8, 143–4, 195; prohibition, 138–9. *See also* okupas; self-managed social centers
Stapell, Hamilton M., 103,
Stepputat, Finn, 36, 37
Swyngedouw, Erik, 195

Tabacalera: history, 17, 63–4; self-managed social center, 15,

61–2, 166, 197, 204–5; la Tabacalera a Debate, 67–8
tonadilla, 82
Tapapiés, 6
Teatro del Barrio, 205–8. *See also* San Juan, Alberto
Teatro Español, 45, 49, 99–103, 219n23
Teatro María Guerrero, 100–1
teatro por horas, 81, 88. *See also género chico*
Teatro Real, 87
teatro de urgencia, 159
Teatro Valle-Inclán, 17, 23, 145, 149, 154, 157, 174, 188; mission and marketing, 104, 231n10; architecture, 105–9; and urban development, 98–9, 110–14, 120–1, 129, 171–2, 208; inauguration and protests, 130–2, 154; as performance space, 112, 174, 185–6. *See also* Centro Dramático Nacional
Teatro de la Zarzuela, 85, 87, 95
Time Out, 15, 171
Toledo, Willie, 155, 158
Torrecilla, Jesús, 74, 227n27
Tuan, Yi-Fu, 58, 108–9

Unamuno, Miguel de, 70, 80, 84, 92, 232n43
Uneven Development, 142. *See also* Smith, Neil
Urban Plan of 1997, 17, 23, 79, 97–9, 110–11, 114–21, 123, 125–9, 169–73

Valle-Inclán, Ramón María del, 24, 105–6, 173, 232n43, 248n80; and the *esperpento*, 170–1, 189; in *Un chivo en la Corte*, 187–93, 196. *See also Luces de bohemia*
Value Added Tax (VAT), 205
Vasquéz Montalbán, Manuel, 159
de Vega y Carpio, Félix Lope, 32–6, 45, 76, 206, 225n6. *See also Fuente Ovejuna*
de la Vega, Ricardo, 89, 91
Vélez-Sainz, Julio, 157, 242n105
verbatim theater, 157
verbena, 25, 66, 77, 89
La verbena de la Paloma, 89–90, 94
Vidania, Carlos, 111, 140
Vilaseca, Stephen Luis, 132, 139, 162, 224n130
violent sovereignty, 54
Vrbo, 15. *See also* short-term rental

Weiss, Peter, 157
Woodward, Keith, 216n40. *See also* flat ontology

Zarate Martín, M. Antonio, 13, 117
zarzuela, 8, 23, 69, 87, 90, 152, 228n64; and *castizo* tradition, 25, 70, 80, 92–4, 168, 196; historical overview, 80–5; and *género chico*, 88, 93; palace, 81, 228n64
Zuccoti Park, 61. *See also* Occupy Wall Street
Zukin, Sharon, 22, 132, 195, 197, 208